From Vietnam
to America

From Vietnam
to America

A Chronicle of
the Vietnamese Immigration
to the United States

Gail Paradise Kelly

Westview Press • Boulder, Colorado

Copyright © 1977 by Westview Press
Published in 1977 in the United States of America by
  Westview Press, Inc.
  5500 Central Avenue
  Boulder, Colorado 80301
  Frederick A. Praeger, Publisher and Editorial Director

Library of Congress Cataloging in Publication Data
Kelly, Gail Paradise.
From Vietnam to America.
Bibliography: p.
1. Vietnam Conflict, 1961-1975—Refugees. 2. Refugees—Vietnam. 3. Refugees—
United States.
I. Title.
DS559.63.K44   361.5'3'0973   77-6383
ISBN 0-89158-326-2

Printed and bound in the United States of America

Contents

Tables

Photographs

Acknowledgements

There are many people to whom I owe a great deal and without whom it would have been impossible for me to write this book. I am grateful to the New York State Council for the Humanities, the State University of New York at Buffalo Foundation, and the State University of New York at Buffalo Institutional Funds for providing the resources that made it possible for me to commute between Buffalo and Fort Indian Town Gap, Pennsylvania, while that camp was open. To the State University of New York at Buffalo Archives and radio station WBFO I am indebted for supplying tape, tape recorders, and invaluable advice on how to use and obtain interview data. Without the State University of New York Foundation Fellowship for the summer of 1976 I would not have had the time to write this book.

There are many individuals who helped me in collecting materials and spent hours reading drafts of the book. I cannot begin to thank the many Vietnamese refugees, American caseworkers, teachers, and members of the Interagency Task Force and camp management who agreed to be interviewed and supplied me with documentation. Lt. James McDaniels of the United States Army was extremely helpful in scheduling interviews and guiding me through Fort Indian Town Gap. John Stephens, who was my graduate assistant through the project, provided invaluable help. His flawless Vietnamese stood us in good stead in the camps. Without his help, the interview data collected at Fort Indian Town Gap would not be what it is.

There are several people who worked in the resettlement agencies who helped me greatly. Among them are Wells Klein of the American Council for Nationalities Services, Robert DeVecchi of the International Rescue Committee, Matt Taylor of Church World Service, and Constance Winters of United Hebrew Immigration and Assistance Service. These individuals allowed me access to their files and reports and gave freely of their time. They are in no way responsible for the interpretation of immigration in this book; they contributed greatly, however, to much of its accuracy.

Six persons read and commented on the manuscript and made it more coherent and readable. There is no way I can begin to thank them enough. I am particularly grateful to David Gerber of the History Department, SUNY/Buffalo; Sheila McVey; John Stephens; Edith Hoshino Altbach; David Kelly, History Department, D'Youville College; Maxine Seller, Department of Social Foundations, SUNY/Buffalo; and Robert DeVecchi of the International Rescue Committee for their time in this regard. They are in no way responsible for the flaws in the manuscript. Without them there would have been far more.

Finally, I would like to acknowledge the assistance of Eileen Raines in preparing the final manuscript and of the Department of Social Foundations, SUNY/Buffalo, for its encouragement and support over the year and a half this book has been in the offing. Jenny K. deserves some praise for tolerating her mother's absences to visit Fort Indian Town Gap and her rigorous work schedule. "Tizzie" too should be thanked for not putting too many demands on my time.

Gail Kelly
1 March 1977

Americans. Over half the refugees were persons like these, closely associated with the war either as policymakers or as employees or relatives of the American military and intelligence community in Vietnam. The remainder of the refugees were persons who had held little power in Vietnam and were not associated with American government or with private agencies. Among the refugees were enlisted men in the South Vietnamese army and navy, frightened fishermen and farmers, and petty traders.

This book is a chronicle of the 1975 flight of Vietnamese from their country. It traces the departure from Vietnam and the resettlement of 130,000 of these refugees in the United States and focuses on the process by which Vietnamese went from refugees to immigrants. Vietnamese came to the United States motivated by events that occurred in Vietnam. When they left their country, most believed their departure was temporary; they were not consciously choosing to become part of another society or culture. They left as Vietnamese, considering their future still to be in Vietnam. In short, they were refugees. Refugees differ from immigrants in that immigrants are persons who seek new roots, and entry into a different social and cultural setting. For immigrants, the country they choose to exchange for their land of birth is a new one where accommodations need be, and are, willingly made. Immigrants to the U.S. traditionally have left their old societies behind for the society either of Americans or of their compatriots, who have also come to this country in search of new roots. Vietnamese were not so motivated when they entered the U.S. They considered themselves part of Vietnamese society and saw their stay in this country as temporary, lasting only until the new government fell. In the refugee camps they all joined Pham Duy, a famous Vietnamese popular and folk musician, when he sang out: "One thousand years of Chinese rule, one hundred years of French rule. Ai-ee Vietnam." In concert at Fort Indian Town Gap, one of the four refugee centers on the U.S. mainland, he sang that communist rule would be as fleeting, if not more so, than French rule. This song and the ones that followed it pleaded with Vietnamese to keep the old ways, for they would surely go back some day. Thousands of Vietnamese in American refugee camps shared Pham Duy's illusions—the illusions of a refugee.

While Vietnamese may have entered the country as refugees expecting to remain part of Vietnamese society and culture, they could not long act upon such assumptions. When they entered the United States they could no longer behave as Vietnamese in a country that was Vietnamese. They were in the United States and had to adjust not only to living with and among Americans, but also to living in a modern industrial society, unlike the Vietnam they had left. For many, this was a painful realization. Before coming to this country they had not expected to be integrated into American society. Many were under the illusion that they would merely pass some time away from home, waiting for the new government to fall. They believed that if this waiting time were long term they would somehow be able to regroup as a Vietnamese community within this country while preparing to return home.

As Vietnamese entered American refugee camps, both in Guam and on the U.S. mainland, it became apparent to them that they had left Vietnam for good and that their future lives would be shaped by American society. In refugee holding centers Vietnamese began to adjust to this perspective; they moved into a world that was run by Americans and in which Vietnamese options were molded by what Americans expected of them and arranged for them. Resettlement in the United States initially involved such conditions, in which Americans set the range of possibilities within which Vietnamese could act.

The transition from refugee to immigrant which this book describes is not only the process by which refugees begin acting within an American rather than a Vietnamese framework but the process in which refugees learn to manipulate American society for their own ends. Those ends may be to further their economic position within American society, to establish an ethnic community, and/or to help the immigrants become Americans. Becoming an immigrant means coping with two worlds instead of one.

I have organized this book according to the stages through which Vietnamese went in their transition from refugee to immigrant. Part 1 describes the departure from Vietnam: why refugees left their country, the conditions under which they left, how they left, and how American policy affected the composition of the population which came to the United States. This first section of the book also discusses which Vietnamese became refugees. This, I believe, is fundamental to understanding subsequent Vietnamese adjustment to American society.

The second part of the book is devoted to the first phase of the transition from refugee to immigrant. Part 2 is about the refugee camps on the United States mainland where Vietnamese waited to be resettled in the United States. Some Vietnamese lived in the camps for as long as seven months, experiencing for the first time life in an American-controlled environment. In the camps Vietnamese learned to conform to American routines and to deal with American bureaucracy. Simultaneously they were prepared for life in America through formal schooling and the daily orientation meetings as well as by articles in newspapers specially written for Vietnamese. In the camps Vietnamese were taught the English language as well as how to fill out job applications, how to shop, budget, and save, and how to interact socially with Americans.

The camps did more than prepare Vietnamese for living in the United States, they also channeled Vietnamese into American society, usually on terms set by Americans rather than Vietnamese. Under the Indochinese Immigration and Resettlement Act of 1975, Vietnamese could enter the United States only if there were a sponsor—an American citizen, resident alien, organization, or corporation—willing to take fiscal and moral responsibility for the refugee and family until that family became self-supporting. Sponsors were found for Vietnamese by voluntary agencies (called VOL-AGs) contracted by the federal government for such purposes.

By December 1975 Vietnamese were settled in America and the camps closed down. The refugees were placed in

American society isolated from other Vietnamese, scattered throughout the U.S. and marginally employed. If Vietnamese had avoided the prospect of accommodating to an American society in the camps, they clearly faced the issue once they had been released into American society. The third part of this book details their life outside the camps. It focuses on the initial integration of Vietnamese into the American economy and the development of a Vietnamese community in the United States. The formation of an ethnic community completes the transition from refugee to immigrant, for it marks Vietnamese coming to terms with American society as individuals who intend to live in it permanently, rather than as transients.

This is the first book on the Vietnamese immigration to the United States. Because of the proximity of the events depicted, the questions addressed here are limited. Neither the persistence of Vietnamese culture nor any assimilation to American culture that may have occurred or will occur among the immigrants, for example, can be assessed in this book. Changes such as these can only be studied after Vietnamese have been in the country for a longer period of time. Similarly, the Vietnamese experience of America cannot yet be compared with that of other immigrants because the Vietnamese experience of this country is just beginning. The aim of this book is instead to lay the groundwork for other scholars to deal with such questions in the future when long-term Vietnamese adjustment to the United States becomes clearer.

While this book is neither a study of cultural change nor a study of resistance to change among immigrants, it does add to our understanding of the immigrant experience. Using materials gathered during the immigration I have concentrated on the process of immigration—the interplay of American policies and Vietnamese responses to them—and on American management of the immigration, particularly on programs developed to prepare Vietnamese to live in this country. I discuss the choices Americans offered Vietnamese in terms of how they would integrate into American life and how Vietnamese reacted to these choices and found their own options.

Among the written and oral documentation for this book, assembled over the past two years, are government reports and Senate hearings. The latest of these to which I had access was issued on 15 June 1976. The documents represent the U.S. government's summation of its efforts in working with Vietnamese.

A second source of information is my own field work at one refugee camp, Fort Indian Town Gap, Pennsylvania. At this camp, which at its peak in 1975 housed 16,000 or more Vietnamese and Cambodians, I interviewed numerous persons: immigrants, camp officials, resettlement workers, volunteers, teachers. Most interviews were tape recorded and are available at the State University of New York (SUNY)/ Buffalo Archives. Many of these interviews were conducted in Vietnamese. I also attended camp events such as orientation sessions, press briefings, elementary and secondary school, and adult education classes. Many of these were also tape recorded for scholarly purposes. At Fort Indian Town Gap I also collected many written materials—school curriculum guides, press releases, cultural orientation materials for refugees, and the camp newspaper, *Dat Lanh*. The field work at Fort Indian Town Gap gave me a "feel" for the immigration as much, I suppose, as any nonimmigrant can have. It also provided me the opportunity to include in this book the perspective of Vietnamese refugees that certainly would be lacking in a work relying solely on written documentation.

While there are merits to working with taped interviews with persons involved in events then current, there are also some drawbacks. For example, refugees were often reluctant to speak out in either English or Vietnamese about their fears and aspirations in regard to settling in the United States. Many Vietnamese were less than honest about their reactions to camp life and American programs or their apprehensions about leaving the camps. Immigrant after immigrant told me how grateful and happy he or she was with his or her present life and future prospects. Only a few Vietnamese mentioned missing Vietnam although they usually referred to it as home. Even fewer talked about their ambivalence about entering American society. These feelings, while not necessarily articulated in the interviews, were obvious in poems Vietnamese wrote for *Dat Lanh*, in songs sung on barracks steps, and in the unwillingness of many to leave the refugee camps and the other Vietnamese who were there.

If Vietnamese were reluctant to reveal their inmost feelings, so were most Americans who worked in the camps. Most felt they were "spokespeople" of their organizations and described their work only in the most glowing terms. The conflicts between voluntary resettlement agencies and government officials, so clear in congresssional reports and subsequent interviews with national agency personnel, were never apparent in speaking to most Americans working in the camps.

The interview materials that I use in this book have been cross-checked against written sources whenever possible. Many of the materials gathered from Vietnamese immigrants could not undergo such verification. They are used to present the feelings and experiences of individuals who lived the journey from Vietnam to the United States. The experiences presented, I believe, are typical of other Vietnamese who came to the United States; I can make no such statements about the individual reactions to those experiences.

Government documents, congressional reports, and the materials—both oral and written—gathered at Fort Indian Town Gap are only two of the bases of this book. I have also used reports, mimeographed materials, and camp newspapers from Fort Chaffee and Camp Pendleton, two of the other refugee holding centers on the American mainland. Post-camp periodicals published for or by immigrants, like HEW's *Doi Song Moi*, form some of my documentation. The last two chapters rely on information obtained outside the camps through interviews with refugees living in the Buffalo, New York, area, observations of adult education classes, and interviews with individuals working for voluntary agencies handling the resettlement. Several of these agencies were so kind as to allow me access to their internal memoranda and general files on the immigration and postcamp life.

Much of the book is based on my impressions of what I saw and heard over the past year and a half while recording and gathering documentation. How I interpret the material has much to do with who I am and what I am. I am not Vietnamese; I am an American. I do not attempt to represent the views of all Vietnamese who came to the United States, their expectations, anxieties, or social or psychological adjustment; immigrants will have to write about this from their own perspectives. Still, I have tried, wherever possible, to include partial transcripts from interviews with immigrants. I hope that my background as a scholar of Vietnam and my knowledge of the Vietnamese language have kept me from distorting these materials too greatly.

Because of my background as an American and the proximity of the events dealt with, I have chosen to look at how Americans have handled the influx of a new group of people to this country, the social and cultural demands Americans have made on Vietnamese immigrants, how Vietnamese have been integrated into American life, and how Vietnamese have coped with American politics and practices. I hope that this study will provide the basis for an analysis of Vietnamese long-term adjustment to American society as well as for a comparison of the Vietnamese experience with that of other immigrant groups.

Part 1

The Departure from Vietnam

Chapter Two

Leaving Vietnam

Vietnamese left their country as refugees. They became refugees for many reasons, most of which were results of the events of the past twenty or thirty years; these events were not necessarily American-made, although they were exacerbated by the American presence in Vietnam. The reasons Vietnamese became refugees, the conditions under which they left their country, and the American planned evacuation are the subjects of this chapter, for they are essential to understanding the nature of the Vietnamese population which came to the United States.

The End of a War

In March 1975, U.S. Secretary of Defense James Schlesinger proclaimed that there would be no major military offensive against the Saigon government that year.[1] He said this despite the fact that two Vietnamese provinces to the north of Saigon had fallen in January of that year to what were presumed to be North Vietnamese attacks. In mid-March, a few days after Schlesinger made his prediction, Pleiku, Kontum, and Ban-Me-Thuot—all cities in the Vietnamese highlands—fell to a military offensive. On 18 March the Saigon government ordered its army to evacuate several provinces including Quang-Tri, which bordered on North Vietnam, and Thua-Thien, in which the city of Hue is located.

Thieu and many of his American advisors did not believe this signaled the end of the South Vietnamese government. Rather, they preferred to view the retreat as a defensive tactic, similar to a plan General Gavin had proposed in 1966. According to Thieu and his allies, the Vietnamese army (ARVN) was regrouping to defend the cities of Nha-Trang, Cam-Ranh, Qui-Nhon, and Da-Nang, all of which were coastal population centers with harbors, air strips, and/or military installations. The South Vietnamese government, as of mid-March, claimed it would also focus its energies on defending the Mekong Delta and the area surrounding Saigon. In the last week of that month, crack airborne troops left Hue for Saigon. Da-Nang was evacuated on 27 and 28 March 1975, and, after Da-Nang fell, Nha-Trang, Cam-Ranh, and other coastal cities quickly followed suit, leaving only a perimeter around Saigon under the control of the South Vietnamese government. The South Vietnamese army lost its last battle at Xuan-Loc in mid-April. Thieu resigned the presidency on 21 April 1975. On 30 April Saigon came under the control of the Provisional Revolutionary Government (PRG).

The military defeat of the Saigon government surprised everyone involved, including the governments of North Vietnam, South Vietnam, and the United States. The military defeat itself was not unexpected; it was the timing of the defeat and the speed at which it came that caught people unprepared. Many people in the American government expected the South Vietnamese army to hold out for a while, certainly for more than six weeks. As one Agency for International Development (AID) official remarked, "They [the ARVN] had enough ammunition to continue fighting for three years," even without continued American military assistance.[2] The American ambassador, Graham Martin, believed the Saigon government would survive. He urged Thieu to try to gain American support by airlifting 2,000 or so Vietnamese orphans to the United States, which Thieu agreed to do.[3] Operation Babylift began on 4 April with the crash of a World Airways C-5A that killed 150 orphans and 50 adults. Babylift might never have been undertaken had

American and South Vietnamese government officials not believed they still had time to get American aid to keep the Thieu government in power. No one would have predicted that within 25 days the PRG flag would fly over the Presidential Palace.

The speed of the ARVN's disintegration was significant in shaping the Vietnamese immigration to the United States. It meant that Americans would not have time for thorough planning and control of an evacuation of the country. The refugees who were to come out of Vietnam were to come out of the panic of the last three weeks of the war, in which many Vietnamese picked up and left the country without thinking about whether the American or any other foreign government would receive them or what consequences would follow their leaving Vietnam.

Refugees and Vietnam

The years of warfare in Vietnam had resulted in thousands of refugees. The first Indochinese war, fought between the French and the Viet Minh, began the refugee movement. Vietnamese fled war zones to escape the death and destruction of living in the middle of a battlefield. Many people returned home to rebuild their villages after battles; others resettled permanently in urban areas where the war was remote. The French also forcibly created refugees by their *agroville* program under which Vietnamese were moved into villages where they could be isolated from guerillas.

With the Geneva Accords of 1954 came political refugees fleeing communism rather than war. About 1 million Vietnamese in 1954 moved from North to South Vietnam. They came from two groups which overlapped considerably: Catholics, and Vietnamese who were in some way closely associated with the French colonial presence. The overwhelmingly Catholic composition of 1954 refugees has been clearly documented.[4] The Catholic church of the 1950s was anti-Communist to the extreme; the Catholic church of Vietnam was even more so. Rumors spread to the effect that the Virgin Mary had gone south. Further, communism was equated by the church with the Antichrist; Vietnamese

Catholics, who had a long history of animosity with non-Catholic Vietnamese, feared for their lives as well as for their religious practices.[5] Catholics of peasant as well as bourgeois origins trekked southward. Whole villages from areas surrounding Hanoi moved south under the aegis of parish priests who doubled as village mayors and judges. Villages like Ho-Nai, located thirty kilometers from Saigon, were transplants from the Phat-Diem area of northern Vietnam. Villages like Phuoc-Tuy, forty kilometers from the port city of Vung-Tau, from which so many refugees left for the U.S. in 1975, were northern villages gone south with their parish priests. Many of these 1954 immigrants set forth for the United States in April 1975, operating under the same assumptions that had resulted in their flight in 1954, and were led, in many instances, again by their priests.

In addition to Catholics, many of the 1954 refugees were persons who served in the French colonial government in capacities ranging from soldiers, school principals, radio broadcasters and producers to assistants to the governor general. Business people, fearing expropriation of their property, also joined the refugees. These persons feared reprisals for their collaboration with the French. Many, but not all, were Catholic. Socioeconomic as well as political position impelled their flight. These people and their children also figured prominently in the 1975 flight of Vietnamese from their country. While the U.S. government issued no information about refugees' place of birth or that of their parents, or place of birth by occupations of refugees coming to this country, there is considerable evidence that these groups joined the 1975 Vietnamese refugees. Interview after interview I conducted with refugees at Indian Town Gap revealed that many individuals were born in northern Vietnam. Either they themselves or their fathers had been associated with the French presence as officials in government or as army personnel. Many were graduates of elite colonial schools.[6] The numbers who went to these schools in the 1920s and 1930s were quite small, never more than 900 for all Indochina (Laos and Cambodia included). Most who went came from wealthy families, which usually served in colonial government.

Many Vietnamese who came to the United States in 1975 represented an extension of the 1954 refugee movement within their country. In all the months I spent at Fort Indian Town Gap, Pennsylvania, in 1975, I scarcely heard Vietnamese spoken without the distinct intonation and pronunciation patterns of the north. Of the sixty or more refugees we interviewed at length, fewer than ten spoke with southern or central Vietnamese accents.

Although the 1975 immigration of Vietnamese to the United States was related to the earlier refugee movement from North to South Vietnam, much of it derived from the events of the twenty years between the 1954 Geneva Accords and the collapse of the Saigon government. The years of warfare within South Vietnam had created millions of refugees. Tens of thousands of Vietnamese had been caught up in war zones. Over the past twenty years they left their homes not because they were Catholics, anti-Communist, associated with foreigners, or upper class, but because the villages they lived in had become free-fire zones, battlefields, and/or razed to the ground by ARVN, United States, and National Liberation Front (NLF) rockets and mortars. They left home because they knew they would be killed or mutilated if they stayed there. Since the early 1960s South Vietnam's population had begun moving to the cities and to refugee camps ringing the cities to escape the war.[7] Saigon's population in 1961 was 300,000; by 1975 over 3 million lived in that city. Da-Nang, Nha-Trang, and Hue experienced similar growth. The cities became filled with people who had experienced the war. Those born in the city who had never seen the war learned of its horrors from them. When mortars began exploding near the cities, many people panicked and began fleeing from their homes, which they assumed would soon be in the middle of a battlefield. The panic increased as President Thieu, up to ten days before Saigon was under PRG control, vowed to defend his government, even in the streets of Saigon, if that became necessary. Many people left the city, going to Vung-Tau or islands off the South Vietnamese coast, intending to return home after

the presumed battle for Saigon was over. Many of these
people found themselves aboard U.S. ships and in Guam,
rather confused about where they were. Coming to the U.S.
was for them a reflex action similar to ones they had taken in
the past to leave the bombing and shelling of the Xuan-Loc,
Ban-Me-Thuot, or the Delta during battles.[8]

The fear of being caught up in the war was only one reason
for the panic-stricken flight to the United States. Many who
left Vietnam believed that the PRG would kill them if they
remained in Vietnam because of their roles in South Vietnam over the previous twenty years. Generals; high and
middle level military officers; government ministers; national policemen; employees of the United States Information
Agency (USIA), the CIA, American corporations and contractors, and the American Embassy; petty Vietnamese government officials—all these people feared for their lives as
well as for their property and social positions. Many, like the
infamous head of the National Police who is currently a
maitre d' at a restaurant in Alexandria, Virginia, had execut-
ed and tortured suspected Viet Cong members in public.
Some had been instrumental in Operation Phoenix, a
program of assassination of persons suspected of disloyalty
to the South Vietnamese government. They expected to be
shot for their past deeds. This expectation was heightened by
their belief that the Viet Cong had shot police and government officials in Hue during Tet in 1968.[9]

The rumors of a bloodbath should the PRG come to
power ran rife not only in the months preceding the fall of
the South Vietnamese government, but for the past twenty
years. American and South Vietnamese propaganda teams
for years had predicted bloodbaths should the Saigon government fall. These rumors were rampant in the last month
of the government's life and Vietnamese sought to leave the
country because they believed them.[10] American embassy
officials helped make the rumors credible. The embassy drew
up lists of people to be evacuated in case the government
should fall. It made it clear that if there were a change of
government people in mortal danger would be taken out of
the country. Embassy officials contacted these individuals

and urged them to join the American evacuation.[11]

Other rumors swept Vietnam, particularly Saigon, before the fall of the South Vietnamese government. It is difficult to gauge how seriously these rumors were taken by the people who fled, but some were cited by Vietnamese who resettled in the U.S. as motivating their decision to leave Vietnam. Paramount among these was one related by a 41-year-old Vietnamese high school teacher of English from Saigon who gave it as her reason for coming to the U.S.:

> I would not leave the country and my mother if they did not tell me the dirty stories about the communists. They said that they are going to give each single girl a huge sack containing a sick or handicapped communist soldier to take care of him, and to marry him, or if the men soldiers "need," the single girls have to give. The children born will belong to the government. I rather die than doing these things.[12]

This rumor was repeated by several refugees at Fort Indian Town Gap and was reported in Terzani's book depicting the fall of Saigon. The correctness of the rumor is irrelevant. No such thing occurred in Saigon or elsewhere after the NLF victory. For people who left Vietnam the rumor seemed as believable as the bloodbath which never materialized.

When Saigon fell many Vietnamese were prepared to leave the country. Their reasons were many, deriving from a Vietnamese rather than an American context. Most left out of fear, acting as refugees. They abandoned their homes not because they wanted to set up roots elsewhere, but because they believed that present circumstances would not allow them to live as they had. Many conceived of their move as temporary and believed that once the battles were over they would return home as they had done many times before.

Americans, the End of the War, and Planning for Refugees

The disintegration of the Vietnamese military was as great a surprise to the American government as to anyone else. It came at a time when the United States Senate had just turned

down a large military assistance request for the South
Vietnamese military. The U.S. was in the worst economic
recession since the 1930s. Unemployment soared, welfare
rolls swelled. Further, the American public was apathetic, if
not hostile, to anything that reminded it of the years of
American involvement in Vietnam. A Harris poll taken in
May 1975 showed that only 36 percent of all Americans
thought the country should admit Vietnamese, Cambodians, or Laotians; 54 percent thought they should be excluded
from the country.[13] Governors, congressmen, and senators
urged the federal government to proceed with caution in
admitting foreigners to the country. Some of their reasons
were blatantly racist. Burt Talcott, a Republican congress-
man from California, reflected this when he urged the
United States not to take refugees because, in his words,
"damn it, we have too many Orientals."[14] These pressures
combined to make President Ford and the Congress reluctant to intervene on behalf of the South Vietnamese government or to commit themselves to receiving large numbers of
refugees.

President Ford first indicated that the United States had a
plan for evacuating Vietnamese on 10 April, nineteen days
before Saigon was in PRG hands. This plan, if it existed,
was never made public. On 15 April Ford repeated his announcement of five days earlier. At this time the American
government still had not planned an evacuation: no one
had worked out how many Vietnamese the Americans would
help evacuate, how these Vietnamese would be selected,
whether all those whom Americans helped evacuate would
be allowed to enter the U.S., and what status those admitted
into the country would have. Further, the U.S. government
had made no provisions for receiving large numbers of
Vietnamese into the country.[15] This lack of planning was
clearest in the undersecretary of state's testimony to the U.S.
Senate's Judiciary Committee's Subcommittee on Refugees
and Escapees in April. Philip Habib of the U.S. State
Department appeared before the subcommittee on 15 April.
At that time he claimed the U.S. government would evacuate
only American citizens and their dependents (3,839 people)

and about 17,600 Vietnamese currently employed by the U.S. government. Habib made no commitments to take out of the country Vietnamese whom the Americans considered potential bloodbath victims. The formula under which Americans were operating at that time limited the evacuation to Vietnamese who were then American employees. It was only on 25 April 1975, four days before Saigon fell, that Americans agreed to help persons formerly employed by the U.S. government or persons whose lives the government considered endangered.[16]

Although officials in Washington did not provide for the influx of Vietnamese refugees, some people in the lower ranks of the State and Defense Departments did. Many Americans felt a deep commitment to Vietnamese with whom they had worked while on tours of duty in Vietnam. They believed the U.S. government had a moral obligation to persons who had supported U.S. policies and should save these individuals from the bloodbath Americans assumed would surely come with a PRG government. These lower-level State and Defense Department personnel developed plans for evacuating Vietnamese in advance of government activity.[17] Several flew to Saigon to escort key Vietnamese and their families out of the country to American bases in the Philippines and returned to Saigon to help speed up the reduction in strength that began on 19 April.

In Vietnam, persons working with the American embassy planned for the evacuation not only of American personnel and their dependents, but also of Vietnamese who wished to leave the country. While the American reduction in force began ten days before the fall of Saigon and the final evacuation about twenty-four hours before the fall of Saigon, plans for it were made in early April, instigated by the deputy ambassador without the consent or knowledge of the American ambassador, Graham Martin.[18] Had the deputy ambassador begun evacuating Saigon openly in early April, he no doubt would have been fired. On 12 April Graham Martin had Brigadier General Richard M. Baughn, the senior U.S. Air Force officer in Vietnam, relieved of his post for secretly arranging transportation out of the country for

Vietnamese employees of the defense attaché's office.[19] Until
Thieu resigned on 21 April, all plans for evacuation of
Vietnamese had to be clandestine. Under the deputy ambassador's direction, a group within the American embassy
began drawing up lists of individuals to be airlifted out of
Vietnam, arranged for bus transportation to Tan-Son-Nhut
Airport, selected assembly points for bus pickups, requisi-
tioned barges and tugs, c-rations, etc. Had it not been
for this sub-rosa planning in the U.S. and in Vietnam, the
number of people who eventually left Vietnam would have
been much smaller.[20] At the same time, because the planning
had so little official support, the evacuation became chaotic
and half of the refugees who ended up in the U.S. came due to
their own, rather than the U.S. government's, efforts. This
meant that those who came to this country were a slightly
different population than had been anticipated by American
officials. Further, because there was so little planning and
what there was was so secret, there were few controls over
who individual Americans would choose to help leave Vietnam. Guidelines for who was to be evacuated, other than
Americans and their relations, were perhaps clear only by 25
April, four days before all Americans left Vietnam. The
persons selected to board American planes were chosen by
Americans who filled out forms at the embassy. These
Americans set up their own guidelines for selecting evacuees,
and these guidelines varied greatly according to the individual Americans making decisions.

As of 15 April, according to Philip Habib of the State
Department, the American reduction in force was limited to
American citizens and their dependents and Vietnamese
currently employed by the U.S. The American government,
Habib told the Senate Judiciary Subcommittee on Refugees
and Escapees, had plans to provide a means of leaving
Vietnam only to these people and to alien dependents of the
U.S. (personnel of other nations' embassies and non-
Vietnamese foreign employees of American firms in Viet-
nam).[21] No decision had been made on whether the U.S.
would assume responsibility for the dependents of its Vietnamese employees or "high risk" individuals. By this time

1,630 children had been evacuated under Operation Babylift and about 220 Americans had left. By 25 April, 4,528 (out of 6,000) Americans and about 17,000 non-Americans (5,587 of whom had flown out on 24 April) had left Vietnam.[22]

Between 15 and 19 April the U.S. government had agreed, under the provisions of the Indochinese Refugee Act, to enable the attorney general to grant parole status to a maximum of 200,000 Vietnamese, Cambodians, and Laotians. This status meant that these individuals could enter the country if they met U.S. Immigration and Naturalization Service (INS) requirements (mainly in the areas of health and security), but that they were not eligible to become permanent residents, either alien or naturalized, of the country. The number of refugees that would be allowed to enter as parolees was lowered on 21 April to 129,000.[23]

The Indochinese Refugee Act set no guidelines on which individuals would be given priority in being granted parole status or being given transportation to the U.S. However, individuals working for the American embassy in Saigon were, as of 19 April, theoretically operating under a set of priorities as to which persons should receive aid in getting out of Vietnam. Priority was to be given to dependents of American citizens and their families and then to current Vietnamese employees of the U.S. government (the embassy, AID, Department of Defense, etc.) and their dependents. No decision was made until 28 April, the day before the U.S. left Saigon, on whether to evacuate Vietnamese who were former employees of Americans and served in sensitive positions or individuals whose lives were considered endangered under a new government.[24] Habib of the State Department had estimated on 15 April that current Vietnamese employees of the U.S. government and their dependents numbered 130,000 persons. Had the U.S. evacuated all its employees and their dependents, the quota would have been filled.

The guidelines issued around 15 April, limiting U.S. evacuation to U.S. employees and their dependents, were not adhered to—because of the individuals who made up the manifests of planes and barges leaving Vietnam. Many Americans processing Vietnamese and giving them permis-

sion to board American transports were persons who had
spent years in Vietnam and had developed personal ties with
Vietnamese, both those who had worked for the U.S. and
those who had not. Many, like J. C., a former military officer
who returned to Vietnam to help with the evacuation, felt
that Americans should assist any Vietnamese who wanted to
leave the country if they thought their lives or livelihoods
endangered. J. C. described his friends' and his own behavior
in dealing with Vietnamese requests to join the American
evacuation as follows:

> I would say that, for those of us that were controlling
> things [the processing of the evacuation], to the extent
> that we were . . . you had two basic types: you had the
> pure bureaucrat who wanted to do everything by the
> letter and then you had a little more humanitarian
> people who would try to get some insight into the
> person [applying for evacuation] and then help him to
> get out if he had a legitimate reason to go. . . . I think
> from the humanitarian side most people felt that there
> would be some kind of bloodbath once the Communists
> took over. And for that reason, I myself and a few of my
> friends were willing to help the most people out that we
> could.[25]

Such selection procedures led the Senate Judiciary Committee's Subcommittee on Refugees and Escapees to charge in its
9 June 1975 report:

> The record is clear that there has been little relationship
> between the categories of Vietnamese targeted for eva-
> cuation and parole into the U.S. and the refugees now
> under U.S. control.[26]

American officials processing Vietnamese on Guam in May
and June 1975 commented: "Half the Vietnamese we intended to get out did not get out—and half who did get out
should not have."[27] This happened partly because planning
was so poor. However, poor planning cannot by itself

explain the discrepancy between the Vietnamese who some Americans would have liked to have immigrated and those who actually did. Who would leave Vietnam and who would stay was in large part a decision made by Vietnamese, who made the choice according to their own imperatives and arranged their own way out of the country. This is apparent, considering how Vietnamese left their country. Wherever possible, I have used accounts of this flight by those who were part of it.

The Journey from Vietnam

The evacuation of Vietnam really began within the country, with the military offensive of mid-March and the ARVN defeats at Pleiku, Kontum, and Ban-Me-Thuot. About 1 million refugees poured out of these areas and headed for the Vietnamese coast. Most traveled on foot following the retreating Vietnamese army; fewer traveled by car, truck, or motor bike. The cities for which many were bound fell in rapid succession—Quang Ngai on 24 March, Hue on 25 March—or were threatened like Qui-Nhon. Because of the large military base at Da-Nang, it quickly became many refugees' destination. Many believed that Da-Nang would be defended, probably at a pass several kilometers north of the city. Da-Nang had received half a million refugees by 25 March.[28]

The first large-scale evacuation of Vietnamese by Americans took place in Da-Nang. The U.S. government chartered Air America and Bird Air to take ARVN, Vietnamese civilians, American officials and their dependents, and the employees of the American government and their dependents out of the city. This air evacuation lasted until 26 March, when the airport became chaotic as Vietnamese soldiers battled with civilians and with each other for places on the planes.

American plans for evacuating Vietnamese as well as Americans from Da-Nang were made quite early. A Vietnamese doctor, working for the British organization Save the Children and reputed to be related to the Vietnamese royal family, pointed out in her account of her departure from the city that the American embassy urged her to leave on 18 March, before it was clear that Da-Nang would not be defended by the Saigon government:

> I had been asked by the American General Consulate on the 18th of March to leave Da-Nang because all of the foreigners [had left]. I myself am Vietnamese. . . . I am in charge of one British mission over there [Save the Children]. Most of the team had to leave by the 18th of March and the American doctors of the Phan Hanh hospital had to leave too and the German hospital had to close their door too. But us, we are the only clinic operating in the refugee camps. You know, we are used to having refugees before and besides this time we don't feel that we are going to leave this place and particularly with the flow of refugees we thought that we had to stay until we had to leave. And by the 24th of March we were asked by the general consulate, the team, particularly the nurse and myself, had to go to [a] marine's house where we were more in security than in our own house which was more exposed to the shelling of rockets. . . . And on the 25th we get the order to move out of Da-Nang. But all of us decide to stay until we really were forced to leave and on the 27th the general consulate really gave us the order to leave the town because there were many communists among the refugees and it is not very safe for us to stay. And, besides that, the British wished later to retreat from Da-Nang center which was completely blocked by soldiers and dead people arriving from Chu-Lai and there was no way to drive back to the city.[29]

This individual did not stay long in Vietnam after leaving Da-Nang. Dr. D. caught a commercial flight from Saigon to Bangkok on 7 April and then proceeded on to Brussels.

Although Americans and Vietnamese began leaving Da-Nang in mid-March, it was not until 26 and 27 March that it became apparent that the city could not be defended against the advancing NLF and North Vietnamese. The South Vietnamese army had become totally disorganized. Individual soldiers panicked and tried to leave the city by any means possible. They fought civilians and each other for scarce seats on the Air America flights; they commandeered boats. On 26 March the American consul general of Da-Nang ordered Americans to leave the city and offered to evacuate by sea Vietnamese employees of American and foreign governments and businesses. He also agreed to take Vietnamese refugees selected by General Truong, the ARVN commander for the Da-Nang area, or by the mayor of Da-Nang. The Americans planned to load those chosen for evacuation onto barges which would then take them out to deep water to American and Vietnamese ships. An orderly evacuation proved impossible partly because the Vietnamese navy, which had promised ships and support, was in disarray, and partly because American ships did not coordinate their activities with the staff of the consul general.

At 4:00 a.m. on the 27th the evacuation began. At first it went as planned. Four to five thousand people were loaded onto a barge in front of the consul general's headquarters on Bach-Dang Street, while another ten thousand persons boarded three or four barges from a deep-water pier across the inland waterway from the consulate. From that point, however, nothing went smoothly. One of the eight Americans who took charge of the evacuation for the consul described subsequent events:

> We began shuttling them [the evacuees] to the Pioneer Contender which was sitting in deep water in the middle of the bay. The marine contingent left with us at that point. . . . What happened was the barges had filled up and the Pioneer Contender filled up and took off. It is still unknown to me [why] the Pioneer Contender did this. He left with a cargo of 600 people and his capacity was about 4,000. I don't know—and there was a lot of complaining about that with people saying odd things, but at any rate, he left with only 600.

So our international shipping was basically gone by the

time we got to the middle of the harbor and we had a couple of tugboats, the Tosi Maroo and also the Oceola, and a bunch of barges, but nowhere to take them. . . . The biggest problem that we ran into was that the barges we were coralling around were filling up by this time. There were probably about four or five of them [barges] of various sizes. [They] were all flat barges and we couldn't take them into the high seas, we couldn't drag them out or tow them out because we were afraid that we'd get into the high seas and we would just lose people over the sides.

The barges were left in the middle of the harbor for three days and four nights waiting for seagoing vessels. While they sat in the harbor, more people got on them. As the same American recalled:

The barges had filled up. The fishing boats—people would commandeer or—when I say people I mean [Vietnamese] . . . would commandeer fishing boats or any type of thing to get out into the harbor and to get on the barges. They would buy their way on—and there were, of course, a lot of fishing boats in Da-Nang. They would buy their way on, they would sneak their way on, they would just steal the boat or commandeer the boat with rifles or whatever and make their way to the barges and get on the barge. Or they would try to get on the tugboat Oceola. The only reason we didn't want any on the tugboat Oceola was that it was impossible with a cargo of refugees to work the tow lines. And we would have become totally invaluable [worthless] to anybody had we allowed the Oceola to become inundated with refugees. There are big heavy tow lines that go up and down the side of the tug and that was the reason that we attempted with some success, and not without the use of fire power, to keep people off the Oceola. No blood was shed, but a lot of shells were expended. The tugs and barges—the largest at this time probably had a capacity of about 6,000 and there were probably 8,500 people on it. There was so little space left so that all body functions, all body needs, took place where you were sitting. We finally put tow lines on these barges just to move them around so that some wind would get to these people, just the movement of the wind was a comfort.

The temperature in Da-Nang rose to about ninety degrees during the day. Those who planned the evacuation had assumed that boats would be waiting for the barges as they loaded up and reached the mouth of the harbor. No one had foreseen the need to provide more than a twenty-four-hour water supply for each barge, nor had anyone anticipated severe overcrowding on the barges. According to newspaper accounts people were on those barges for four nights and three days.* Overcrowding, the extreme heat, and the lack of water meant that most of the refugees were dehydrated by the time they were picked up by Lebanese and several Vietnamese boats on the fourth morning. The emptied barges stood as a testimony to the suffering of the past days and nights. One American described the sight:

> I myself witnessed, saw, and took pictures of one of the largest barges after it had been evacuated and I saw on the barge that had had a population of 8,000 or so, of what I could just see walking across it, no less than seventy-five [dead] bodies, mostly of children, of women, of children and small babies, and that sort of thing.[30]

The evacuation of Da-Nang illustrates poignantly how American planning was less than perfect, and how those whom the Americans ended up evacuating from Da-Nang included persons Americans had not intended to provide for.

---

*Tape 37, sides 1 and 2, V.I.C., contains a graphic description of the four nights and three days on the barges. For reasons unbeknownst to me, the individual who described the events on this tape refused to give me permission to include the tape transcript in this book. See the censored original draft, chapter 2, V.I.C., Box 10.

The barges in Da-Nang were overcrowded with South Vietnamese soldiers who had commandeered small craft and had boarded the barges at gunpoint. This pattern was to some degree repeated in the final evacuation of South Vietnam. Many of the boats that set out to sea from coastal Vung-Tau were filled with soldiers who had taken them at gunpoint.

On 28 March, Da-Nang was in PRG hands. Other coastal cities followed suit. By 7 April, almost half a million refugees from these cities and the northern provinces of South Vietnam crowded into Saigon and Vung-Tau. Arrangements for the evacuation of Saigon began on 15 April. At that time, the American embassy started taking U.S. citizens and their dependents, and Vietnamese employees of the American government and private corporations out of the country by air. The American embassy drew up lists of individuals to be evacuated, drew up their papers, and, until 27 April, when Tan-Son-Nhut Airport was bombarded and 500 people were killed waiting to board planes, loaded them on airplanes in an orderly fashion. The air evacuation lasted from 21 to 28 April. Between 24 and 28 April 5,000 to 6,000 persons per day left from Tan-Son-Nhut.[31]

The atmosphere in Saigon turned to panic as rockets began falling sporadically inside the city. The American embassy was surrounded by thousands of Vietnamese begging for transportation out of the country. On 29 April the shelling increased. Word spread that the Americans were leaving and the Viet Cong would soon be there. Whatever plans Americans had to bring Vietnamese out of the country became unworkable. Once Tan-Son-Nhut Airport closed, the only way to get out of the country was by helicopter or boat. On the twenty-ninth the embassy did arrange for barge transportation down the Saigon River for 16,000 persons. The chaos in Saigon, however, made this plan less than a full success. One of the Americans who was in charge of the barge evacuation explained why only 6,000 out of 16,000 persons for whom space was available managed to board the barges:

I told 500 people at Doan Thi Diem at the deputy ambassador's house to make it [to the Khanh Hoi docks] by either hook or crook or any way they could, because there weren't any buses coming and there weren't any planes leaving, and if you wanted to leave you could go with us on the boats. So a number of them did make it. . . .*

We loaded the barges, there was no roll call or anything like that, it's just that if you wanted to go, you just got on. There was plenty of room. . . . These barges were much different from the ones at Da-Nang. These were the ones that were the ones that were carrying ammo up to Phnom Penh and they were sand bagged on the side so that they offered sufficient security we thought for going down the river at least on barges. . . .

And I went back and I checked the dock and there was some looting of American cars going on that had been left and all that sort of thing. But there was nobody left on the dock of any—the barges were sitting there half empty, there was no attempt to keep anyone off and there was no attempt for anyone to get on. And I came back and I can remember my exact words to him [the tugboat captain]: "The only people I can see on the dock at this moment are cowboys and cops." There were a lot of cops. And they didn't seem too prone to leave. You've got to remember at this point that a lot of people, including a lot of Americans probably didn't think the last day had come yet. And I was surprised. I had thought that we could get down to Nga Bay and drop a group off and then come back to Saigon and pick up another group. I was told by the embassy at that point

---

*I was denied permission to include in this book the part of the tape which discusses why a number of Vietnamese did not make it to the barges. For a full explanation, see tape 37, side 2, V.I.C. See also V.I.C., Box 10, for the original draft of chap. 2, the censored manuscript, and the letter from the individual denying permission to use information he supplied on the tape.

that . . . I don't remember the time exactly, that
this was a one-way trip, that you weren't coming back
and it was only at that time that I really realized this
was it.[32]

In all, between 21 and 29 April Americans managed to
provide the means for about 65,000 Vietnamese to leave the
country by air and by boat.[33] Much of this, except in the case
of the sea evacuation of Da-Nang, went with a minimum of
physical hardship and duress for those who left this way.
Most of these refugees left by air, flying from Saigon to
American bases either at Clark Airfield in the Philippines or
at Subic Bay. They were then taken, again by air, to the
refugee holding center at Guam. Many paid dearly to leave
Vietnam; some paid more than $2,000 (U.S. currency) to
obtain papers giving them permission to join the American
evacuation. Sen. Edward Kennedy charged that there was
"considerable corruption in the decision as to who is going
to leave and who is not."[34]

The American government provided transportation for
only half of all Vietnamese refugees. The rest arranged their
own transportation. Vietnamese air force pilots took their
planes, loaded them with friends, family, and often people
whom they charged more than $10,000 (U.S. currency) per
person, and flew them to U.S. bases in Thailand.[35] South
Vietnamese navy ships at sea headed for Subic Bay. Many of
those on them had no idea they were becoming refugees since
officers, rather than sailors, made the decision to sail away
from Vietnam. Vessels of the Vietnamese navy stationed in or
about the Saigon area evacuated families of crew members
and friends, sometimes for a price. N. T. D., originally from
the Hanoi area and a former professor of English at universities in the Saigon area, arranged for his own and his father's
and brothers' transportation out of Saigon. They left on a
Vietnamese naval vessel on 30 April, the day the PRG flag
went atop the Presidential Palace. N. T. D.'s story, like that
of many other Vietnamese, reveals how the ability to leave
depended on Vietnamese connections and sheer luck. He
happened to have a girl friend who had a brother who had a

friend who knew of a way out of Saigon. Here is N. T. D.'s account of how he left Saigon:

> It is very sad for me to talk about that [the departure] because the situation in Vietnam, it changes so quickly that we do not have any time to prepare our departure. Even now I still have my mother and six sisters of mine remain in South Vietnam, you know. And, you know, it is on April 30 and it is about ten o'clock in the morning and Saigon has been overrun by the Communists and since there is no plane . . . there is no boat, we really think that there is no way to go to the United States any more. It is too late. And, as I have told you before, I was a university teacher in South Vietnam and I have a student of mine. . . . She is a girl. And it seems to me that she is a little fond of me, she loves me a bit . . . and she would like to bring me to the United States. But, of course, I refuse to go to the United States in case I do not manage to bring along all members of my family. So she wanted to bring all the members of my family to the United States.
>
> She has two brothers. Her first brother is a pilot and the second brother . . . he is working for the American Embassy in South Vietnam. Her first brother, the pilot, he has a friend, and his friend is an officer in the Vietnamese navy. And this officer in the Vietnamese navy, he has the last boat and he still remains in Nha-Bay. This is a small district which is rather far from Saigon. And this man . . . would like to stay in Nha-Bay in order to wait for his father and mother, and this student of mine, she's a girl, and she has a brother. And this brother knows the officer in the navy and he can manage to bring along the members of the family to this place, to his naval base, and we wish to ask the men to bring us to the Pacific Ocean because there is an American boat which is waiting for the Vietnamese refugees in the Pacific Ocean. But when I brought my family along to his house . . . he doesn't want to bring along my mother and my sisters, maybe because we are

too numerous, our family is a little large. . . . We are
twelve peoples.

And already the daughter, the girl . . . of the house, she
fall in love with me, but the man doesn't know me, you
see. So he doesn't want to bring my family along. He
would like to do his best to escape by himself. And . . .
because the situation is very dangerous, there is much
shooting and many men die. . . . And, so he would like to
go as fast as possible. But he doesn't want to bring along
my [family] members and so he should like to go alone.
And so he tries to keep, to run away, and we have only
two Hondas . . . the Honda bicycles, not the Honda cars,
the Honda bicycles. And my mother is very afraid that in
case we cannot all go together . . . it will be big trouble
for the man who stayed in South Vietnam because my
father he is a South Vietnamese governmental official,
my oldest brother he is a captain and he is the chief of a
battalion, and I am a teacher. . . . There is no big thing to
be finished, to be killed. But because I was a university
teacher and because the major field that I taught was
English, and just because I taught English it might be a
little dangerous and so I need to go. And my second
brother . . . was a lieutenant and he was in the air force.
And this man, the younger brother of mine, the young-
est, he was working in a directorate of taxation. And he
was a government official too, you see. And so in case we
would like to stay in South Vietnam, it would be a
danger. And there is no way for us to go together, all the
members of my family. So my mother she hurries us to
go, she pushes us to go, because in case the other guys,
they run away. And if we are in delay we do not know
where to go. So my mother told my father: "Please go
and bring along your sons. In case we cannot go, we may
stay because we are women. So you have not to worry
about us, please go at first." And, you know, just
because I did not have any time to think about how I
love my mother and I am like a blind man, you see, so I
went away along with this man. I have my father and

three other brothers with me because we have only two Hondas. The maximum of the number of people we can bring along is five. And so I still have my mother and six sisters remain in South Vietnam. And my sister-in-law she is pregnant eight months and she cannot go along with us. It is very sad to see.

And, after, you know, eight days on the boat we came to the Philippine Islands and Subic Bay. I wish I can die because I am so sad and so responsible for the loss of my mother and my sisters.[36]

N. T. D., his brothers, and his father left in a panic. They acted in blind fear and left behind half the family. They were typical of many who arranged transportation on their own. What makes N. T. D.'s tale unusual was his good fortune in being able to locate a fully provisioned boat that could take him and members of his family to Subic Bay. Most Vietnamese were not as lucky. Many Vietnamese, like B. T., formerly minister of primary education in the South Vietnamese government, could not find naval transport or obtain American aid in leaving the country. Instead, he purchased his way on to a small boat that took him and members of his family down the Saigon River to the ocean. He, his family, and the people on that boat lived through an experience more like that experienced by those on the Da-Nang barges than like N. T. D.'s comfortable ride on a seagoing vessel. Here is B. T.'s story:

I escaped from Saigon in April, it was exactly the twenty-ninth, the twenty-ninth at night when Saigon fell. We call this in French the twenty-five hours. Very difficult to escape from Saigon. So many people, very very numerous. They are fighting there to have a place in the aircraft. So many aircraft, many helicopters land on the street of Saigon in many places to save the life of man, to save life of human being. But very very critical situation. And too many people so that it is very very difficult to reach up there. And in this time heavy

mortars [were] sent in by the Communists. So many
men, many men die. And myself, I feel that it is very
difficult to reach the airplane, I must go up the long
river and I reach a boat, a small boat. And there are many
people who try to take the boats and run. And it is very
difficult. So myself I can go to this boat, my wife and one
of my child [sic] and my sister go with me. She lost her
child. She has only one child, her son who is fifteen
years old. She lost her son because he didn't get to reach
the boat. . . . [After being on the boat for a while] we try
to count members of our families and we find out we lost
one man, one sister, one children, or one nephew. That
is very normal because it is a big problem to be saved.
And on the ocean many people die of thirst or hunger.
First children, boys, small boys first, and . . . we were
very numerous. So we lost many people [on the boat]. If
you had luggage, you put it in the ocean [to stay afloat].
I escaped by boat and we were aboard seven days and six
nights on the ocean like that and [there was] no wind.
We died ourselves. [After seven days] we change our boat
and big boat bring us to Guam.[37]

B. T. quite consciously chose to come to the United States
and despite the hardships he lived through he had few
regrets. Other refugees unintentionally left their country.
T. V. C., a former South Vietnamese government official, a
Catholic, and a native of North Vietnam, was one such
refugee. He had not planned to leave his country when he
did, as the following excerpt from an interview with him on
25 September 1975 indicates.

On the twenty-ninth of April, as the Communist offensive was nearing Saigon, my brothers and I boarded a
Vietnamese naval vessel—things were very chaotic.
When we boarded the ship we didn't think of coming to
the U.S. We thought we were going to Con-Son Island.
The naval officer told us that we would regroup there in
order to return to Saigon and back up the failing Americans.[38]

This individual would no doubt have chosen to leave Vietnam had he realized that the end of the Saigon government had indeed come. Others perhaps would not have made such a choice. Over 1,500 Vietnamese who found themselves in the U.S. demanded to return home in August 1975 and did so. Most of these returnees were rank and file members of the Vietnamese navy and air force who had not made a conscious choice to leave Vietnam and ended up in the U.S. because they happened to be on ships at sea or planes at the time of the PRG victory.[39] Other persons, not in the Vietnamese military, gave American officials "the impression of not understanding where they were or why they were there. Some simply fled in panic from conflict and violence as Vietnamese have for years."[40]

Leaving Vietnam and How It Affected Who Came to the U.S.

The rapid disintegration of the Vietnamese army; the panic that seized the population of South Vietnam, many of whom were already refugees either from North Vietnam or from the war; and American hesitancy in planning and executing the evacuation of Vietnamese civilians all affected which Vietnamese would come to the U.S. The U.S. government committed itself to helping evacuate only American citizens and their dependents and Vietnamese who worked for Americans. These people, who constituted much of what American officials came to call the "first wave" of refugees, were individuals who were relatively well prepared to live in the United States. Those who were dependents of Americans had someone to care for them upon their arrival in America, and they would not become a burden to the government. The "second wave" consisted of employees of the U.S. government and firms. They also were persons that the American government believed would cause few problems. Vietnamese employed by Americans spoke English well, were relatively well educated, had skills presumed marketable in the American economy, and were, for the most part, urbanized and westernized. As one report stated, "some INS officials believe that these early groups were better prepared for life in the

U.S. than either the Hungarian or Cuban refugees."[41]

Not all Vietnamese who were invited to evacuate actually left Vietnam. The chaos and press of events was such that many simply refused to believe the end of the war was at hand and made no effort to leave, or tried to leave but could not make it through the crowds in the streets of Saigon to the assembly points, or were restrained by Vietnamese police at the docks for money they may not have had on hand.

The "third wave" of refugees were persons who left Vietnam on their own and were not persons the American government would have chosen to evacuate. They made up the majority of those who came to the U.S. They were lower-level Vietnamese government officials, teachers, rank and file members of the Vietnamese army and navy, petty traders, farmers and fishermen. They were not necessarily urban, had few skills that were usable in the United States, spoke little or no English, and were totally unacquainted with life outside their parishes or villages in Vietnam. Many in this "third wave" of refugees owned the small crafts that took wealthier Vietnamese out to sea. Among them also were the individuals who had commandeered boats and aircraft. This "third wave" consisted of persons many American officials believed "should have not gotten out" but did. They did because it was impossible for Americans to control precisely who would leave Vietnam.

About 130,000 Vietnamese entered United States territory by mid-May. These 130,000 were not the sum total of people who left Vietnam then and after the PRG gained control of the country. As of July 1975 over 60,000 Vietnamese were in refugee camps in Hong Kong and Thailand and were requesting permission to enter the United States. This was denied until fall 1975 when 10,000 additional individuals were admitted if they were members of the immediate families of refugees already in the United States or were American citizens. In spring 1976 an additional 11,000 refugees were granted parole status to come to the U.S. Most of these persons were Laotian, confined until then in Thai camps. The U.S., in short, had set a limit on the number of Vietnamese to be allowed in the country in April 1975. The 130,000 that came were, on the whole, a group not anticipated by American officials. Because of the Vietnamese population that immigrated, the U.S. government established a set of resettlement policies that were to some extent specific to Vietnamese refugees arriving in the midst of a recession.

Chapter Three

Who Immigrated: A Profile

The preceding chapter argued that because of Vietnamese history and the circumstances underlying the collapse of the South Vietnamese government, the Vietnamese who came to the United States represented a different population than the American government had anticipated. To substantiate this point, I will describe the immigrant population as a whole: its age, sex, family, educational, and occupational characteristics. The nature of the immigrant population in large part explains why the American government set up a series of holding centers on American soil, made sponsorship by Americans a condition for Vietnamese being granted permission to enter the United States, and adopted a resettlement policy that entailed dispersion of Vietnamese throughout the country.

There are many ways one might go about describing a group of people, depending on what one wants to know about them. When I first entered the refugee camps, I was anxious to find out which Vietnamese had left their country. Did these people represent a continuation of 1954 refugee patterns? Were they from northern Vietnam? Were they Catholics? Were most of them government employees who began their careers serving the French and then took employment with the South Vietnamese government or with the Americans? To what extent were they part of a substantially

new refugee movement in Vietnam? Were they merely
members of the cliques that had ruled South Vietnam over
the past twenty years? Were they part of the southern
landowning gentry that emerged in South Vietnam under
colonialism and became versed in western culture and
western ways, and so not northerners at all? If they were not
from these groups, were they people who had been part of the
South Vietnamese and American war effort? Were they
members of the national police, the Vietnamese special
forces, the people involved in the various rural pacification
programs to "win the hearts and minds" of the Vietnamese
people as many Americans thought they were? Perhaps the
immigrants were not any of these, but rather represented a
cross section of Vietnamese society which for a variety of
reasons ended up in the United States. Certainly the American government led the public to believe the immigrants
were representative of Vietnamese society and were persons
who were "voting with their feet" against communism.
Many public relations officials at the refugee centers harped
on how many poor fishermen and peasants had entered the
U.S. looking for freedom and democracy.

These questions concerning the composition of the Vietnamese population entering the United States are answer-
able only insofar as information was collected about people's pasts—their places of birth, their parents' places of birth,
educational institutions attended, employment histories,
jobs performed, religion, where they had lived in Vietnam,
etc.—and was made available. Some of this information was
collected by the INS. From MCBCP-3305/4 (5-75), known as
the ADP ID card, INS collected such data and fed it into a
computer. The form, which INS officials filled out for every
Vietnamese in United States holding centers abroad and on
the American mainland, asked about family size, last place of
residence in Vietnam, job skills, religion, whether the immigrants had been civil servants or worked with the Vietnamese military, whether they were employees of American
government agencies or private corporations, where they
were born, where they wished to resettle in the U.S., how
much money they had, if they had friends or relatives in the

U.S., etc. The form also recorded the results of medical examinations and resettlement efforts.[1]

Although data were collected by INS and the Interagency Task Force (IATF) on Indochinese Refugees, not all of them became public information. Government reports describe Vietnamese only in terms that would be useful in setting immigration policy or providing for immigrants' future welfare. Thus, descriptions of the immigrant population as a whole are limited to information about family size, age, sex, religion, job skill classifications relevant to the American economy, educational levels, English language abilities, and place of resettlement. Information pertaining to individuals' pasts—their former employers, birth places, last residences in Vietnam, etc.—were buried in government files. Given American right-to-privacy laws, they will remain there unless the U.S. government chooses to produce aggregate statistics on them.[2]

Because of the type of information gathered and released by American officials, many of the questions raised earlier about the composition of the immigration are difficult to answer definitively. On the other hand, it is possible to provide a portrait of the immigrants that will in part explain what elements of Vietnamese society came to the United States.

Profiles of Vietnamese Immigrants

Vietnamese who came to the United States tend to be young, part of a family group, and Catholic. The age and sex composition of the immigrant population is reported in table 1; household characteristics are depicted in table 2. Table 1 indicates that 45.9 percent of all immigrants were under the age of 18 and, therefore, likely to be dependents of a family. (There were 729 unaccompanied children in the immigration.) Another 35.6 percent were between ages 18 and 34, roughly the ages of military service. It is among these age groups that the disparity between the numbers of men versus women becomes greatest. Among 18- to 24-year-olds about 4,000 more men than women came to the United States; among 25- to 34-year-olds about the same disparity exists.

The difference between the number of men and women narrows down in the 35- to 44-year-old age groups, almost evens out among 45- to 62-year-olds, and, among those over 63, the number of women far surpasses the number of men.

Table 1 tells us much about who immigrated. As was pointed out above, it shows that many more men than women left Vietnam and that the predominance of men was strongest in the age groups affected by military service. Probably many men in this age range came to the United States alone. Of all the people in this age range, only 3,316 are women. Many of the 13,502 men are former Vietnamese military, both officers and rank and file. These were individuals who were most in a position to leave Vietnam without American assistance. Many had access to transportation out of the country (planes or boats) or were armed and could commandeer transportation. About 10,674 refugees were members of the Vietnamese armed forces, not including the national police. Of these, 6,047 were officers; 4,627 were enlisted men.[3]

The statistics in table 1 indicate that Vietnamese came to the United States in family groups; table 2 substantiates this. Table 2 describes immigrant household size. Household size, as reported in the table, is not synonymous with family size, even though it can be taken as an approximation of immigrant family size. If we interpret the table as roughly indicating family size, we see that Vietnamese immigrated in family groups. Only 16,819 out of 124,493 refugees came without family members. Vietnamese households, according to the table, range in size from 2 persons to somewhere over 17. One household processed at Fort Chaffee numbered 100 persons or more. What tables 1 and 2 do not indicate is the extent to which Vietnamese immigrated as households consisting of large extended families. INS officials defined a household as a nuclear family spanning, in the main, two generations— mother, father, and children. Vietnamese would make no such definition. Vietnamese, both urban and rural, rich and poor, Catholic and non-Catholic, lived in households composed of many nuclear families. Even in middle-class Saigon

Table 1

Age and Sex of Indochinese Immigrants

(Sample size, 123,301) Data Correlated as of December 15, 1975

Age	Male		Female		Total	
	Number	Percent	Number	Percent	Number	Percent
0-5	10,572	8.6	9,817	8.0	20,389	16.6
6-11	9,704	7.9	8,611	7.0	18,315	14.9
12-17	9,519	7.7	8,296	6.7	17,815	14.4
18-24	13,591	11.0	9,105	7.4	22,696	18.6
25-34	12,063	9.8	8,821	7.2	20,884	17.0
35-44	6,364	5.1	5,068	4.1	11,432	9.2
45-62	4,706	3.8	4,569	3.7	9,275	7.5
63+	980	.8	1,515	1.2	2,495	2.0
Total	67,499	54.7	55,802	45.3	123,301	100.0

Source: Interagency Task Force for Indochina Refugees, Report to the Congress, 15 December 1975 (litho), p. 11. (Available also at V. I. C., Box 2.)

neighborhoods there were households consisting of grand-parents, their sons and sons' wives and children, their single daughters, their grandsons and wives and their children. In collecting statistics on household size, the INS placed into this category groups that fit the American definition of household limited to a nuclear family unless it meant leaving an individual over 18 or minors outside a household unit. Thus, INS counted an adult with spouse, regardless of age, a household. If Vietnamese had come to the United States with married children over 18, these children were considered separate households. Minors who might be cousins, nieces, or nephews of a family so defined were considered part of their aunts' or uncles' household only if their parents or a sibling over 18 did not accompany them. Thus, INS considered a household in some cases a 60-year-

Table 2

Immigrant Household Size by Sex of Head of Household

Household Size	Male Head of Household				Female Head of Household			
	Number of Households	% of Households	Number of People	% of People	Number of Households	% of Households	Number of People	% of People
1	13,502	35.68	13,502	10.85	3,317	8.77	3,317	2.66
2	3,174	8.39	6,348	5.10	1,350	3.57	2,700	2.17
3	2,172	5.74	6,516	5.23	994	2.63	2,982	2.40
4	2,173	5.74	8,692	6.98	779	2.06	3,116	2.50
5	1,892	4.99	9,460	7.60	645	1.70	3,225	2.59
6	1,681	4.44	10,086	8.10	504	1.33	3,024	2.43
7	1,323	3.50	9,261	7.44	340	.89	2,380	1.91
8	1,127	2.98	9,016	7.24	230	.61	1,840	1.48
9	786	2.08	7,074	5.68	174	.46	1,566	1.26
10	551	1.46	5,510	4.43	69	.18	690	.55
	28,381	75.00	85,465	68.65	8,402	22.20	24,840	19.95
Over 10	905	2.39	12,102*	9.72	156	.41	2,086*	1.68
Total	29,286	77.39	97,567	78.37	8,558	22.61	26,926	21.63

Source: HEW Refugee Task Force, Report to the Congress (litho), 15 June 1976, pp. 27, 28.

*Calculated figure based on an average of 13.3722 persons in a household of over 10 persons by the HEW Refugee Task Force.

old woman and her 17-year-old daughter, regardless of whether the woman had come to the U.S. with her 6 adult sons, their spouses, and her grandchildren. Households reported in the statistics (and also resettled as families) often consisted of two male cousins over 18, a child under 18 and his 20-year-old sister or brother, etc. All this means that table 2, which presents household size statistics as INS defined household and collected data on it, underestimates the extent to which Vietnamese immigrated as large extended families.[4] In this respect the immigrants were typical of Vietnamese whose major social, economic, and political ties resided in the family, not in other institutions. Less typical of Vietnamese, however, is the extent to which households that immigrated were headed by women. About 22.61 percent of all households had female heads while 77.39 percent had male heads.

Despite the underestimate of household and therefore family size in table 2, the table still indicates that Vietnamese households are substantially larger than American households. Over 27 percent of all households contained more

Table **2** — Continued

Household Size	All Households			
	Number of Households	% of Households	Number of People	% of People
1	16,819	44.45	16,819	13.51
2	4,524	11.96	9,048	7.27
3	3,166	8.37	9,498	7.63
4	2,952	7.80	11,808	9.48
5	2,537	6.69	12,685	10.19
6	2,185	5.77	13,110	10.53
7	1,663	4.39	11,641	9.35
8	1,357	3.59	10,856	8.72
9	960	2.54	8,640	6.94
10	620	1.64	6,200	4.98
	36,783	97.20	110,305	88.60
Over 10	1,061	2.80	14,188	11.40
Total	37,844	100.00	124,493	100.00

than five persons. Households over five persons, however, accounted for roughly 62 percent of all immigrants. Average household size computed from table 2 is 3.3 persons. However, if one were to deduct one-person households from such a computation, average household size emerges at 5.1 persons as against 3.1 for American households.

Although Vietnamese households that immigrated seem large by American standards, they are small by Vietnamese standards. Vietnamese families, even when defined only in terms of mother, father, and their children, had at least eight persons. Six children per nuclear family was the rule rather than the exception. Immigrant families, however, tended to have about four children.[5] This smaller family size reflects to some extent the conditions under which many people left Vietnam. Those who left the country on their own often left children. Many children died en route to the U.S. in small crafts that put out to sea. What is amazing about the statistics in table 2 is that so many families did manage to come to the U.S. bringing many members of their extended families with them.

Those who came to the United States alone are, to some extent, persons who have abandoned Vietnamese traditional concepts of the family. These people left on their own without making provisions for relatives. This break with the extended family tradition is evident not only among the single immigrants, it also exists among those who came in groups defined as families. Mr. D., whose story of his departure from Vietnam was recounted in the last chapter, came to the U.S. with only four members of his family, leaving behind his sisters and mother. Mrs. A., a former secretary in the U.S. embassy, left home with only her young daughter and had few regrets about so doing. Mr. Q., a Vietnamese government official, fluent in both French and English, brought only his two younger brothers; an elderly woman from the Mekong Delta brought only her daughter and granddaughter, etc.[6] Most of these individuals were part of Vietnamese urban life. One American official estimated that over two-thirds of the immigrants were from the cities.[7] In urban areas, factors such as the war and westernization had weakened family ties to some extent so that leaving home without all family members became possible.

Some of the families who came to the United States did not abandon Vietnamese family traditions and did travel to this country in extended familes. This is the case with the Vietnamese families of seventeen persons or more, which numbered at least sixty-two.[8] These families tended to be from rural areas or were recent immigrants to Vietnamese cities. One family that I saw at Fort Indian Town Gap numbered over thirty persons. The women were unusual in that they wore the black peasant dress (*ao ba-ba*). Their teeth were darkened from lacquering. No one in the family spoke English; most were illiterate. When I saw them the first time, a caseworker from the U.S. Catholic Conference, one of the agencies responsible for resettling immigrants in the U.S., was trying to photograph them in groups of three or four for the purpose of finding them sponsors as households of that size. The attempt was unsuccessful since the family refused to come out of their barracks until they were assured that only one picture would be taken and it would include all the members of the family. There were other families like this in the resettlement camps. They all were from rural, rather than from urban, areas and tended to be farmers or fisher people. They were, as the household size statistics indicate in table 2, exceptional. Table 4, which describes occupational classifications of the immigrants and which is discussed later in this chapter, also shows how unusual these people were.

The size of Vietnamese families probably has little to do with religious beliefs or practices, despite the fact that over 40 percent of all refugees are Catholic.[9] Family planning was virtually nonexistent in Vietnam where disseminating birth control information, much less birth control devices, was a crime.[10] Even though Catholicism was not a major variable predicting Vietnamese family size, it should be pointed out that the immigrants are more heavily Catholic than a cross section of Vietnamese society would be. Catholics comprise less than 10 percent of the South Vietnamese population, compared to 40 percent of those who immigrated to the U.S. It is hard to estimate how many of these people, particularly the Catholics, were remnants of the 1954 refugee movement from North to South Vietnam. The public affairs officer at Fort Indian Town Gap claimed that most of the residents of that camp came from families that were part of the 1954 refugee movement or had been refugees in 1954.[11] My own impression, based on the people interviewed at Indian Town Gap in fall 1975, is that most were. Over three-quarters of the Vietnamese who agreed to be interviewed were Catholic and were born in North Vietnam. Judging from the camps, the immigration seemed more heavily Catholic than the statistics collected by the IATF and the INS indicate.

If those who came to the U.S. were unlike Vietnam's overall population in terms of religion, they were even more atypical when it came to education. Table 3 provides a breakdown of educational levels for heads of households and for immigrants over age eighteen. Table 3 indicates that over 27.4 percent of all heads of households (or 19.5 percent of all immigrants over eighteen years of age) had some university education or more. Another 47.8 percent of heads of households (or 37.9 percent of immigrants over eighteen) had some secondary education. Only 18.0 percent of heads of households (or 20 percent of immigrants over eighteen) had less than secondary schooling. The disparity between the educational levels of heads of households and all immigrants over eighteen is due to several factors. First, women as a whole had less educational opportunity in Vietnam than men. This shows up in the statistics since women were only 22 percent of heads of households. Second, the statistics include the older generation of Vietnamese, those forty-five years old and above (about 9.5 percent of all immigrants). These persons were educated before the French left Vietnam when less than 10 percent of the school-aged population entered school.[12] The older generation was less well educated than those who went to school after 1954 when educational opportunities expanded appreciably. Third, the category of immigrants over eighteen includes those still going to school who are not heads of households. Many in the eighteen to twenty-four age group had been students at the time they came to the U.S.

Table 3
Educational Levels of Immigrants

	Heads of Household Only		All Immigrants 18 Years of Age or Older	
	Number	Percent	Number	Percent
None	407	1.3	1,384	2.1
Some Elementary	5,120	16.7	11,979	17.9
Some Secondary	14,632	47.8	25,432	37.9
Some University	7,004	22.9	11,150	16.6
Post-graduate	1,375	4.5	1,955	2.9
No Information	2,090	6.8	15,133	22.6
Total	30,628	100.0	67,033	100.0

Source: Interagency Task Force for Indochina Refugees, Report to the Congress, 15 December 1975 (litho), p. 12. (Available also at V. I. C., Box 2.)

Table 3 probably contains some distortions. It reports educational levels according to whether individuals *entered* primary, secondary, or higher education; it does not indicate whether individuals *completed* primary, secondary, or higher education. Because this distinction was not made by INS, the table in many cases may report educational levels higher than immigrants actually possess. Some of the reporting in table 3 may tend to inflate educational backgrounds; yet it may also tend in some cases to deflate educational levels. Table 3 assumes Vietnamese and American educational levels are equivalent. To some extent, part of the South Vietnamese school system, especially after 1964, was equivalent to American school organization. American advisors and AID reformed the public schools to the American primary-secondary school pattern.[13] However, less than half of Vietnamese children who went to school attended public schools. Private schools grew much faster than public schools after 1954 and many of these private schools, such as Marie Curie, the Lycée of Dalat, and Lycée Jean Jacques Rousseau, were modeled on French institutions. In many cases they were attached to the French cultural mission in Vietnam and were French schools.[14] Finishing *lycée* in the school system of Vietnam was equivalent to finishing American junior college, not American high school. Despite the distortions that table 3 probably contains, the table does describe the approximate educational levels of immigrants and can serve as a basis for comparing their educational levels with those of South Vietnam's population as a whole. This will provide some indication of how typical immigrants are of South Vietnamese society.

The immigrants, as table 3 points out, are relatively well educated, even by American standards. Vietnamese heads of households look not too terribly different educationally from American heads of households. While educational levels of immigrants look "average" by American standards, when these levels are compared to the educational levels of all South Vietnamese, the immigrants emerge as an educated elite. Some statistics on education in South Vietnam over the past decades will show this to be the case.

In 1954/55, the years in which the twenty-seven to thirty-two-year-old immigrants went to primary school, less than 16 percent of all children ages six to eleven went to primary school in South Vietnam. In the same year, only 3 percent of twelve- to eighteen-year-olds were in secondary school (these are the years in which the thirty-three- to thirty-eight-year-old immigrants went to secondary school) and less than 1 percent of nineteen- to twenty-year-olds (the thirty-nine- to forty-two-year-old immigrants of 1975) were attending institutions of higher education. By 1965/66 educational opportunity in South Vietnam had expanded appreciably. In that year 64 percent of children aged six to eleven were in primary school (this is the age cohort of 1975 immigrants aged seventeen to twenty-two); 16 percent of those twelve to eighteen years old were in secondary school (the age cohort of immigrants twenty-three to twenty-seven years old in 1975); and still less than 1 percent went to university.[15] These figures, although they do not aggregate the educational levels of all Vietnamese over eighteen years of age, do show how highly educated the population who came to the United States is. Of the immigrants educated while the French ruled Vietnam and 90 percent of the population went unschooled, about 98 percent of immigrants received some primary education and over 37 percent had some secondary education while 19.5 percent entered university. Even by 1970 standards for Vietnam, these people are extremely well educated. By 1970 less than 2.5 percent of nineteen to twenty-one-year-olds entered university.

The educational levels of immigrants indicate that they are not only highly educated but also that they tend to be urban and from relatively well-to-do families. Schools in both colonial and postindependent South Vietnam were concentrated in urban areas—in cities like Saigon, Cho-Lon, Dalat, Da-Nang, and Hue—and in provincial capitals like Can-Tho and Quang-Tri city. Access to education depended on living in these areas or on rural families having sufficient funds to board their children in the cities where there were schools. Living in or moving to the cities was not the only prerequisite to attending school. Equally important was family income, for after 1954 school expansion was most rapid in the private rather than public sector so that by the mid-1960s only 40 percent of Vietnamese children attending school were in public institutions while 60 percent were in private tuition-charging schools. Going to school meant being relatively affluent. The number of immigrants who went to French-language private schools in Vietnam is unclear. The IATF and the INS never inquired what schools individuals attended; they merely wanted data on the quantity of schooling an individual possessed. An appreciable number of Vietnamese I interviewed at Fort Indian Town Gap had gone to private French-language schools: the Lycée of Dalat, Lycée Jean Jacques Rousseau, Ecoles des Jeunes Filles of Saigon, Lycée Marie Curie, etc., were some of the schools mentioned in interviews.[16] All are prestigious private schools with ties to the French Cultural Mission in Vietnam after 1954. To some extent this is reflected in the numbers of immigrants who spoke French fluently. At Camp Pendleton, the only refugee holding center which collected statistics on French language capabilities of those processed there, about 30 percent of heads of households were fluent in French; another 30 percent spoke some French. Less than 41 immigrant heads of households spoke no French. Roughly 25 percent of all immigrants over eighteen processed at Pendleton were fluent in French. Such French language skills, especially among those under about thirty, could be obtained only by going to private French schools in Vietnam, for by 1962 English had replaced French as the second language offered by public secondary schools.[17]

The fact that many of those who came to the United States were from the South Vietnamese elite is apparent not only in the educational backgrounds of immigrants, it is also clear in their occupational skills. Table 4 describes the primary employment skills of heads of households. The table does not necessarily indicate what jobs individuals held in Vietnam; rather, it lists the skills they possess as translated into U.S. Department of Labor job skill categories. Table 4 shows that about 31 percent of immigrant heads of households had professional, technical, or managerial skills. The second largest category of skills is transportation and miscellany, into which 16 percent of refugees fell, followed by clerical and sales skills (11.7 percent), and the machine trades.

Table 4

Primary Employment Skills of

Heads of Households* (N = 30,628)

	Skill Categories	Number	Percent
1.	Medical Professions (includes M.D.s, Dentists, Pharmacists, Midwives, and Nurses)	2,210	7.2
2.	Professional, Technical and Managerial	7,368	24.0
3.	Clerical and Sales	3,572	11.7
	Service	2,324	7.6
4.	Farming, Fishing, Forestry, and Related Areas	1,491	4.9
5.	Agricultural Processing	128	0.4
	Machine Trades	2,670	8.7
6.	Benchwork, Assembly, Repair	1.249	4.1
7.	Structural and Construction	2,026	6.6
8.	Transportation and Misc.	5,165	16.9
9.	Did Not Indicate	2,425	7.9
	Total	30,628	100.0

Source: Interagency Task Force for Indochina Refugees, Report to the Congress, 15 December 1975 (litho), p. 13. (Available also at V. I. C., Box 2.)

*Table does not necessarily indicate individual's past occupations.

More than anything else, table 4 shows that immigrants were part of the "modern" urban sector of the Vietnamese economy. People with professional, managerial, and technical skills make up close to one-third of the immigrant population. Individuals with skills relating to a modern industrial economy—the machine trades, bench work skills, construction, agricultural processing—make up another 19.4 percent. In all likelihood many of those in clerical and sales job skill categories were businessmen or accountants, lower-level government civil servants, or secretary/translators for American concerns. In Vietnam, 60 percent or more of the population is employed in agriculture (what the Department of Labor would have classified as farming, fishing, and forestry skills); only 4.9 percent of all immigrants had agricultural or fishing skills.

Table 4 does not indicate the jobs that immigrants held in Vietnam. A precise statistical breakdown of jobs held is not available. The IATF, as was pointed out at the beginning of this chapter, did not release this kind of information. Several things, however, can be said about the jobs these people held at home. First, 10,674 men over 18 were members of the Vietnamese military at the time they left their country. They were probably scattered among the skill categories in table 4. Second, the bulk of those in category 2 (professional, technical, and managerial) were high ranking Vietnamese government officials (including top rank military officers), journalists, editors, professors, and businessmen. Third, those listed in the medical profession represent about half of all Vietnamese doctors, dentists, and pharmacists. Finally, a considerable number of immigrants are former employees of the U.S. government and American firms operating in Vietnam.[18] Over 600 of the 30,628 heads of household were employed by American private corporations like ESSO, TWA, Mobil, Firestone, and Caltex, and charitable organizations like Friends for All Children, Catholic Relief Services, and the Pearl Buck Foundation. The U.S. government had about 17,600 employees in Vietnam; at least half of these came to the U.S.[19] It is not out of the realm of possibility, then, that about 9,000 of the people listed in table 4 were employees of American public and private agencies in Vietnam, serving in capacities ranging from secretaries, drivers, clerks, and translators to computer operators and security specialists. Thus, about two-thirds of those who

immigrated could have been Vietnamese army personnel or
U.S. government employees. Another 8 percent were medical
practitioners working either in foreign hospitals or with the
Vietnamese military. An unspecified number of high ranking government officials—ministers, mayors, police administrators, etc.—are also hidden in table 4, probably in the
managerial classifications.

From the foregoing analysis of the Vietnamese population
which came to the U.S., it is hard to understand statements
made by various American government officials that the
"wrong" Vietnamese were evacuated. The statistics issued by
the IATF point to the immigration being composed primarily of the South Vietnamese elite and their families. As this
chapter has shown, many immigrants were extremely well
educated, came from relatively wealthy families, and were
employed in the "modern" sector of the Vietnamese economy. Despite this, however, the immigrants did not necessarily represent the group that the U.S. government had planned
to evacuate. The 4.9 percent of the immigrants who were
peasants or fishermen were not people who would readily
adjust to American life. They came in large families, and had
no inkling of what life in a modern industrial economy was.
The ARVN rank and file—at least 4,500 men, some with
families—were also an unwelcome, unanticipated group of
immigrants who had few skills marketable in the United
States. Similar to the ARVN foot soldiers and officers were
the South Vietnamese lawyers, professors, journalists, government bureaucrats, etc. Within Vietnamese society they
were the socioeconomic elite. Within American society, they
probably faced exclusion from the elite, at least in the short
run.

As was stated in the preceding chapter, Americans had
expected only those Vietnamese employed by Americans and
the dependents of American citizens to immigrate to the
United States. This was all the U.S. government officially
provided for in its evacuation programs. If the immigrant
population had been confined to these two groups, the way
the resettlement in the United States was handled might have
been different. Vietnamese could have been processed by INS

Two rural women at Fort Indian Town Gap. *Fred Friedman*

in Guam quickly and been allowed to resettle with their families already in the U.S. or where their former employers could find work for them. This is, in fact, what occurred as refugees began to pour into the U.S. before Saigon was evacuated. Chase Manhattan Bank, for example, brought its employees by charter flights from Saigon to Guam to New York and found them housing in Queens as well as jobs with the parent company.[20] ESSO Corporation and American Express Corporation had similar programs. Before 25 April, about 5,000 Vietnamese had been paroled into the United States without having gone through the lengthy security checks and search for sponsors that were required of immigrants who arrived in Guam after 25 April.

As Vietnamese began to be processed in Guam after the evacuation of Saigon, it became clear that Vietnamese seeking entry to the United States were not, for reasons explained in chapter 2, confined to those with ties to American families or corporations—groups which would involve the U.S. government least in costly resettlement. By 26 April 1975 it became apparent that many immigrants who were not connected with the U.S. government or American corporations could not be integrated immediately into American society. Security checks would become time consuming as individuals appeared whose names and backgrounds had not been researched by the American embassy in Saigon. Further, many immigrants, despite their educational levels, spoke little English. In fact, as of March 1976, almost a year after the immigrants left Vietnam, 27.1 percent of all heads of households and 64.7 percent of all immigrants spoke no English at all. Only 35.5 percent of heads of households and 21 percent of all immigrants spoke some English, while 36.7 percent of all heads of household and 13.9 percent of all immigrants could speak enough English to function effectively in the United States—for example, work at a job requiring English literacy skills and communicate on their own with Americans.[21] The language skills (or lack of them) indicated to American authorities that some sort of mediating institutions would need to be established for most of the immigrants. Sponsorship by Americans, handled by

American voluntary organizations, was the clearest way to proceed. These voluntary organizations, although they were consulted before 25 April, were not seriously involved with the immigration until after it was clear that the immigrants could not be placed in the United States directly without causing major political and social problems. It was after 25 April that Camp Pendleton was opened in California to take up the processing of immigrants that could not be handled on Guam. After Pendleton, centers were established at Eglin Air Force Base in Florida and Fort Chaffee in Arkansas. As of 31 May, Fort Indian Town Gap, Pennsylvania, became the fourth and last center to open on U.S. soil. These centers existed because, given the unanticipated nature of the immigration, time would be needed to find Americans willing to take responsibility for the immigrants, to do security checks, and to prepare Vietnamese culturally to live in this country.

Part 2

From Refugee to Immigrant

Chapter Four

Being Processed: The Refugee Camps and Their Organization

Vietnamese did not travel directly from their country to the place they ultimately settled in the United States. Most, when they left Vietnam, either landed in or were brought to American overseas bases like Utapo in Thailand (where Vietnamese air force pilots flew their planes) and Subic Bay and Clark Field in the Philippines. From these bases most were flown to Wake or Guam, where Americans, as of 22 April, had set up a reception center to house 50,000 refugees for a maximum of 90 days. By 26 April the facility at Guam had become severely overcrowded. Further, because of the unanticipated numbers of refugees who arrived at U.S. bases, it was apparent that processing and resettling of immigrants could not be done from Guam within three months. The center at Guam was considered unsafe over the long run because of typhoons that could hit the island. Thus, four centers, or camps, were established on the U.S. mainland to house Vietnamese while they waited for clearance to enter the United States or some third country. Camp Pendleton, outside of San Diego, California, opened on 29 April with a tent city capable of housing 18,000 immigrants. On 2 May Fort Chaffee opened in Arkansas, with barracks that could accommodate 24,000 persons. Eglin Air Force Base, with a capacity for housing 5,000 persons, was the third reception center, opening on 4 May 1975. On 28 May, the fourth and last reception center, Fort Indian Town Gap, near Harrisburg, Pennsylvania, opened with the capacity to house more than 16,000 refugees.

In the camps, Vietnamese were "processed" into America: they were interviewed, examined, given identification numbers, registered with American agencies, introduced to American society and culture, and found a place to live and work in the U.S. Vietnamese went into the camps as refugees; they came out of the camps as immigrants. As refugees they were a chapter in Vietnamese history and culture; when they emerged from the camps, they had begun a series of painful adjustments that severed them from Vietnamese life as they knew it and were on the road to becoming Vietnamese-Americans. The camps were the places where systematic efforts began at resocializing Vietnamese to live in America and accommodate to the country and its culture.

For structural and bureaucratic reasons the camps were by no stretch of the imagination "little Vietnams." They were conceived, organized, and controlled for American needs. The purpose of the camps, as articulated by the IATF, was to see to it "that the possibility of their [the refugees] becoming a public charge is reduced."[1] This goal, which entailed having immigrants quickly and quietly absorbed into American society, necessitated certain types of organization, procedures, and staffing within the camps that left very limited, if any, roles for Vietnamese.

The camps paved the way for Vietnamese entry to the United States; they also introduced them to American life, often in well-organized programs. The nightly movies and daily newspapers put out by camp management as well as public school for children ages six to eighteen, adult classes in the English language and vocational skills, and "orientation" meetings all tried to prepare Vietnamese for the United States, informing them how to date, prepare food, speak to Americans, work, and play.

The camps prepared people to live and work in American society; they also settled Vietnamese throughout the country. Camp management, the arm of the IATF, pursued a policy of diaspora. Resettlement was aimed at preventing large clusters of Vietnamese, Cambodians, or Laotians from building

Faces. Fort Indian Town Gap. *Fred Friedman*

up in any given area in the country. After the immigrants were found sponsors, the camps closed.

Most of what I say in the next three chapters about the camps is based on what I saw at Fort Indian Town Gap, Pennsylvania. To some extent, the four camps did vary in their particulars. But their control, organization, and programs were so similar that what can be said about the camp at Fort Indian Town Gap applies to all the camps.

Camp Organization and Personnel

Each refugee camp was run jointly by the IATF and one of the military services. Camp Pendleton was a marine base; Forts Chaffee and Indian Town Gap, army bases; and Eglin, an air force base. The division of labor in administration was theoretically functional: the armed services were responsible for logistics and security; the IATF oversaw cultural programs, government policy implementation, processing, and resettlement.

The IATF was set up on 18 April. Nationally it was composed of twelve federal agencies including the departments of State; Health, Education and Welfare; Housing and Urban Development; and Justice and Labor "to coordinate . . . all U.S. Government activities concerning evacuation of U.S. citizens, Vietnamese refugees and resettlement problems relating to the Vietnam conflict."[2] The task force's personnel both nationally and in the camps came from the twelve cooperating federal agencies.[3] In Washington the task force had the responsibility for setting general policy. It was the task force which, encouraged by Congress, decided to scatter Vietnamese through the country. Likewise, it was the task force which set closing dates for the camps and pressured voluntary agencies to speed up resettlement and accept as sponsors individuals who, under other circumstances, would have been rejected.[4]

The task force in Washington set overall policy. It appointed a senior civilian coordinator to administer each camp according to guidelines that the task force established. These guidelines provided for a division of labor between the military and civilians. They also provided for the operation within the camps of various government and private agencies to care for the refugees. The guidelines provided for processing through the INS bureaucracy, for security clearance and for future social services and resettlement in the country. Beyond this, the day-to-day operation of the camps and the coordination of activities among agencies within legal limits was up to the senior civilian coordinator and his staff.

The senior civilian coordinator was the chief administrative officer of each camp. Most of the people who served in this position were State Department careerists. Donald G. MacDonald, the only person to serve as senior civilian coordinator at Fort Chaffee, was called out of retirement from the State Department to serve in his post. MacDonald had, before his retirement, been chief of AID in Vietnam. Nick Thorne was the senior civilian coordinator of Camp Pendleton. Before taking the post, he had been in the Foreign Service. Thorne had come to the foreign service relatively late in his life, having been a career marine colonel who went into the foreign service after he retired from the marines. The first civilian coordinator at Indian Town Gap was Richard Friedman of the Department of State. He was assisted by Alan Francis who had been consul general of Da-Nang until the Americans evacuated the city in March 1975. Alan Carter, who was Friedman's successor as senior civilian coordinator at Indian Town Gap and who served from 11 July to the time the camp closed in December, was a twenty-year veteran of the United States Information Service (USIS). He had served that agency in Japan, Pakistan, and India and, for eight months—up to the day before the U.S. evacuation of Saigon—had headed the USIS in Vietnam. Carter was assisted by a deputy, Clifford Nunn, who had been a senior AID official in Vietnam for about fifteen years. Carter's senior staff included several persons who had served with the consul general in Da-Nang.[5]

The senior civilian coordinator and his staff's task was to implement the policies set by the IATF in Washington by directing and coordinating the work of the various government and private agencies operating in the camps. He and his staff meshed these efforts with those of the camp's military. In addition, the senior civilian coordinator was responsible for the camp's civil governance.

The work of coordinating all the government and private agencies in the camps was no easy task. Twelve government agencies were involved in "in-processing"—a government term which covered everything from INS interviewing, finger printing, physical examinations, and security checks, to distribution of social security numbers by the Social Security Administration and registering for employment with the Department of Labor. The work performed by these government agencies was legally prescribed and carried out by individuals on loan from their respective agencies either on a rotational basis or for the entire time the camps were open. At Fort Indian Town Gap these individuals were confined to a quonset hut outside the area in which Vietnamese were permitted to move freely. Most were professionals at this work and, with their agencies' backing, followed procedures they have always followed; most had never worked directly with immigrants before.

The senior civilian coordinator did have some control over the work of these agencies, mainly in the areas of work pace and of forcing cooperation among agencies not necessarily used to working together and/or sharing information. The coordinator and his staff set the hours of work, depending on the influx of immigrants into the camps. They also ironed out some problems created because similar functions were assumed by several agencies resulting, especially at Fort Chaffee, in a log jam in resettlements. Security checks for each individual were carried out by INS, the CIA, the Department of Defense, the Department of Treasury, and, if the individual had ever visited the United States before, the FBI. The security checks initially took so much time that at Fort Chaffee people who had been found sponsors and jobs in the U.S. were detained as each agency duplicated the others' efforts. The civilian coordinator forced a speedup of the security checks and a pooling of information among agencies to cut down time spent on this part of U.S. government paperwork.[6]

The senior civilian coordinator also oversaw the work of state agencies that operated within the camps. At Fort Indian Town Gap, the Pennsylvania State Department of Public Instruction provided education to all children aged six to eighteen and ran English language classes for adults. The senior civilian coordinator set the boundaries of what state agencies could or could not do in the camp. Several state agencies did operate within the camps, depending on state initiatives—and only with the agreement of the senior civilian coordinator. The Pennsylvania Commission on Women, for example, ran a series of programs for Vietnamese women; the Pennsylvania Department of Labor ran an employment registration service. Except at Fort Indian Town Gap, state government involvement was minimal. States in which the other camps were located, California and Arkansas, were none too eager to get involved with the camps. Governor Brown of California, for example, was very concerned that California not become a center for Vietnamese resettlement and urged camp authorities to relocate refugees held at Camp Pendleton in other states. He did not send officials to register Vietnamese for employment; neither did the governor of Arkansas.[7]

The most touchy task of the civilian coordinator was supervising the work of the voluntary agencies involved in resettlement. In late April the IATF contracted seven voluntary agencies, all of which had extensive experience with refugees and immigrants, to relocate Vietnamese, Laotian, and Cambodian refugees in the U.S. The agencies were to find individuals or groups willing to assume fiscal and moral responsibility for individual immigrants or an immigrant family for at least two years. The agencies were to be given a $500 per person resettlement grant. It was up to each agency to determine how this grant was to be spent. The resettlement agencies represented in the camps were: The United States Catholic Conference (USCC), the Lutheran Immigration and Refugee Service (LIRS), the International Rescue Committee (IRC), the United HIAS, the Church World Service (CWS), the Tolstoy Foundation, the American Fund for Czechoslovak Refugees (AFCR), the American

Council for Nationalities Services (ACNS), and Travelers'
Aid–International Social Services.

To some extent conflict between these organizations and
the IATF was unavoidable if only because of their conceptu-
alization of what resettlement entailed and the type of
personnel agencies recruited to do their work. HIAS, USCC,
LIRS, and CWS, long-standing organizations for immigrants and refugees, connected to religious social service
agencies, had on their staffs professional social workers who
had firm professional convictions and experience in resettlement. They resisted as much as possible pressure to place
Vietnamese without careful person-to-person checks with
prospective sponsors and preferred group (in the case of the
churches, parish) to individual sponsorship.

IRC is a secular organization whose experience with
immigrants predates World War I. Unlike the religious organizations, except for USCC, IRC had long been active in
Vietnam. IRC's work in Vietnam began in the mid-1950s
when it became heavily involved with the American Friends
of Viet-Nam, which lobbied for American aid to the Diem
government. IRC developed within Vietnam refugee relief
services, including orphanages and medical aid.[8] Its camp
staff, for the most part, contrasted with that of the religious
organizations. At Fort Indian Town Gap close to half its
staff had appreciable experience in Vietnam either with
voluntary organizations like the International Voluntary
Service or with IRC or AID. Several staffers at Fort Indian
Town Gap spoke Vietnamese. At Fort Chaffee, IRC's initial
staff was similar and included a former foreign service officer
with no experience in Vietnam. The effect of all this was to
have a staff that was somewhat sensitive to Vietnamese
culture, if not to the difficulties of adjusting to American life
(which the religious groups were).

The other secular resettlement organizations and their
staff working in the camps did not share the social work
orientation of the religious organizations or the direct
familiarity with Vietnamese that IRC staffers had. Organizations like the Tolstoy Foundation and the AFCR were staffed
by former immigrants and/or individuals with no prior

overseas work or social work training. They were nonprofessionals, many of whom had little concept of either the Vietnamese with whom they were dealing or of the broader task of resettlement. Organizations like these had neither the extensive social welfare apparatus of HIAS, LIRS, CWS, or USCC nor a national network like Travelers' Aid–International Social Services or IRC.

The staffing of most resettlement organizations is crucial, I believe, to understanding not only some of the difficulties in resettlement after the camps closed and the nature of services each agency could offer refugees, but also of the interaction between the IATF authorities and resettlement agencies in daily camp life. The task force personnel, who implemented as well as helped formulate policy, were administrators concerned primarily with efficiency models—getting refugees resettled quickly and cheaply. As one task force spokesman put it, it cost the U.S. government $10.50 a day to house, feed, and tend to each immigrant.[9] Speed in resettlement became the task force's major priority. This was reflected in the final report at Fort Chaffee which contains tables charting each agency's productivity and efficiency on a monthly basis.[10] The resettlement agencies were not as keen as the government to do their job fast. Most openly resented the civilian coordinators' attempts to speed up their operations, putting professional or experiential judgment against the task force's pressure.[11] However, while they resented the pressure to resettle Vietnamese rapidly, they were affected by it and, in the end, acceded somewhat to it. The civilian coordinators, after all, had some power over the organizations. From the opening of the camps the IATF made it clear that it would not use the voluntary organizations as the sole resettlement channels. The IATF generated state and other voluntary agencies to serve as resettlement organizations. Among the states that did this were Maine, New Mexico, Nebraska, and Washington.[12] The voluntary agencies never before involved in immigration that became resettlement agencies included the Chinese-American Benevolent Association and the Christian Missionary Association. To some extent this was a threat to some of the older

voluntary organizations' conceptions of "proper" resettlement and encouraged the agencies, as a lesser evil, to step up
their pace of operations. A second means the task force used
to speed up the resettlement agencies' work was the forty-
five-day limit imposed in September 1975. Each agency was
given but forty-five days to find an immigrant who had
registered with it a sponsor and get that immigrant out of the
camp. If the agency failed to meet the deadline, the task force
threatened to shift the immigrant to another organization
for the purposes of resettlement.[13] The result, several caseworkers pointed out, was an increasing tendency not to look
too closely at sponsorship offers, to reconsider offers previously considered "inappropriate," and to pressure
Vietnamese who were hesitant about being resettled in a
particular geographic area or with a particular individual or
group sponsor into accepting that form of resettlement.[14]
The pressure was there and it affected agencies' work paces
and individual reactions to immigrants' desires and problems. One caseworker summed it all up in mid-October
when the pressure had really built up for rapid resettlement.

> Everything has changed from the beginning. . . . I came
> here [to Fort Indian Town Gap] because of the feelings I
> have for people . . . In the beginning it was all good vibes
> and all that stuff. And now it is more, "How come all
> these bodies aren't out of here?" It's the numbers game
> from the army's standpoint and from the civilians' too.
> . . . I feel more alienated from the [Vietnamese] people
> because of the pressure from above to get them out.[15]

The resettlement agencies were not the only nongovern-
ment organizations operating within the camps. American
service groups, at the invitation of the senior civilian coordinator, ran extensive programs which complemented the
work of resettlement agencies and helped in the day-to-day
operation of the camps. Organizations like the Red Cross
and the YMCA offered many services to immigrants. The
Red Cross, for example, held baby-care classes for mothers
and expectant parents; it ran a college placement and an

educational credentials translation service; it also, with the YMCA, staffed recreation halls in the camps that ran ping-pong tournaments, organized teenage dances and art shows, provided sewing machines for individuals to use, and furnished reading rooms with English language tutors. One of the Red Cross' most extensive services was family reunification. At Fort Indian Town Gap, two individuals working full time for the Red Cross interviewed individuals who had lost family members in the evacuation of Vietnam, took down the names of these lost relatives and checked them against lists of Vietnamese in camps in Thailand, Hong Kong, and within the U.S. If it located individuals, the Red Cross would notify the State Department, which decided whether the family should be unified. The State Department would provide for reunification only if it involved bringing together members of nuclear families. No more than seven members of a family would be reunified. Over 300 Vietnamese families at Fort Indian Town Gap were reunited through Red Cross efforts.[16]

The nature of the services offered by organizations like the Red Cross depended on the division of labor among agencies in the camps decided on by the senior civilian coordinator and his staff. For example, the Red Cross handled family reunification at Fort Indian Town Gap until late October. The State Department assumed this role directly at Fort Chaffee. At Fort Indian Town Gap, reunification services were taken over by the agencies involved in resettlement after late October when their work load had evened off. At all the camps volunteers organized by the Red Cross and the YMCA provided day care, English language instruction, and cultural programs. In the fall education was contracted out to state and county agencies. In late November at Forts Chaffee and Indian Town Gap, the only camps remaining open, the YMCA and Red Cross once again took over English language education when camp authorities closed down the schools for children and adults.

In addition to allocating the work of private organizations working in the camps, the civilian coordinator also worked closely with the armed services, which maintained camp facilities, took over camp security, and handled "logistical problems" like food services and distribution of supplies to the camp population (pillows, towels, sheets, blankets, etc.). The military was not necessarily subject to the civilian coordinator's office. Decisions considered logistical were simply the military's province and, according to the public affairs officer at Fort Indian Town Gap, most decisions that needed to be made in the camp were logistical.[17] The distinction between logistical and nonlogistical matters was by no means clear-cut. The U.S. Army psychological operations unit at Fort Indian Town Gap produced the camp's daily newspaper *Dat Lanh* which not only informed Vietnamese of the rules and regulations of the camp, but also ran article after article on life in the United States. It was the army at Fort Indian Town Gap which decided who would have access to the camp from the outside and handled much of the public relations for the camp. The army also made the rules about the hours during which civilians, including those employed at the camp, could be present in areas of the camp in which immigrants could move freely, and kept school personnel, resettlement agency case workers, etc., apart from the immigrants they theoretically served.

The civilian coordinator, in addition to coordinating the work of the various government and private agencies, had an organization all his own which, in conjunction with the military, governed Vietnamese in the camp. Except for Eglin Air Force Base in Florida, which held a relatively small number of immigrants (about 5,000 at its height) and was open for but a short time (less than two months), the camps were small cities housing more than 26,000 persons over several square miles. Each camp was divided into "areas" or districts for the sake of day-to-day governance; each area was superintended by an area coordinator appointed by the senior civilian coordinator and a military officer who handled security and logistics. Each area coordinator's office had a staff of secretaries and interpreters who were assisted in their functions by immigrants.[18]

The manner in which immigrant assistants were selected varied from camp to camp. At Fort Chaffee and Camp

Pendleton, within the first two months of their existence Vietnamese assistants were chosen through camp-wide elections. Fort Chaffee had a Vietnamese mayor and council for superintending the barracks and the distribution of clothes for the area coordinators. This created a parallel government in the camp which proved unsettling to authorities for several reasons: first, independent of the IATF it set up a power base for Vietnamese that could affect control over camp life and the pace of resettlement; it also created a sense of permanency in the camps that obscured their transitional nature. According to area coordinators, parallel government in the camps created conflicts among Vietnamese themselves, making it more difficult for these area coordinators to do their jobs. Several area coordinators opposed any form of Vietnamese organization in the camps on the basis that it presented a barrier to Vietnamese learning to live in the United States. As one area coordinator pointed out, Vietnamese were going from camps to a country ruled by Americans, not Vietnamese. The sooner they got used to that, he maintained, the better.[19] Thus, at Fort Chaffee and Camp Pendleton, Vietnamese shadow governments were allowed to dissolve as Vietnamese elected officials left the camps and were relocated in the United States. At Fort Indian Town Gap, no Vietnamese government was ever instituted. One of the area coordinators at that camp had, before working there, visited Camp Pendleton and the refugee center at Guam as a representative of the senior civilian coordinator and had concluded that such an organization was unwise.

Vietnamese assistants at Fort Indian Town Gap and, after the end of Vietnamese self-government, at other camps, were selected by the American area coordinators. Each area, especially at Forts Chaffee and Indian Town Gap, consisted of barracks, each of which housed up to 100 persons. At Indian Town Gap, five such areas existed with about 44 barracks per area. The area coordinator had each barracks meet and nominate three individuals for "chief" of the barracks. The area coordinator then assigned one of the three the post. The choice was arbitrary and usually based on the respect an individual seemed to command among his barracks mates, his language abilities (those who spoke English were usually preferred by area coordinators), and whether the individual seemed cooperative.[20]

The Vietnamese assistants, or barracks chiefs, had little authority of their own. Their role was to organize individuals to maintain their barracks (clean toilets, take out garbage, sweep stairs, etc.) and inform Vietnamese of clothing supply and meal ticket distribution and any other information that area coordinators needed to have distributed to each individual living in the camp. The barracks chief also was theoretically the immigrants' representative to each area coordinator. He was supposed to bring problems to the attention of area coordinators who would then attempt to solve them. These problems ranged from interfamily conflicts over noise, lights, or property within a barracks or tent to intrafamily difficulties and fights such as wife beating. Sometimes the barracks chiefs identified troublemakers (thieves, dissidents, noncooperators, etc.) for area coordinators.

The area coordinator's role was to tend to the daily physical needs of immigrants. One area coordinator described this work as that of "handing out toothpaste."[21] But in fact the job was never that mundane, partly because of area coordinators' backgrounds and their conceptions of their work. The area coordinators at Fort Indian Town Gap were all former AID employees who had worked together for several years in Vietnam out of the consul general's office in Da-Nang. At least two were fluent in Vietnamese. All had served as district or provincial advisors either in land reform programs or political organizing projects. One had been in Vietnam since 1967; another since 1968; and a third since 1972. Area coordinators at other camps had similar backgrounds. One area coordinator commented that the people in these positions at Fort Indian Town Gap all had worked together in Vietnam for years

> as the people in the other [refugee] camps. They know each other, too. Everybody knows everybody else. . . . They were from all over the country [Vietnam], but we

had the same boss, AID, and we'd all been there for several years, so a lot of us knew each other. We knew each other from conferences that were held in Vietnam on various problems.[22]

These individuals' experiences in Vietnam shaped their behavior insofar as they all had clear conceptions of problems peculiar to Vietnamese and believed that the method of camp management should respond to these problems. One area coordinator firmly believed that it was camp management's job to reconstruct social values among Vietnamese. As he put it,

one of the basic problems they [the Vietnamese] had before they left their country was there was a general lack of discipline in almost all areas of life. So one of the most immediate things for us [camp management] to try to reestablish was discipline. I'm not talking about discipline in the sense of people walking in lines, in the military sense, but I am talking about just the normal discipline that is necessary for people, peoples, to live together which would mean that you would have to have a certain amount of community responsibility when you're living in a single building that has one hundred other people in it. When I talk about discipline I talk about the amount of self-control that a person must have to be comfortable and make other people comfortable when he lives in a community situation. For example, people in Vietnam were not too much experienced at community living, the part of community living that involves joint projects. For example, people didn't care as much about picking up trash, because it wasn't really a problem [for them] . . . they really didn't care if you wanted to dig a ditch, it really didn't affect the person next door. And so there was very little necessity for getting into detail as far as asking another person if you did something how it would affect him. But the biggest thing is when you live in a community like this [the camp] and you're talking

about a supercommunity because you've got a very high
density of people, that you have to be much more careful
about the things you do, how they will affect other
people.[23]

Through the years of warfare, he continued, Vietnamese had
no sense of community responsibility and were, in fact,
unable to live among themselves without a foreign intermediary who could keep peaceful relations among them. The
camps, as far as he was concerned, were a place where Vietnamese would learn to live together under the auspices of
camp management. Presumably this would serve as a transition to living in the United States under the guidance of an
American sponsor.[24]

Although the opinions expressed by this particular area
coordinator were his own, they were shared to some extent
among some Vietnam "hands" in camp management and
elsewhere. The attitude was perhaps born out of roles these
individuals had played over the past decades in Vietnam as
district and provincial advisors and military personnel. In
Vietnam their job had been to restore order among Vietnamese and develop Vietnamese society. It had extended
from helping organize Thieu's Democratic Party to rede-
signing land tenure patterns and school systems. It had
involved handing out money just as toothpaste was handed
out in camps, with directions on how to use it. The difference between Vietnam and the camps was that in the camps
Americans had a great deal more control over their own
efforts. In the camps Americans did not have to work
through a Vietnamese organization; they could impose their
own.

The area coordinator's official role was to maintain order
within the day-to-day life of immigrants and to provide
immigrants with housing, clothing, and food. Their role
also was to support the overall camp effort of resettling
Vietnamese in America. The area coordinators encouraged
Vietnamese to attend camp activities believed to speed
resettlement, particularly English language classes and
cultural orientation sessions. Through the barracks chiefs,

the area coordinators announced the classes and events and eventually singled out refugees who needed to be encouraged to attend such functions. The area coordinators also assisted in decisions on the pace of resettlement. They pressured Vietnamese into accepting sponsorship offers by explaining to them the reality facing them. This often amounted to pointing out that the camps were going to close down soon and that the immigrants would not be able to continue living in them.[25]

The area coordinators helped speed up resettlement in another way. They were almost the only officials in the camps who had extensive experience in Vietnam, spoke Vietnamese, and had any claims to knowledge about Vietnamese society and culture. The area coordinators became the major source of information about Vietnamese for many resettlement agency case workers, YMCA and Red Cross employees, army personnel, school teachers, and volunteers. They conducted cultural orientation sessions for Americans working in the camps and told them about how Vietnamese supposedly thought, their fears and their problems and how these should be handled. The area coordinators helped create a climate in the camps conducive to pushing Vietnamese out of the camps and into American society rapidly. They told caseworkers that Vietnamese reluctance about accepting any resettlement offers had little to do with the offers, but rather stemmed from Vietnamese patterns of dependence on the "little Vietnam" the camps had become. Vietnamese cultural traits, several pointed out, were such that Vietnamese were hesitant to try anything new and were unable to live among themselves without foreign intermediaries. Information of this sort justified the task force's resettlement policies. It also helped insulate resettlement workers who believed it from their Vietnamese clients and made them more amenable to following the task force's goals of speedy resettlement for immigrants. Many caseworkers were influenced by the area coordinators' interpretation of Vietnamese culture, desires, and needs, simply because they had few other sources of information. The immigrants could not serve as this source primarily because many spoke no

English and could not communicate with caseworkers or teachers, and because as was pointed out earlier, the camps were organized in such a way as to minimize contacts between Vietnamese and Americans. The Americans who had the greatest contact with the immigrants were the area coordinators; in reality they had great influence both in setting camp policy and in seeing that other Americans followed it.[26]

The resettlement camps were American-created institutions geared to serve American-defined needs. Their sole function was to settle Vietnamese in the United States according to policies made in Washington with American political and economic problems in mind. These policies were made without consulting Vietnamese. Some—like the dispersal of Vietnamese through the country to make them invisible and, therefore, not a political problem or an undue economic burden to local governments—were opposed vehemently by many Vietnamese.[27] Private resettlement agencies also were unenthusiastic about, if not against, this policy. Their experience with other refugees and immigrant groups had shown that not only did dispersion create more problems than it solved, but that it did not work in the long run and necessitated two resettlements rather than one.[28]

The camps were organized and administered in such a way as to minimize the impact of persons or organizations, whether American or Vietnamese, hesitant about government policy. The camps were firmly in the hands of the American government and the military, who coordinated and defined the resettlement agencies' work as well as the daily lives and, to a large extent, the futures of Vietnamese. Real power within the camps lay in the hands of the senior civilian coordinator, his staff, and the military. The resettlement agencies and the refugees had little official power. Thus, no Vietnamese self-government was permitted to last long within the camps and voluntary agencies found themselves unable to make policy, but rather were hustled along despite themselves by the IATF and the armed forces.

A description of the organization, administration, and personnel of the resettlement camps does not recreate life in the camps. The resettlement camps did have a sociocultural life and routine of their own that reflects not only the organization and ultimate goals of the camps in the minds of American government authorities, but also to some extent Vietnamese reactions to them.

Routines, Daily Life, and "Processing"

Americans ran the camps; Vietnamese lived in them. Camp routines were what over 130,000 people lived for anywhere from ten days to six months of their lives. Living in the camps was not living in Vietnam, nor was it living in the United States. Each day was arranged by American authorities for Vietnamese.

Every immigrant who entered the camps underwent "in-processing," a government term for collecting information about individuals that paved the way to gaining entry to the United States. Vietnamese arrived in mainland U.S. on airplanes. Except for Camp Eglin, which was an air force base, the immigrants landed at major airports nearest the camps. At Fort Indian Town Gap flights landing from Guam arrived at the Harrisburg, Pennsylvania, airport. There they were met by the army, Red Cross volunteers, and ITAF representatives, and their paid Vietnamese interpreters. This delegation from the camp loaded the newcomers onto army buses and took them the hour or so journey to Fort Indian Town Gap, an army reserve training base. Upon arriving at Fort Indian Town Gap, with tags around their necks bearing identification numbers assigned them in Guam and their names, refugees, arranged by households, were unloaded at the two-story structure labeled "in-processing." This building stood outside the official boundaries of the camp. (The boundaries of the camp were defined by a series of white ropes. Vietnamese could not go beyond these white ropes without passes and escorts.)

In reality refugees went through two government screenings. When they arrived at Fort Indian Town Gap, the military did some preliminary interviewing. Refugees received either a snack or hot meal (depending on the time they arrived) and were shown their living quarters. Each was handed a pillow, a pillow case, two sheets, two blankets plus toiletries, and meal tickets. At this time each refugee received a camp number. The next day after they arrived, refugees were escorted back to the in-processing building where HEW and INS began paper work necessary before the Vietnamese would be allowed to relocate within the United States.[29]

HEW and the INS together had a staff of over 160 persons at Fort Indian Town Gap for their paper work. At Fort Chaffee over 200 of their personnel worked collecting data the government required about refugees. For the Vietnamese the procedure was boring as well as grueling. They stood on interminable lines waiting for Americans to ask them questions, take their finger prints, and photograph them. INS officials assisted by Vietnamese interpreters (usually a refugee who had already been resettled in the U.S. and was paid for his or her work) filled out the lengthy ADP form described in chapter 3. INS was particularly interested in determining immigrants' occupational skills and gathering information necessary for Department of Defense, Department of State, CIA, the Drug Enforcement Agency, and FBI to do security checks on each immigrant. This initial data collection, finger printing, and photographing took about two and one-half to three hours for each person.

Either on the same day or on the next one the immigrants were taken to the quarters of the HEW Center for Disease Control, usually located at the military field hospital on base. There they received immunizations, were x-rayed, given TB tests, and examined by a doctor who was screening them for communicable diseases. After the examinations, Vietnamese were recalled to INS/HEW in-processing headquarters and lined up behind the Social Security Administration and INS desks. There they were assigned social security numbers and alien numbers. At this point they were asked to declare their financial resources and sign a statement to the effect that they had never been involved in drug trafficking. Next Americans registered Vietnamese with the Department of Commerce, which took job histories of all persons over seventeen and signed them up for work.

The final step in American government data collection was registration with a resettlement agency. At Fort Indian Town Gap from May to August 1975 refugees were free to sign up with any agency they pleased. Most tended to choose the USCC. For Vietnamese Catholics the choice was logical simply because they perceived the agency as an extension of their church and looked to it for leadership. By August, however, no such choice was given to Vietnamese at the camp. The assignment was made on the basis of the work load each agency was presumed to have. Many refugees were upset about being assigned to agencies Americans picked for them. Vietnamese Catholics, in particular, feared that Protestant or Jewish agencies would resettle them among Americans who would try to change their religious beliefs. Many Vietnamese, registered with agencies not of their choosing, kept refusing sponsorship offers until they were reassigned by the task force to an agency they found more acceptable.[30]

Government interviewing and data collection took anywhere from twenty-four hours to three days, depending on the numbers of immigrants arriving in the camps at any one time. The procedure the government called in-processing involved shuffling Vietnamese back and forth among lines, barracks, and agencies. It was bewildering to many Vietnamese not used to American bureaucratic routines. In-processing to some extent was a harbinger of camp life. It involved Americans shifting Vietnamese about. The Vietnamese role was passive: things were done to them; they did very little. And, like much of the camp life that followed, they stood in interminable lines waiting for something to happen.

In-processing involved Americans taking data. Much of the information gathered at the camps was forwarded to federal agencies for security checks. The security checks included computer searches of American agency and South Vietnamese national police files in American possession. The U.S. government was particularly interested in identifying Communists, known criminals, and drug traffickers. The results of the checks were never made public; apparently a handful of refugees failed to gain clearance for reasons the

Waiting. Fort Indian Town Gap. *Fred Friedman*

American government has kept to itself.[31]

Once the American government had finished collecting its data and examining and registering refugees, immigrants entered camp life and followed a routine of getting up in the morning, standing on meal lines for breakfast, going back to barracks to await notices from voluntary agencies to report for interviews. Waiting was the major camp activity. Vietnamese sat around waiting to be interviewed and waiting for information about what was to become of them. The boredom was broken by meals dished up by military cooks and their staffs, by daily church services, and by entertainment Americans arranged for refugees.

In the camps Vietnamese lived at close quarters with little privacy. At Camp Pendleton they lived in army tents with wooden floors. Each tent housed twenty-five people. Often several families shared a tent. At Forts Chaffee and Indian Town Gap, Vietnamese lived in two-story wooden barracks. Each barracks housed up to one hundred persons. Families were given privacy by a five- to six-foot wooden partition. This partition, which did not reach up to the ceiling, set aside a space for ten to fifteen people. Each partition came equipped with cots. No other furniture was supplied. There were two communal bathrooms in each barrack. Many people stayed inside the barracks all day long, emerging only for meals. Most families left at least one person in their living quarters at all times to guard the family's personal property. Many immigrants feared their personal property would be stolen. Some had come to the United States with their life savings in gold leaf or currency only to have it stolen in the camps before they had a chance to deposit it in banks. How common this was is a mystery, but the rumor that it occurred meant that refugee living quarters were always occupied by a family member.

If an immigrant chose, he or she could always participate in a host of American-sponsored activities: volley ball, soccer, and ping-pong matches were continually announced over the loud speakers. The Red Cross held daily safety, health, and sewing classes in recreation centers. TVs were always turned on in the recreation halls. Every night there

The barracks at Fort Indian Town Gap. *Fred Friedman*

were movies shown in each area of the camps. At Fort Indian
Town Gap, "The Sting," "Airport," "White Lightning,"
"Slither," "Something Big," and "Sugarland Express" were
among the films shown. Occasionally concerts were held. At
Camp Pendleton, for example, Herb Alpert and the Tijuana
Brass entertained over the summer months; at Fort Indian
Town Gap, Pham Duy, a Vietnamese popular singer (asso-
ciated with General Lansdale and the U.S. military/intelli-
gence community in South Vietnam) evoked many strong
emotions from his audience when he sang about home.

In addition to these activities, American holidays became a
time for special events. On the Fourth of July, Vietnamese
witnessed parades and fireworks at all camps. Thanksgiving, Memorial Day, Halloween, were the occasions for
special dinners and parties at recreation halls.

Americans planned all these activities for Vietnamese to
fill time. There was little for Vietnamese to do all day in the
camps. Americans supplied Vietnamese with clothes, meals,
and clean linens. Vietnamese were not assigned to work
other than keeping the barracks clean by washing the
communal bathrooms, sweeping stairs, and taking out
garbage. Many American officials feared that Vietnamese
would become depressed if they were not kept busy. Movies,
special events, parades, art shows, and the like were supposed to keep up camp morale. It is questionable whether all
this entertainment did accomplish what it was intended to
do. Many Vietnamese felt that these activities did not fill the
void left by having everything done for them. As one immigrant remarked, "Let me say this, the Americans have done a
lot for us, but whatever we think we need, they don't provide,
and whatever we don't need, they provide."[32]

While Americans tried to entertain Vietnamese, Vietnamese entertained themselves, sometimes in ways that camp
officials found unacceptable; other times in innocuous ways.
Card games were frequent in the barracks as was folk
singing. Many immigrants who had cash purchased radios,
tape recorders, record players, tapes, and hot plates at camp
PXs. Several people rewired barracks so that they could use
their appliances, much to the dismay of camp officials and

An ex-soldier at Fort Indian Town Gap. *Fred Friedman*

the alarm of fire inspectors. Radios and record players often blared at night after ten o'clock when the lights were supposed to be turned out and immigrants asleep. The noise led to disputes within barracks and area coordinators tried to ban music with little success. Fire inspectors tried to confiscate hot plates, fearing they would overload barracks circuits and cause fires.[33] The existence of hot plates in the barracks was less a sign that Vietnamese were displeased with the camp cuisine than it was a sign that they wanted to do something for themselves.

Another major form of recreation for many refugees was "hanging around" Americans. The voluntary offices were filled with Vietnamese young people, most of whom were men. They spent a lot of time gossiping with Vietnamese employees of the resettlement agencies who were no longer living in the camps, such as interpreters and secretaries. They also chatted with American volunteers, paid camp staff, and anyone else who happened to be present, including reporters and researchers.

Many volunteered their services as interpreters if they spoke good English or as runners to fetch other immigrants for interviews with resettlement agency caseworkers. Others typed for Americans or collated materials written for distribution in the camp. Hanging around filled time; it also gave Vietnamese an opportunity to find out about the U.S. first hand through contacts with Americans other than the area coordinators and the military. Those who "hung around" practiced their English. They asked whomever had time to talk with them about dating and marriage, cars, housing, and the weather in various parts of the country.

Hanging around was more than recreation, it was a way for Vietnamese to make contacts with Americans on their own and, to some extent, through these contacts, control their resettlement. Mr. V., formerly of Vietnamese military intelligence and a photographer for the South Vietnamese National Police, spent his days at the Red Cross headquarters at Fort Indian Town Gap. He volunteered his services to the organization as a photographer and did publicity shots for them. Red Cross people with whom he worked went out

of their way to find Mr. V. a job in his trade. The director of
the office cornered newspeople and photographers who
came into the camp, including members of the *Philadelphia
Inquirer*'s staff. Finally, they found him a job working for a
small town newspaper in Pennsylvania in a photo lab and
arranged for his sponsorship through a resettlement agency.
Mr. V. had turned down several sponsorship offers that the
resettlement agency had found for him. Mr. V. was not the
only person to get results from hanging around.[34] Miss H., a
former U.S. embassy employee, got her sponsor and a job
with a resettlement agency by volunteering at that agency's
office at Fort Chaffee. There she translated and did office
work for them. She ultimately found a sponsor who was on
the staff of that agency. He got her a job working in the agency's national office.[35] The pattern was common and it offered
those who could hang around not only something to do, but
more control over where they would resettle in the United
States, what kind of work they would end up doing, and
which Americans they would have close contacts with.

Camp routine reflected in large part the organization of
the camp in which Americans were actors and Vietnamese
were acted upon. In the camps Vietnamese were "processed"
into American society, both literally and figuratively. The
camps paved the way for entry into the United States
through INS/HEW red tape. But the camps were more than
holding centers for INS clearance; they were also places
where many Vietnamese received their first exposure to
American society and the demands they would have to meet
to survive in it. The mode of camp management made it clear
to Vietnamese that Americans, not Vietnamese, held power
within the country and that Vietnamese would have to
conform to American ways of doing things. While this is
apparent in camp organization and routine, it is clearest in
the cultural programs in the camps which, more than
anything else, tried to define for Vietnamese their future
patterns of life, thought, and culture. These patterns suggested very little possibility of Vietnamese maintaining their
own communities. Rather, they emphasized Vietnamese
becoming Americans. In this sense, Vietnamese were being

asked to transform themselves from refugee to immigrant. Refugees were persons who remained closely allied to the culture from which they came and were away from home for political reasons. A refugee is a temporary resident abroad. An immigrant, however, is a permanent resident of a new country not his or her own who, because of this permanency, develops new cultural roots—not necessarily those of his new country's mainstream, but not those of his home country either. The camps' organization, routines, and educational programs promoted the transformation from refugee to immigrant.

Being Taught about America: Education and Cultural Orientation in the Refugee Camps

Most Vietnamese refugees had thought very little about the social or cultural consequences of leaving their homeland at the time of their flight. Most came to the United States, not because they wanted to become Americans, but because they felt their lives and livelihoods threatened by the war and/or by the new government of Vietnam. In the camps Vietnamese became painfully aware that they were immigrants, not refugees. While they expressed the hope that they would somehow return to Vietnam, most began to face the reality that they had come to the United States for a very long time, if not for good. Somehow, they believed, they had to prepare for a new life, one which would be different from the one they had known in Vietnam.

The desire to prepare for a new life was evident in N. V. S.'s family register. N. V. S., a forty-five year old ARVN officer, born in northern Vietnam, made up the register (or diary) while at Fort Indian Town Gap awaiting to be resettled in the United States. He began it with the quote, "what is past is past." It contained pictures of himself and his family and a description of his journey from Vietnam to the United States. These Mr. S. called "Di Vang," or the past. Most of the pages of the register were blank, signifying the unknown future. While Mr. S. showed his register to us, one of the refugees huddled around the tape recorder burst out with the well-known Vietnamese proverb:

DUONG DI KHO KHONG KHO VI NGAN NUI
CACH SONG, KHO VI LONG NGUOI NGAI NUI
E SONG

> The road is difficult not because it is blocked by a
> mountain or a river
> It is difficult because people are afraid of the river and
> the mountain.[1]

Many refugees we interviewed at Fort Indian Town Gap
told us that Vietnamese would have to change in order to live
in the United States; however, few had any conception of
what that change would entail. Within the camps, however,
they were exposed to American notions of the changes
Vietnamese would need to make in order to become members
of American society. Children were exposed to these notions
in compulsory schooling; adults in English language classes
and in the camps' many cultural orientation programs and
bilingual reading materials. The preparation of Vietnamese
to enter American society is the subject of this chapter.

My discussion focuses on the curricular content of educational programs and the cultural messages transmitted
within classrooms by teachers and administrators. It is based
on the instructional materials used at Fort Indian Town
Gap, observations of classroom instruction in that camp,
and interviews I conducted with teachers, curriculum specialists, school administrators, and persons developing and
conducting cultural orientation programs. The programs
for refugees at Fort Indian Town Gap were similar to ones
offered at Camp Pendleton and Fort Chaffee. HEW funded
the adult and children's schools, as well as a series of cultural
programs, and helped develop their curricula. Persons who
were involved in these programs at the various camps
consulted with one another. For example, individuals from
West Arkansas Community College, the institution HEW
contracted to run adult and children's schools at Fort Chaffee, visited Fort Indian Town Gap to observe classes and
share instructional materials. The Fort Chaffee team collected complete sets of curricular materials from the Fort Indian
Town Gap schools.[2]

Vietnamese Boy Scouts welcome American scouts to their first roundup meeting at Camp Pendleton.
American Red Cross

Being Taught About American Kids: Compulsory Schooling for Children

Formal education for school-aged children began in all refugee camps after Labor Day. Until that time no formal instruction for children existed, although activities like organized sports, day care and teenage dances were arranged for them. Volunteers, who were untrained and could not be counted on to appear in camp regularly, taught children American songs and attempted to teach them rudimentary English over the summer months. At Camp Pendleton, several bilingual Vietnamese held classes for children, teaching them phrases such as, "hello, my name is——" and "how are you today?" But this instruction was neither systematic, sustained, nor representative of educational efforts that schools and their professional educators made in the fall when the IATF, through HEW, contracted for educational services for school-age children.[3]

The agencies that operated camp schools were not consistent among the three camps that remained open as of fall 1975. At Camp Pendleton, the San Diego County Public Schools ran the center's schools for the month and a half they were open; at Fort Chaffee, the West Arkansas Community College held the HEW contract; while at Fort Indian Town Gap the Pennsylvania State Department of Public Instruction took over this task. Three million seven hundred thousand dollars were allocated to both adult and children's education in all three camps.[4] The school at Fort Indian Town Gap was probably the best organized of the camp educational systems. It existed for about three months and became the model for efforts at Fort Chaffee. It employed at its height over 100 persons, 66 of whom were teachers certified to teach in the state of Pennsylvania and, given the scarcity of openings in the field, more than happy to have any teaching job.[5] Several teachers were experienced and had been recent victims of cutbacks in the Pennsylvania educational system. Although the teachers were trained to teach in American schools and were experienced, few had worked with Vietnamese or with children coming from culturally different backgrounds. They were, for the most part, young

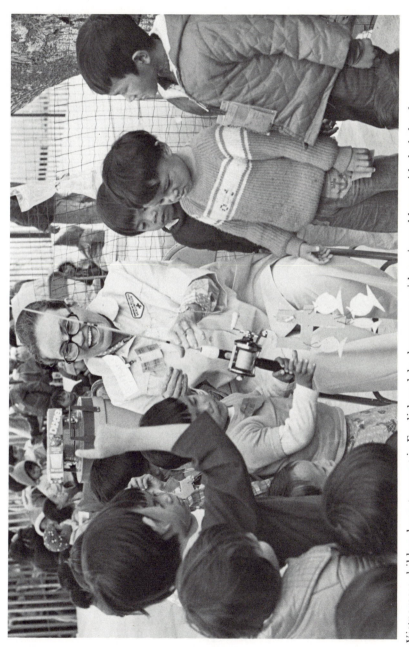

Vietnamese children learn to count in English and do elementary arithmetic problems with the help of a fishing pole, a Red Cross volunteer, and some weighted wooden fish. Camp Pendleton. *American Red Cross*

women and their previous teaching jobs had been in suburban or small town schools.

The school at Fort Indian Town Gap employed twelve resource people, five counselors, and various administrators and secretaries. The twelve resource people were curriculum coordinators, language arts specialists, an expert in English as a second language (ESL), art and music instructors. In the elementary grades the curriculum coordinators were both persons who had considerable experience abroad, one as the wife of an air force officer, another as a teacher of children on American military bases in the Panama Canal Zone. The high school curriculum coordinators had similar backgrounds: one had been a chemistry teacher and had lived in western Europe; another, formerly with the military, had taught English in Japan and worked for six years in a rural Pennsylvania school district. The resource personnel had long service records in the American public schools. A language specialist, for example, had taught fifteen years in inner-city schools and had worked for Project Head Start. The ESL expert, an eighteen-year veteran of the army's active reserve, had a master's degree in linguistics and in foreign language education. He got his job at the Fort Indian Town Gap school through his duty at the officer's candidate school at Fort Indian Town Gap that summer. The school counselors, most of whom were male, had been retrenched in the Pennsylvania schools' budgetary cutbacks.

At the head of the school system at Fort Indian Town Gap were two principals and a superintendent. The two school principals, one for the elementary, the other for the secondary grades, were called out of retirement to work at Fort Indian Town Gap and supervise the fifty or so people who comprised their staffs, fill out the numerous forms required by HEW and the Pennsylvania Department of Public Instruction, and do public relations. The superintendent of schools was on loan from the Pennsylvania Department of Public Instruction. He had taught for fifteen years in a rural Pennsylvania school district and worked his way up to coordinating a resource center at a state college before working for the state. He had initially come to Fort Indian

"Color Me Proud." Fort Indian Town Gap. *Fred Friedman*

Town Gap to coordinate the summer adult English language classes which had been staffed by volunteers.[6]

The school staff was made up of professional American educators who knew a lot about teaching in American schools and the American educational bureaucracy which was reproduced at Fort Indian Town Gap. These people knew nothing about Vietnam and Vietnamese children; most had never even worked with children who came from culturally different backgrounds. The school, while it operated among Vietnamese, teaching Vietnamese children, was divorced from the refugees. No teacher, administrator, or specialist spoke Vietnamese. Their only possible communication link with parents or students, few of whom spoke English, was through other Vietnamese who spoke English.

The school system hired two Vietnamese, former residents of Fort Indian Town Gap who had been relocated nearby, to work as aides. One was a former minister of primary education in Vietnam; the other had taught English literature in several Vietnamese universities. Their role was hardly one of giving Vietnamese a part in developing the school program.[7] According to them, their jobs were limited to serving as models for Vietnamese schoolchildren learning to speak English, to reinforcing the ban against speaking Vietnamese during school hours, and to disciplining children. They also were supposed to translate for teachers in the classrooms and to explain to teachers Vietnamese culture at appropriate times. They conducted in-service training for teachers on the organization of the Vietnamese school system, Vietnamese school curriculum, student/teacher relations, the Vietnamese child's psychology, and the Vietnamese family. Finally, these two Vietnamese handled all parent/school relations. They claimed they were instrumental in getting reluctant parents to send their children to school. Both stressed that they had no part at all in developing school curriculum. Their job was simply to facilitate the work of the American school bureaucracy.

These two Vietnamese were the only refugees employed by the school. Teachers used Vietnamese refugees as volunteers to translate in the classroom. Very few bilingual refugees worked at the school since, by the time school opened in September, few English-speaking Vietnamese were left in the camps.[8] Those who were preferred to volunteer their services to the resettlement agencies since they could gain some control over where they were resettled by so doing. As a result, teachers taught in English without the help of translators. Because of this, communication between English-speaking teachers and their Vietnamese-speaking students and their parents was almost nonexistent. This distressed several teachers who were frustrated by the blank stares they got in class and by their inability to do anything to explain class work to their students.[9] While some teachers, accustomed to getting through to their students, were dismayed by the lack of communication between themselves and those they taught, school administrators and curriculum experts had no such feelings. As did most people trained in ESL, they firmly believed that these children needed total submersion in English and would learn the language only if no Vietnamese was spoken for the six-hour school day. At daily meetings teachers were criticized for trying to teach a standard school curriculum, for requesting translators in the classroom, and for getting "too close" to their students, which was considered a breach of Vietnamese cultural norms.

School Curriculum: Teaching a New Culture

The curriculum of the schools at Fort Indian Town Gap and the other camps was not a reproduction of standard American school curriculum. Few of the materials used in the class could be found elsewhere.[10] They were especially designed for Indo-Chinese children by the Fort Indian Town Gap school curriculum coordinators in conjunction with ESL experts and HEW consultants. The purpose of the schools was to "teach the children about America" and get them "ready for American schools."[11] To carry this out, schools emphasized the teaching of English and accustoming children to the routines typical of American schools. Thus, the school day without fail began with attendance taking, the pledge of allegiance, the singing of patriotic

songs like "America the Beautiful," God Bless America,"
and a piece beginning, "We love our flag, our country's flag,
our own red, white and blue." This was followed by teachers
asking students, "what day is today?", an enumeration of the
days of the week in English, and a monologue by the teacher
on the weather ("today it is raining," etc.).[12] These opening
exercises mirrored the rest of the school day, for the classes
would launch into repetition of common English phrases
("I'm a man, I'm a girl," etc,) and look-say drills in which a
teacher would present a picture of some object like food and
point to it, say its English name, and try to get the children to
repeat the English term in unison after her. Math instruction
followed a similar course as did social studies and anything
else the school taught.

Most language instruction was grouped around central
themes which curriculum coordinators maintained were
critical to the children's adjustment to American schools and
the world in which they were to live, which, they all believed,
would be American, not Vietnamese. The three themes
emphasized in the elementary grades (kindergarten through
grade six) were school, family, and community life and
behavior. The first, on the school, consisted of learning
names for classroom objects (scissors, books, pencils), class
activities (story telling, sitting down, standing up), and class
behavior (raising one's hand to ask a question, asking
permission to go to the bathroom, coming to school on time,
helping clean up after classroom activities). The second
theme, unlike the one on the school, went beyond the
boundaries of the school and the child's acclimatization to it
and impinged on one of the fundamental aspects of his
culture—the family, its life and behavior. The theme, which
curriculum coordinators acknowledged was not too well
received by the children or their families, consisted of
teaching children what a family is, what "other" people live
in "my" house, family fun and activities, work father does,
work mother does, care of the home and toys, and the rooms
and furnishings of the home.[13]

That this material represented an unnecessary imposition
of American cultural norms is clearest in the way the

curriculum defined family, households, and each member's roles. A "finger game" which students in grades one through three were taught and drilled on daily exemplifies this:

> This is the mother so happy and gay (point to thumb)
> This is the father who works all day (point to the second finger)
> This is the brother so strong and tall (point to the middle finger)
> This is the sister who plays with her doll (point to the fourth finger)
> This is the baby the sweetest of all (point to the little finger)
> This is the *whole* family great and small (point to all fingers)[14] [author's italics]

The curriculum never deviated from defining the family as father, mother, sons, and daughters and the household as coextensive with this nuclear family. The "other" people who lived with the family in the household were persons Vietnamese of all classes considered part of their families and households—cousins, aunts, grandparents, uncles—as well as persons not in Vietnamese or American families—nurses, maids, cooks. A household was a nuclear family; the Vietnamese household consisting of the extended family simply did not exist in English in the classroom or in America as portrayed by the schools. The finger game cited above not only defined the family, it also presented sex role divisions of labor deriving from American stereotypes: father works to earn money, mother works to keep the home (if she does any work), brother is tall and strong, sister plays with dolls.

The family depicted by the school at Fort Indian Town Gap behaved like any American nuclear family, even in its leisure, celebrating Christmas holidays, Halloween, birthdays, going to picnics and parties, taking rides in the country, swimming, etc. Children were also depicted as doing tasks that American middle class children do in their own homes. They were to clean up the toys, make the beds, and care for their own rooms while helping younger sister or brother tend her or his room. The unit on the family extended the school's mission outside of acclimatizing Vietnamese children to American schools or teaching them about America; rather, it was depicting "my" or "our" family as American in structure, outlook, and sex role division of labor and activity.

The school at Fort Indian Town Gap taught Vietnamese children about the community as it might to any white, middle-class American child. The curriculum emphasized the benevolence of the policeman, the mayor, and the fireman and told children about services available in the community. No Vietnamese-American community existed.

The sex role divisions the schools presented are not necessarily typical of American families, nor are they universally accepted by all Americans. Over half of all American women work outside the household; most work out of economic necessity, including married women with children.[15] Not only are these sex role stereotypes at odds with many Americans' beliefs and practices, they also contrast with most immigrants' practices. Most Vietnamese women had been part of the money economy in their own country. Rural women, especially if from farming or fishing families, earned money through either petty trade, crafts, or working the family plot or in fishing. Their economic importance to the household increased as a result of the war. Inflation was rampant over the past twenty years; this alone forced women into the cash economy. Further, the war changed the occupational structure of Vietnam significantly, opening up women's work, while obliterating men's work. That is, farmers who had been relocated through the various rural programs aimed at rooting out the Viet Cong found themselves unemployed or unemployable except as soldiers, whose pay and disability benefits if maimed and discharged were notoriously low. They became dependent on their wives and daughters who could find work as prostitutes, bar girls, laundresses, maids—all war-created work, much of which was, until recently, related to the American presence.[16] Not only had rural women, even as urban immigrants, become an economic mainstay of Vietnamese families, so had urban middle class women. Wartime inflation had forced them into wage-earning occupations. Middle-class Saigon families found they could not survive without the women's wages. Mrs. H., an immigrant with five young children, had worked as a teletype operator; her husband had been manager of a radio network in South Vietnam. N. T. D.'s mother opened a knitting shop in Saigon to help make ends meet, even though her husband was a highly paid government official, two sons were army officers, one was a customs inspector, and another a university teacher.[17] The school, in short, was teaching Vietnamese children about family sex role divisions of labor that were foreign to immigrant children as well as widely challenged in the United States in both theory and practice.

The curriculum of the secondary school differed in some ways from that of the primary grades. The high school at Fort Indian Town Gap was not set up by grade level, determined by students' chronological age, as was the primary school. Rather, it was divided into groups depending on students' English language ability. Those students who knew no English, some English, or could make themselves understood relatively well in English were placed in separate classes. There were about eight hundred students taught by thirty-four teachers in the secondary school.

The secondary school tried to approximate American schools with defined class periods, home rooms, and special subjects like math, art, music, physical education, social studies, and English. Most of the time was spent on English instruction based, as was English instruction in the primary grades, on specific themes. The themes used in the secondary grades varied in some ways from those of the primary grades. Instead of stressing life in the family, the curriculum tried to prepare Vietnamese children for young adult life and work. In all, eight themes were used in the secondary school in basic, intermediate, and advanced classes. They included language used in school, health and safety, jobs, youth culture, daily activities (entertainment, jobs, getting apartments), holidays, food and clothing, and institutions in the community.[18] All these topics emphasized the child as an

In the school library at Fort Indian Town Gap. *Fred Friedman*

autonomous individual detached from the family as perhaps only American teenagers are. For example, the unit on jobs stressed student choice in becoming engineers, lawyers, nurses, radio repairmen, etc. Students in intermediate and advanced classes were assigned to write a few sentences on what occupations they wanted to pursue and why. Part of the week's lesson included looking at film strips about prospective jobs and introduced vocabulary relevant for teenagers finding an apartment of their own.[19]

The unit on youth in America had but one aim: to fit the Vietnamese teenager into the American teenage subculture of pizzerias, cokes, dances, dating, and dope. In the week of 20-24 October, students were taught the following vocabulary:

scene	acetylene tank	joint
stoned	"going ape"	grammar school
juvenile hall	"pot"	to stutter
groove	a lid (of pot)	overdose
cool	convulsions	heroin
gets high	parole officer	addict
"reds"	"speed"	

as well as vocabulary designated "typical teenage expressions" like "gimme," "coke," "aw," "say baby," "you rate."[20] This type of vocabulary seemed to be preparing Vietnamese teenagers for urban teenage culture where the adolescent takes drugs and gets in trouble either by overdosing on them or by being arrested by the police.

A dialogue for advanced classes assured teenagers that they would fit right into the American youth scene. Brian, Thanh, and Doug hang around snack bars, bored, discussing whether they'll spend Friday night at the "Y" dance, get themselves dates, or watch TV. Thanh's reactions, of course, are the same as Brian's and Doug's as he slurps down hamburgers and cokes and bemoans the lack of anything to do.[21] The assumption, of course, is that Vietnamese families make no greater or different demands on youth than do American families. Thanh, after all, is a free agent. The school, in some ways, was encouraging this by normalizing teenagers "hanging around" in an American peer group. Such teaching, in short, represents resocialization of some Vietnamese teenagers, particularly those from rural families. Schooling at Fort Indian Town Gap was preparing them to be "American kids" while adjusting them to American educational institutions. It did this with primary school children through instruction on the family; in the secondary school this was done through preparation for jobs and the adolescent subculture.

Because the schools taught Vietnamese about American life styles and culture does not mean that children learned and accepted what was presented to them. Most students did not understand what was going on in class, especially in the primary grades. They sat impassively while teachers went through their paces. Occasionally they talked to one another in Vietnamese despite the school ban on the language. (Several teachers pointed out that the students did not know they were supposed to refrain from speaking Vietnamese.[22])

The lack of communication between teacher and students was obvious in classrooms I observed at Fort Indian Town Gap. In October, the curriculum coordinator who escorted me to a fifth grade class picked up an orange crayon and asked a child who was busily coloring a carrot purple: "What color is this?" She pointed again to the orange crayon and repeated, "What color is this?" The child looked confused and turned to one of his classmates, asking him in Vietnamese what this person was saying. The curriculum coordinator responded immediately with, "Speak English only." "What color is this?" she repeated, pointing again to the orange crayon. The child, smiling, finally answered, "I am a carrot."[23]

In the high school students responded similarly. In one social studies class for students whose English was considered good, the teacher was trying to discuss elections with her students, showing them how the American political system works. The students sat at their tables and the teacher lectured to them about voting and elections. Few students took notes, but they assiduously watched their teacher. After a while she began questioning them. There was no response, even from students on whom she called. Thinking that the students found the discussion too removed from their experience, she began asking about elections in Vietnam. "Who was the first president of Vietnam?" she inquired several times. Silence reigned. "Who elected Diem President?" she persisted. Diem's name evoked a response. "He's dead," a student answered.[24] The school may have been trying to prepare children for American life, but it could do so only insofar as students could follow classroom instruction and curricular materials.

The school curriculum was by no means bicultural. It presented American culture to Vietnamese children. As far as the school was concerned, there was no need to incorporate elements of Vietnamese culture into its curriculum. The role of the school was to make Vietnamese children aware of American culture and prepare them to work within that context. Vietnamese students, most school people thought, knew about their own culture and how to behave within a Vietnamese context. What they did not know was what to expect from American life or how to behave in an American context.[25] The school's mission was to shape students' expectations of the future by introducing to them what American teachers and curriculum experts believed would be the world in which these children would be placed. The primary school's conception of that world contrasted sharply with that of the secondary school, and teachers of adults had their own idea of what Vietnamese needed to know in order to live and work in the United States.

Preparing Adults: Teaching English, Teaching Culture, Teaching Roles

Schooling for children was a relatively small part of the refugee camp's educational enterprise. Adult education was far more extensive and was part of every camp's life from almost the day it opened to the day it closed. From May through September English language classes were held day and night. At Fort Indian Town Gap up to 320 Americans, volunteering their services, were rotated weekly through 38 classrooms running five days a week providing two one-hour sessions each morning, afternoon, and evening. About 9,700 adults attended these sessions teaching basic English.[26] These classes were designed for heads of households only. Women and children were automatically excluded from them for "lack of space" and fear that men would lose face if a woman or child learned the language faster. This would, according to school officials, disrupt family life.[27]

English instruction before September 1975 at all refugee camps was based on "survival" and the course, consisting of sixteen lessons in all, was called "Survival English." It was developed by professional linguists from the Departments of State and Health, Education and Welfare, assisted at Fort Indian Town Gap by the Pennsylvania Department of Public Instruction. Emphasis was on oral English and not on reading or writing. It taught what its authors believed would be the bare minimum of English skills necessary for functioning in the United States.

The course consisted of sixteen lessons covering topics that included meeting strangers, finding a place to live, occupations, renting apartments, shopping, visiting the library, and applying for a job.[28] These lessons taught Vietnamese what constitutes politeness in American society and how to talk about the weather with friends or talk about food (lesson #11, for example, was about whether Mr. Jones wanted black coffee or coffee with cream and how much he should eat for breakfast). This course also taught Vietnamese some functional English—foods, parts of the body, and job names.

While Survival English taught rudimentary vocabulary and phrases, it also taught Vietnamese American sex role divisions of labor and prepared many members of Vietnam's former elite for new social and occupational roles. The lessons covering occupations illustrate this. Survival English lessons consisted of vocabulary introduced in isolation and then presented in sentences and phrases, usually in the form of a conversation between a "Mr. Brown" and a "Mr. Jones." Mr. Jones was no doubt the refugee, for he was forever asking Mr. Brown questions about shopping, finding a place to live, and job hunting. In the unit on jobs, Mr. Jones wanted to find a job that would allow him to support his wife and two children. The kinds of jobs he was looking for were, for the most part, on the lowest end of the American occupational spectrum: room clerk, salesman, cashier, laborer, cook, cleaning person, plumber, brick layer, secretary, typist, seamstress, and nurse's aide. Mr. Brown assured the refugee he would make more than enough money in these jobs for his family to live comfortably.

American stereotypic sex role division of labor was also clear in the Survival English course. Women were almost totally absent from curricular materials as well as classrooms due to American rather than Vietnamese initiatives. Women entered the dialogues only twice in the sixteen lessons: in a lesson called "conversation" and in another lesson on budgeting and shopping. In the former, women appeared in but two sentences: "Miss Jones missed the bus to the Miss Universe competition" and "she is an attractive girl." In the lesson on shopping, women went to the store only to purchase cosmetics, foods, baby needs, and aspirins; men shopped for shirts, houses, cars, and furniture. Women could purchase only small items without consulting their husbands.[29]

While women were almost absent from course materials and, when present, were depicted as pretty and interested in beauty contests, and as purchasers of small commodities, the Survival English course tended to place Vietnamese men in roles usually reserved for American women. In the lesson on occupations, men could be seamstresses, typists, cleaning persons, secretaries, and nurse's aides—traditionally women's occupations in the U.S. Further, the men, in subsequent lessons, find doctors for their families, locate stores for buying food and clothing, take care of children's schooling and select a church. This variation on American sex role stereotypes may well have been tailor-made for Vietnamese immigrants. Americans involved in designing the programs believed all efforts should be made to preserve the sanctity of the Vietnamese family by reinforcing patriarchal relations they assumed central to the family. Vietnamese women, I was told, never ventured out of the house and were subordinate to their husbands in a way American women were not. Thus, several curriculum coordinators presumed the men would take over what Americans thought were women's roles.[30]

The Survival English classes lasted only until late August. At that time the Pennsylvania State Department of Education received a contract to set up an adult school staffed by paid professional teachers and with a more "scientific" curriculum. With the HEW funding came a new curriculum taught by a group of individuals trained to teach foreigners and, unlike the volunteer teachers of the summer, less curious about Vietnamese culture and life. By the fall, twenty-six classrooms had been set up teaching English in two-hour-and-fifty-minute lessons three times a day five days a week to between twenty and forty adults in each class. The classes were segregated as to ability level with illiterate non-English speaking (about 120 Vietnamese in all), literate non-English speaking, literate persons who spoke a little English, and those who were literate and had substantial English language backgrounds taught in separate classes.

The adult school did not use Survival English curriculum. Rather it used a standard text, designed to teach English to non-English speakers—whether Arab, Italian, Chinese, German, French, or Vietnamese. The text was the three-volume MacMillan 900 Series. Fluency in the language—reading, speaking, and writing—clearly was the goal and the program was a long-term rather than a short-term affair. It was not designed to teach minimal language skills rapidly so that within six weeks a person could purchase food, ask directions, fill out job applications, or seek medical care. Rather, it focused on building a proper foundation for total mastery of English. Thus, the texts were full of words for colors, enumerations, weights, measures; for objects, for making requests, getting information; for talking about family, relatives, and marriage; for chatting with neighbors and friends; and for talking about the future and the weather. Eight weeks into the course (assuming that the classes covered one unit per week, which most did not), the text introduced vocabulary on sickness and health. Vocabulary related to occupations, finding jobs, shopping, and dealing with school or government authorities was totally lacking in the text and was absent in all classrooms, where teachers felt obliged to follow strictly the prescribed curriculum.

The MacMillan 900 Series taught social roles and culture as well as language, although it did this in a manner quite different from that of the Survival English course which it replaced. The series made no attempt to adjust Vietnamese to a new and lower occupational and social status than they had held in their own country. The world of work was nonexistent. Rather, the series presented a world of personal life—gift giving, relations with neighbors, work around the house, getting married, family celebrations, the weather, getting dressed, etc., all within the context of a suburban middle-class existence. In the series men work, women keep their suburban homes, have coffee breaks with neighbors, shop for and attend weddings and showers, bake cakes, etc. Much of the series dwells on depicting private social life and thus strongly delineates sex roles and social roles, not occupational roles. For this reason women are more visible in the MacMillan 900 Series than they were in the Survival English courses—in every lesson women are present baking cakes, shopping, chatting with neighbors, getting advice on children's health habits, preparing parties, etc. Men's roles, likewise, are delineated only in terms of social behavior, leisure, and household tasks (mowing the lawn, hammering nails in the wall, watching TV). Language curriculum based on these texts presented only one American lifestyle.

Textual materials, regardless of whether they were organized as in the Survival English or in the MacMillan 900 format, seemed aimed at teaching Vietnamese how to act and think as Americans while learning English. The conduct of class for the most part emphasized this even more, although in more subtle ways, for teachers elaborated on the texts, trying to make them more "useful" to Vietnamese. Two adult classes that I observed at Fort Indian Town Gap exemplified this. One was a class for illiterate Vietnamese with equal numbers of men and women in it—which was quite unusual, for in most classes the overwhelming majority of students were men. The women in the class were among the most traditional in the camp. They were from rural extended families—all had lacquered teeth and were dressed in the black peasant *ao ba-ba*; several had fished for a living. The teacher, a former anti–Vietnam war activist, discarded the MacMillan text because his students couldn't read. He opted instead to teach his own version of Survival English centering on learning the English terms for parts of the body and pains, things to eat, and jobs. His classes were chaotic. Students rarely understood him; he in turn did not understand what they said. His method consisted of pointing at objects and naming them, and pantomime. To introduce the word "chicken," for example, he clucked and crowed for the class. He then drilled them in the sentence "I want some chicken to eat."[31]

This class established occupational/social choices for Vietnamese that were not necessarily consonant with Vietnamese culture or with those Vietnamese were to face once resettled in America. This was apparent when it came to teaching about jobs. The instructor began the lesson with the phrase, "what kind of work do you do?" He then drew stick figures on the blackboard showing different kinds of work—ditch digging, selling, etc.—naming them all. After introducing phrases like "I am a ditch digger," "I am a mechanic," he asked each of his thirty or more students: "What kind of work do you do?" The first student to respond was a young man who replied, "I rat-a-tat-tat" while pointing his fingers like a gun. The teacher corrected him with, "I work with my hands," which the man repeated. Next to recite was a middle-aged woman. She made a motion that looked like casting nets. The teacher retorted: "I am a housewife." The woman looked puzzled. The teacher then drew a stick figure holding a broom inside a home on the blackboard and repeated "I am a housewife." She and the women sitting with her began a lively discussion in Vietnamese and started laughing. The teacher then drilled these former fisherwomen and petty traders as a group with the phrase, "I am a housewife."

A second class at Fort Indian Town Gap for students whose English was reasonably good was more subtle in imposing American cultural norms, for the class had pretenses of being bicultural. Each session was divided into three one-hour segments. The first segment used the Mac-Millan 900 Series. Students read, both individually and in unison, phrases and conversations in the text, with the teacher interrupting to correct their pronunciation or some of the text's cultural biases. One evening, for example, after students read a conversation aloud in which Mr. James purchased a new house, the teacher stopped the class to explain to her students that the book gave the impression that all houses in the U.S. were new houses, and that it was desirable to buy a new home.[32] Vietnamese, she pointed out, probably wouldn't be able to afford to buy a new house. This, she added, was not a tragedy since old houses were nice, too. Besides, she ended, most people from Fort Indian Town Gap would live in apartments and would be happy in their new apartments. Her message was clear: you don't need a new house to be happy.

The second hour of class tried to bring a bit of Vietnam into the classroom. Tea and cookies were served, the ban against speaking Vietnamese was lifted, and students socialized with one another and their teacher. The teacher frequently invited refugees who owned guitars to class so that students could sing folk songs and Vietnamese popular ballads.

The third hour of class was devoted to student compositions. The teacher had students write about themselves in English and read these essays aloud in class. Two to three essays per night were covered. These autobiographical sketches were often emotional outpourings of despair. In one class a student, a former sailor, spoke about how sad he was to have left Vietnam and how he wanted to kill himself. He read this to a rather stony-faced audience of fellow Vietnamese who disapproved of his venting his emotions in front of strangers and in English. More typical of the essays was one that a student read rather quickly about how he was born in Saigon, went to school, and is now in the United

States. The teacher suggested he rewrite his essay to include more of his feelings about being in the United States. In this class, the teacher assumed that Vietnamese needed to express their feelings in the same manner as Americans. The teacher stated this explicitly as did the counselor of the adult school, who thought Vietnamese reserve was "unhealthy." English class became a way for Vietnamese to learn not only how to speak English, but also to deal with their emotional lives on American terms.

English language classes were, in short, classes that taught American culture as they taught pronunciation and vocabulary. The teachers and programs, like the day school for children, were divorced from Vietnamese culture. They were run by Americans, with Americans determining what Vietnamese needed to know to live in this country. Because of who set up and controlled curriculum and format, Vietnamese had no say as to what they were being prepared for, what they would learn, or how they would learn it.

Vocational Education and Cultural Orientation

English language classes were, by far, the most heavily promoted and attended of all educational programs in the camps. Learning English for Vietnamese adults was the key to leaving the camps and earning a living in the future. Those who might have been reticent about attending were "encouraged" by area coordinators and barracks chiefs. Formal education in the camps other than English language classes consisted of vocational courses, a series of cultural orientation programs called "Transition America" developed by camp management in conjunction with HEW, and, at Fort Indian Town Gap only, a program called "Women in America" sponsored by the Pennsylvania Commission on Women. These efforts, like English classes and other educational programs in the camps, tried to set the terms on which Vietnamese would adjust to America. They were consistent with school programs only to the extent that they involved Americans selecting these terms, not Vietnamese.

Vocational Classes

Every camp theoretically ran vocational courses for its

residents. These courses, however, as the ones at Fort Indian Town Gap, should not be confused with vocational training. Rather, they were courses designed to teach Vietnamese the specialized English terminology necessary to work at skills individuals already had. There were five such vocational courses operating at Fort Indian Town Gap including ones on electricity, plumbing, and carpentry. About ten persons attended each of these classes regularly.[33] Skilled workers were few in number among the immigrants, as shown in chapter 3. Further, those who had a skilled trade found sponsors relatively easily because they appeared to have greater potential for becoming self-supporting than the bulk of the refugees. These classes began in late September when only the "problem" cases—Vietnamese who had difficulty in finding relocation opportunities, usually those who had no skills useable within the American economy and who could speak no English—remained in the camps. This perhaps best explains poor turnout for the classes.

The only vocational course at Fort Indian Town Gap that taught a skill other than language was the home economics class. In it the teacher showed Vietnamese how to use electric stoves and appliances like refrigerators, mixers, blenders, etc. Much of the instructional time was devoted to describing prepackaged foods and in cooking demonstrations. Among the things the class prepared were pickled beets, chili con carne, jello molds, and gingerbread.[34] The course, in short, taught the techniques of operating an American kitchen and how Vietnamese might buy, cook, and eat American style. Despite its "practical" value, only eight to ten persons steadily attended it.

Orientation Sessions

At all camps three-hour Transition America classes were held for Vietnamese who, having found sponsors, were about to leave the centers. These classes were conducted by Americans—assisted by translators—with whom HEW specially contracted. The sessions, which began in late May, had one purpose: to present Vietnamese with the basic features of

American life "so that refugees, when they leave the camp, will have a better understanding of what is expected of them as well as a better understanding of American behavior."[35]

Classes were not open to all; refugees were personally invited to attend the three-hour meetings. At Fort Indian Town Gap, the HEW representative obtained lists of all persons who had found sponsors and whose "out-processing" papers (for example, clearance by INS and HEW) were ready for them to leave camp. He then sent a written invitation to attend Transition America to those on the lists over 18 years of age. Attendance was voluntary and strongly encouraged by both camp management and resettlement agency case workers.

Transition America was supposed to supply the minimum of "practical" information its organizers thought necessary for Vietnamese to have about America. The assumption, with good reason, was that Vietnamese had little conception of American ways of doing things and what kinds of demands they could and could not make on sponsors or other Americans with whom they would have contact. According to the director of Transition America at Fort Indian Town Gap, his program focused on four things which he presumed Vietnamese lacked knowledge of and/or were essential for them to know to "get by." These were: (1) how to get a job and what kind of job to expect; (2) how to find housing; (3) differences between American and Vietnamese family structures that Vietnamese must learn to "respect;" (4) whom to rely on in case of need or emergency. The last two items were deemed important because they impinged on sponsor/refugee relations, particularly in cases where individual Americans rather than organizations or groups like churches became sponsors. Vietnamese, who were to live with their sponsors, needed to be aware of American family structures and live within them at least temporarily and learn what kinds of demands they could make of American families. Particularly important, the program organizer pointed out, was for Vietnamese to understand that many social services were government-rather than family-provided and that refugees should know to ask the government rather than the sponsor for medical care and certain types of financial assistance.

Transition America's program was originally based on American concepts of difficulties Vietnamese would face, which were initially defined in terms of financial independence and daily survival. According to the HEW contractor for the program at Fort Indian Town Gap, the program was modified as needs of Vietnamese became more clearly defined through relocation and problems both refugees and sponsors brought to the Interagency Task Force and resettlement agencies. In May the program consisted almost exclusively of "how to" advice: how to shop at a supermarket, rent a place to live, find a job, register children for school, etc. By October, when friction between refugees and sponsors came to the IATF's attention, "cultural" concerns became paramount as did the issue of readjusting Vietnamese expectations of jobs, sponsors' ability to help them, and their lifestyle possibilities in America.

Transition America was the official cultural orientation program in the camps. There were, however, other organized programs. At Fort Indian Town Gap, the International Rescue Committee (IRC) held its own version of Transition America for Vietnamese it was resettling. The program was held Friday afternoons by a caseworker for the agency who spoke Vietnamese fluently. In his orientation sessions he gave practical information similar to that presented in Transition America. The IRC program ended in late October when the caseworker left the camps for a job in the agency's San Francisco offices. It was never too well attended, possibly because it duplicated Transition America and the information given to Vietnamese in the camp school, in meetings with resettlement agency caseworkers, or through camp newspapers.[36]

Formal cultural orientation was not confined to dealing with practical aspects of adjusting to America as HEW defined it or developing modes of behavior appropriate to getting along with one's sponsor. It also extended to teaching new roles for Vietnamese in their private lives. To some extent this was clear in the school programs where children and teenagers were taught about American nuclear family life and roles they could comfortably assume in it and in the adult English language classes that delineated sex role behavior and social relations in which Vietnamese could expect to engage. American efforts at teaching new roles perhaps was clearest in the Pennsylvania Commission on Women's six-class series called "Women in America," held at Fort Indian Town Gap in fall 1975.

Women in America

Women in America was perhaps the most controversial cultural orientation program at Fort Indian Town Gap. It was consciously designed to change what the program's organizers perceived to be Vietnamese family behavior and sex role divisions of labor.[37] The series was controversial not because it presented Vietnamese with roles perhaps at odds with ones they had assumed in their own country—all Americans in the camp did that in one way or another— but because it was presenting roles different from those school authorities and IATF officials thought appropriate for Vietnamese or Americans. The Pennsylvania Commission on Women representatives criticized camp management and the adult school for reinforcing patriarchal relations that they assumed persisted among immigrant families. They pointed particularly to the exclusion of women from English language classes up to the fall and the emphasis on attracting men to cultural orientation classes.

The Women in America program began in mid-October. Initially six successive meetings were planned, but by the second meeting it became clear that the refugees would not be able to attend all six meetings. The program was then rearranged to give the same presentations each week. The purpose of the program, according to the director of information of the commission, was to give Vietnamese women some idea of the diversity of roles they might assume in the United States outside the family by showing them how men might help with household tasks and child rearing and the kinds of jobs women could find. The commission also wanted to use the program to explain to immigrant women their rights and the various government agencies and private organizations to which they as women might turn to safeguard their rights.

The Women in America program was presented by four American women assisted by a translator.[38] The first part of the program discussed American family life and showed photographs of men bathing children, changing diapers, cooking, and washing dishes. The second presentation explained that women had a right to hold property, get divorced, obtain abortions, use birth control, and vote. This was followed by a description of jobs women could hold accompanied by photos of women driving tractors and bulldozers and working as nurses, teachers, and corporate executives. The final part of the program talked about organizations that served women, mentioning groups like the YWCA, the League of Women Voters, Planned Parenthood, and the National Welfare Rights Organization. The conduct of the meetings changed each time due to Vietnamese response. At several meetings, discussion centered on weather and/or shopping as women, perhaps more comfortable in classes designed just for them, asked about things that concerned them the most at the time.[39]

At other meetings, Vietnamese openly objected to the program's presentation of women's roles. Several men openly challenged the wisdom of the roles the Pennsylvania Commission on Women presented. At some meetings they snickered and groaned when pictures showing men doing housework were shown. One middle-aged Vietnamese man told the organizers that "women in this country [the U.S.] have too much power." A Mr. Vinh, a forty-one-year-old accountant, believed that the careers for women would result only in women being overworked.[40]

The men were not always the ones to object to the content of the program. Several women also let their disapproval be known. A middle-aged Vietnamese woman, dressed in the peasant *ao ba-ba* and wearing a crucifix, grilled the program director on monogamy at a meeting I attended. She kept asking why her husband couldn't have two wives in the U.S.

and, if he couldn't, which wife retained her status in the U.S.
The woman was hardly serious. She was a devout Catholic—
and she was her husband's only wife. She did, however, seem
to take great pleasure in making the program coordinators
uneasy. The women sitting with her enjoyed the interchange, laughing and talking among themselves while the
questions were being answered.[41]

Whether Vietnamese found the roles presented by the
Pennsylvania Commission on Women offensive is perhaps
irrelevant. Some did, some did not. What is relevant is the
fact that, regardless of whether they agreed or disagreed with
the program, many Vietnamese who attended clearly resent-
ed American intrusion into their life-styles. They made this
resentment felt at the Women in America sessions more than
they did elsewhere, partly because they were fully aware that
camp authorities disapproved of the program and they
risked nothing in challenging it, partly because the roles
presented were offensive to many Vietnamese, and partly
because the program coordinators, unlike school teachers,
invited Vietnamese response to their presentation. The very
same woman who baited the Pennsylvania Commission on
Women program director about the husband with two wives
and laughed so heartily at pictures of men doing housework
made fun of her English teacher when he asked her to recite
the phrase "I am a housewife." In English class she was not
asked to respond; she could only laugh. In Women in
America she could let her anger be shown—which she did
both by laughing and by repeating irksome questions and
groaning loudly at American answers to them.

Women in America to some extent represents some of the
ironies of the cultural orientation programs for refugees in
the camps. The program's content contrasted sharply with
sex-role divisions of labor presented in English language
classes or in the primary school. Of this the women running
the programs were well aware, as were school officials and
other Americans in the camp. The program became controversial precisely because it underscored deep divisions
among Americans as to what the American way of life, if
there is such a thing, is and how aspects of it should be

presented to immigrants. The programs merely underscored American confusion and division.

Images of America in the Daily Newspaper

Each camp published for its residents its own newspaper, which was bilingual and devoted not only to informing Vietnamese of camp rules, special events, and American law relating to them, but also to providing Vietnamese with information about American institutions and customs and how Vietnamese would be expected to behave in American society. To a great extent the newspapers—*Dat Lanh* at Fort Indian Town Gap, *Thong Bao* at Camp Pendleton, and *Ton Dan* at Fort Chaffee—duplicated the work of the schools and Transition America in preparing Vietnamese to live in the U.S. To some extent they elaborated on them. A look at the camp dailies, especially the cultural articles they contained, will complete my description of efforts within the camps to prepare Vietnamese for life in America. The analysis that follows is based primarily on *Dat Lanh*, the bilingual daily of Fort Indian Town Gap published by the U.S. Army's Psychological Operations Unit, and *Thong Bao*, Camp Pendleton's newspaper. I have not had access to a complete collection of *Ton Dan*. In the discussion that follows it is possible to assume that *Ton Dan* varies little from the other two papers in their content if only because the publishers of the papers were similar, as were their functions. There is basically little difference between *Dat Lanh* and *Thong Bao* in news stories, the publication of camp regulations, and in the columns they contained: "Life in the U.S.," "The American Way of Life," "New Life," etc.

The newspapers began publication almost immediately after the camps opened. *Thong Bao's* first issue was on 9 May 1975 (the camp opened 1 May); *Dat Lanh's* inaugural issue was on 28 May. The first two or three issues were published only in Vietnamese; thereafter the paper became bilingual. At Fort Indian Town Gap, where a substantial number of Cambodians awaited resettlement, occasional Cambodian language editions appeared. The early issues of the newspapers had almost no cultural articles in them. Rather, they explained camp organization, barracks rules at Fort Indian Town Gap, and rules regarding tent sharing at Pendleton; explained the resettlement agencies' functions and immigration law as well as services available in the camps; and published lists of incoming refugees. At Fort Indian Town Gap, *Dat Lanh* in its second issue provided instructions on how to work the camp's telephones. The paper also announced camp events: classes, movies, sports matches, clothing distributions, clinic hours, etc. Informational pieces relating to camp regulations and events dominated the first ten issues or so of the newspapers; they made up close to 50 percent of all items published in *Dat Lanh* and *Thong Bao* throughout their six-month lives. These informational pieces were much in keeping with the primary stated purpose of the papers, which was to help communication between the Interagency Task Force and the refugees.

While the newspapers were a vehicle for camp management's job in running the camps, they were never solely announcement sheets. From about their second week of publication, the papers began to assume the task of orienting Vietnamese to American life and reassuring them they would have no difficulties fitting into the country's social and economic life. *Thong Bao* as early as its fourteenth issue on 29 May ran a front page article entitled "Vietnamese Settlers, Can They Adapt?" answering the question in the affirmative. On 3 June it carried an article assuring Vietnamese they could easily find jobs. These assurances were also backed up with information about repatriation stating that the new government of South Vietnam would reject anyone wishing to return home. This, by the way, was one of the few pieces of information published on Vietnam in *Thong Bao*.[42] *Dat Lanh*, like *Thong Bao*, ran very few articles on South Vietnam. It never carried a column called "News on Vietnam." The only camp newspaper that carried significant news about Vietnam was *Chan Troi Moi*, the Guam daily, the only newspaper edited and published by Vietnamese refugees. The camp newspapers, by such news selection, in essence argued that Vietnamese were in the United States to stay and should get on with the task of accommodating to what the paper heralded as the "new life." *Thong Bao*, on 9 June, three days after it had announced that the South Vietnamese government would not allow refugees to return home, began publishing a series of articles called "Life in the U.S.," or sometimes "Choosing a New Life," "American Customs," and "American Ways," in almost every issue.

Dat Lanh, the Fort Indian Town Gap paper, had a similar progression. On 14 June, the second week of its publication, the paper began a series of articles designed to teach Vietnamese about American history, geography, and the political system as well as to describe American customs in its column sometimes called "The Experience of Living in America" and "The American Way." *Dat Lanh* was somewhat more systematic than *Thong Bao* in this regard. On 14 June *Dat Lanh's* front page was printed in red, white, and blue ink with an American flag underlying the bilingual text. The whole issue was devoted to a history of the U.S. armed forces. Thereafter, every day the Fort Indian Town Gap paper carried either a minibiography of an American president (they appeared in alphabetical rather than chronological order) or a spread on one of the states in the union. Whenever there was a holiday, these articles were replaced with almost full issue coverage of the holiday. The Fourth of July, Labor Day, Thanksgiving, even Halloween were explained in detail: why they were holidays and what Americans did to celebrate them. From 1 July to the day *Dat Lanh* ceased publication, these kinds of articles filled up about one-third of each issue.

Informing Vietnamese about the United States as *Dat Lanh* and *Thong Bao* did, when taken against the blackout of news about South Vietnam, encouraged Vietnamese to become immigrants, rather than refugees, for the U.S. was now to be their country, their "new land." Learning about American holidays, presidents, and states and their histories was a first step in such socialization. Vietnam simply ceased to exist in the papers except as a place to which the immigrants could not return.

Carrying article after article on American presidents,

holidays, and states and omitting news about Vietnam was a subtle form of cultural reorientation. Less subtle were the numerous articles called "The American Way" in *Dat Lanh* and "New Life" or some similar title in *Thong Bao*. These articles told Vietnamese how they would have to live to survive in the U.S. Article after article, often on the front page, talked about renting houses, buying cars, getting insurance, shopping in supermarkets, the American diet and how food is prepared, how much to tip waitresses at restaurants, how to register at hotels, dress appropriate to particular occasions, etc.[43]

Dat Lanh published several articles on social behavior in its "American Way of Life" columns. The lead article of 7 September 1975 was entitled "Men and Women" and provided Vietnamese men with advice on their relations with women. Men were told, if they were married, to take their wives on trips. All men, the article continued, should rise when a woman enters the room; they should open doors for women and pay all bills. Vietnamese men, the article went on, should not be "frightened" by American women, especially those who seem "noisy, aggressive and domineering." Most American women, *Dat Lanh* pointed out, are "quiet, content and gentle," and enjoy being taken care of by men. *Dat Lanh* also counseled women on how to behave toward men and encouraged young girls to join sports clubs or take ballroom dancing courses in order to meet eligible young men. It cautioned women against asking men out. "In this country the man . . . does the inviting and planning," *Dat Lanh* told its audience. Women, however, could invite men to their homes for dinner. Most of these articles were written in the second person, suggesting that you, the refugee, need to behave in the manner *Dat Lanh* suggests, to get on in this society. American customs, in short, were not merely things Americans did, they were things people who lived in America did.

Cultural Orientation in the Camps and the Immigrants

Cultural orientation in the camps, regardless of whether it consisted of the formal teaching of English to adults, the schooling of children ages six through eighteen, meetings describing women's rights, or articles written in camp newspapers, was designed to prepare Vietnamese to live in America. The programs existed to get Vietnamese used to the idea that they were going to remain in this country for an indefinite period of time and would need to begin functioning within an American rather than a Vietnamese context. The programs introduced Vietnamese to American culture and social norms. They described to Vietnamese the type of behavior expected of persons who lived in the country and what Vietnamese might expect when they left the camps. The programs covered a range of American cultural and social life. They described American families, teenage subcultures, American food, houses, and jobs, and sex role divisions of labor.

The programs did more than inform Vietnamese about American life, they also tried to mold Vietnamese expectations of their future lives in the United States. The elementary school taught about households consisting solely of nuclear families, as if they were the child's own, rather than Americans' families. The high school introduced Vietnamese adolescents to the teenage drug subculture—and tried to teach them the vocabulary for participating in it. It attempted to prepare Vietnamese teenagers for a world in which they would be autonomous, detached from their families in ways American rather than Vietnamese youth have been.

Adult expectations of their futures in the U.S. were also part of cultural orientation programs in the camps. English language classes became places where Vietnamese learned about a range of occupations corresponding more to the types of work Americans assumed Vietnamese would take in the U.S. than to the type of work that Vietnamese had in fact done in the past. Many former government ministers, lawyers, journalists, and businessmen were told about how they could support their families working as dishwashers, cooks, nurse's aides, and, as the Survival English courses tried to point out, these occupations were "respectable," ones about which Americans, and by implication Vietnamese, had few qualms. Vietnamese women, many of whom had been in the labor force in Vietnam, were prepared to give up this role in favor of one in which they became housewives, mothers, and shoppers.

The kinds of lifestyles for which English language classes, newspaper articles, and orientation sessions prepared Vietnamese were not necessarily consistent. Survival English introduced immigrant men to a world of work at the lowest end of the American occupational structure and women to roles as housewives; other textual materials oriented Vietnamese to the suburban lifestyles and leisure of the American middle class. Women's social roles were expanded on and not necessarily confined to shopping or household tasks. The Women in America program presented different and contradictory roles for women, preparing them for the world of work and a family life in which household tasks were shared by men and women.

These cultural orientation programs were a mass of contradictions. They presented what various Americans thought Vietnamese ought to know about the country in order to live in it. There was, however, little agreement among Americans about which aspects of American life Vietnamese needed to be informed of. Thus, Vietnamese were presented with varying aspects of American life and encouraged to adapt to them, regardless of whether those aspects contradicted one another or were at odds with Vietnamese lifestyles and culture. Americans were not clear about what their own culture was—and they had even less of a conception of Vietnamese culture. There simply was no way to resolve these contradictions.

Most Vietnamese accepted, or began to accept, their futures as being in the United States. Most knew that eventually they would somehow have to change their lifestyles and accommodate to American society. But they had little conception of what those changes would involve. Many found the changes Americans proposed in the orientation programs confusing, and more often than not, reacted passively. This passivity derived, to some extent, from their inability to comprehend what was being proposed for them. Other immigrants rejected almost every new way of life the programs described, like the fisherwoman from Vang Tau who mocked both the image of woman as housewife and as worker. She seemed to resent being prepared for an American world, either because she was unwilling to concede that she was breaking with a Vietnamese world, or because she was not yet able to conceive of her place in American society.

Perhaps this underscores some of the problems inherent in the whole idea of attempting to prepare Vietnamese immigrants for American society in advance of their entry into it. Americans can only prepare immigrants for the contexts in which they as Americans live, which in this country are many. They cannot possibly have lived and worked in the context of newcomers who still perceive themselves as part of Vietnamese society and culture.

Chapter Six

Being Sponsored and Resettled

The U.S. Immigration law specifies that each immigrant have a sponsor—resident relatives, a citizen or a group of citizens—who will be responsible for the newcomer's welfare until he can assume the responsibility himself. The law states more specifically that the immigrant must have this sponsor *before* he can enter the U.S.

"Bao Lan Cua Ngo vao Hoa Ky,"
Dat Lanh, vol. 4, no. 2
(25 October 1975), p. 1.

Camp life centered on getting Vietnamese out into American society. In-processing, camp routines, educational programs, and the very organization of the camps had but one end—to prepare Vietnamese to live within an American community. There were only four ways Vietnamese could leave the camps: by seeking and getting third-country resettlement through the embassy of that third country; by seeking repatriation; by showing a family's ability to be immediately self-supporting with proof of a cash reserve of at least $4,000 per family member; or by finding an American sponsor—either a resident alien, citizen, or group of citizens willing to undertake fiscal and moral responsibility until the refugee became self-supporting.

The American government encouraged third-country resettlement. From the time planning the evacuation and

resettlement began in mid-April, the U.S. Senate charged the
IATF to involve other countries in assuming responsibility
for Vietnamese and to work as closely as possible with the
United Nations High Commissioner on Refugees.[1] The
IATF did everything within its power to encourage resettlement in countries other than the United States. It provided
facilities within the camps to representatives of the Canadi-
an government and assigned State Department personnel to
facilitate arrangements for resettling refugees in countries
other than the U.S. Camp newspapers also encouraged
Vietnamese to think about resettling elsewhere. *Dat Lanh,*
the bilingual daily at Fort Indian Town Gap, at one point
ran a headline on its front page "And Why Not Malawi?"
This article was accompanied by a map of Africa and a long
description of how well suited Malawi, given its climate, was
for Vietnamese.

Third-country resettlement, while encouraged by the
U.S., was not a major resettlement option for Vietnamese. In
all, 6,632 Vietnamese made their way to other countries. By
far the largest number (3,926) went to Canada, followed by
France (1,877), Australia (161), Taiwan (120), and the Philippines (115).[2] The number was small because third countries
were not willing to grant blanket acceptance to Vietnamese.
Nations like Canada, Iran, Australia, Ivory Coast, and
Malawi sent delegations to the camps to encourage Vietnamese to resettle. They attempted to attract only highly
skilled individuals who spoke English or French and focused their efforts on recruiting engineers, medical doctors,
dentists, etc. These individuals were relatively few in
number and had no problem finding sponsors in the U.S., if
they chose. The state of Nebraska's offer to help Vietnamese
medical doctors obtain American licenses by paying them a
yearly salary while they prepared for examinations was
certainly more appealing than an uncertain future in Malawi or Iran. Countries like France allowed entry only to those
individuals who had relatives already in the country, spoke
French well, and had a job awaiting them.[3] Canada accepted
Vietnamese who were related to residents of the country as
well as those who were skilled professionals. Taiwan opened

its doors to 120 ethnic Chinese leaving Vietnam.

Repatriation was a second route out of the camps. By October 1975, 1,546 persons had returned to Vietnam.[4] These individuals were men, categorized by the U.S. government as single. Most were members of the Vietnamese military who had come to the United States either on ships or planes whose commanders decided to leave Vietnam, or who had "made a mistake." Most were characterized as lonely, missing wives, children, and/or mothers left behind. The 1,546 who repatriated did so from Guam.

Requests for repatriation began as early as May. At Fort Chaffee alone by 29 May, 265 Vietnamese signed up with the United Nations representative to return home.[5] By 20 June, 80 of these individuals demonstrated against what they believed was American unwillingness to allow them to go home. They demanded that they be transferred to Camp Pendleton and then sent to Vietnam. On 22 June 164 were sent to Camp Pendleton and eventually transferred to Guam, where on 30 September the U.S. agreed to outfit a ship for them. On 16 October the ship *Vietnam Thuong Tin I* set sail. This occurred after several demonstrations on Guam, including a scuffle between American military police and refugees.[6]

More than 1,546 Vietnamese requested repatriation. By December 1975 another 403 Vietnamese and 183 Cambodians had registered with the United Nations High Commissioner on Refugees to return home; 115 of these people (most of whom were Cambodians) refused to accept interim sponsors and ended up in a halfway house in Philadelphia.[7] The problem, according to American officials, was that the Vietnamese government refused to commit itself to accepting repatriates. The Vietnamese government did receive the 1,546 persons who sailed from Guam, but has made no provisions for another 403 refugees who wish to go home.

Most Vietnamese—129,729 in all—went through the refugee camps and were "sponsored" into the United States primarily through voluntary agencies contracted for such purposes.

Sponsorship: What It Is and What It Entails

Vietnamese could not officially enter the U.S. until a U.S. resident, citizen, or group of citizens agreed to assume fiscal and moral responsibility for them to ensure that they "do not become public charges."[8] According to an IATF pamphlet prepared to generate offers of assistance for Vietnamese, an individual willing to sponsor a Vietnamese

> makes a commitment to feed, clothe, and shelter a refugee family until it is self-supporting. The sponsor assists the refugee head of household in finding a job, enrolling the children in school, and in understanding our customs. Ordinarily the health care costs are all the responsibility of the sponsor. However, unemployed refugees are eligible for Medicare coverage which will protect the sponsor from unusual medical liability.
>
> When the refugee becomes self-supporting, the sponsorship obligation is basically one of friendship.[9]

Sponsorship implied a large financial obligation. The LIRS, one of the nine agencies involved in finding sponsors for the immigrants, estimated that resettlement costs were $5,601 per household. LIRS arrived at this figure by considering the minimal needs of a family of four adults over 18, two of whom would enter the American work force. The sum included furniture for a living room and two bedrooms as well as minimal clothing,* rent and utility deposits, one month's rent, $50 worth of food, and medical and hygiene supplies (Band-Aids, aspirin, soap, etc.). About $1,150 of the LIRS budget was earmarked for support services to immigrants: help in finding jobs, apartments, language instruction, etc. These figures, LIRS's David Johnson maintained, were "quite conservative."[10] They did not provide for medical care and assumed that Vietnamese would be able to pay for their own food after one week and their rent after one month.

---

* For a woman, the budget provided for two winter dresses, two skirts, two blouses, one coat, one sweater, stockings, etc.

A sponsor did get some financial assistance from the government. The government provided a $500 resettlement grant for each refugee. Between $50 and $500 of this sum was retained by the voluntary agency which arranged the sponsorship for the refugee.[11] They used this money to cover their administrative costs and followup work. This left the sponsorship organization or individual with up to $1,800 for resettling a family of four immigrants. The sponsors' expenses would be $5,160 at a minimum. The costs, however, were usually much greater since Vietnamese households averaged over five persons.[12]

The financial commitment sponsorship entailed was indeed great. It had several implications for the pattern of resettlement and the types of persons or organizations willing to become sponsors. The costs thrown on individuals and organizations meant that Vietnamese resettlement would be scattered. Few individuals could afford to lay out at least $3,000 for a family of four. Organization sponsorship in which this responsibility was shared was far more viable. The number of these organizations within any community was bound to be limited. The sponsorship requirement and the financial obligations it implied encouraged scattering Vietnamese throughout the country.

Second, because of the financial obligations that came with sponsorship, employment possibilities for an immigrant became a major consideration in the relationship. Job offers became confounded with sponsorship offers and led, according to Donald Anderson of LIRS in his testimony to the U.S. Senate's Judiciary Committee Subcommittee on Refugees and Escapees in July 1975, to these offers being "little more than requests for indentured servants, bed mates, or cheap labor."[13] The lack of government financing of the Vietnamese increased the possibility of immigrant exploitation at the hands of a sponsor since the financial pressures of taking care of a stranger, especially in a severe economic depression in which jobs were scarce, led to sponsorship tied to contract labor. By July the IATF began defining sponsorship as either "an offer of support, employment, or both."[14]

Connecting sponsorship with employment also tended to

increase the pressure to disperse Vietnamese throughout the country. The country was in recession; jobs were hard to come by; and no one community was willing to welcome large numbers of foreigners who might take jobs away from Americans. This fear was expressed countless times, by members of the Senate Judiciary Subcommittee and in the pressure towns exerted against individuals and churches who offered to sponsor Vietnamese families. The case of Island Pond, Vermont, illustrates this. Three families in the town offered to sponsor a Vietnamese family of fifteen. The head of the Vietnamese family had been the former minister of ethnic affairs in the Thieu government. The town select-men and the mayor, expressing fears on the part of some of their constituency, pressured the families who had made the offer to withdraw it. The first selectman summed up the town's feelings:

> Who the hell is going to hire Vietnamese people when there aren't enough jobs for our own? I don't believe the federal government should bring a bunch of people and then dole them out on welfare at our cost. We've got nothing against the Vietnamese, but why should a town like this bear the burden of people the federal govern-ment brought over here?[15]

In the case of this town, no immigrants were allowed to settle. In other towns one family numbering four or five persons seemed the upper limit.

The sponsorship system as practiced by the federal govern-ment increased local fears that they would have to support immigrants resettled in their communities. It was not until August 1975 that the federal government provided for any assistance to refugees, including medicare for major ill-nesses, despite the fact that it had more or less committed itself to reimbursing states and localities for medicaid given to refugees earlier. By this time almost half the refugees had found sponsors. Several states including Michigan and Texas had refused to enroll immigrants in their medicaid program since the federal government had no procedures for reimbursement.[16] If any public assistance were to be necessary, it would fall on local resources and, until the federal government came up with procedures for paying welfare costs, Island Pond, Vermont, echoed the concern of other towns and states about whether it was advisable, given the recession, to allow a community organization or a church or individual within that community to sponsor Vietnamese. If they did, the pressure was to take not only a small family, but also only one family.

Sponsorship was not exclusively a relation between immigrants and individual Americans or organizations. It also involved agencies which arranged the sponsorship. These agencies, called VOLAGs, were: The United States Catholic Conference (USCC), the American Fund for Czechoslovak Refugees (AFCR), Church World Service (CWS), the Lutheran Immigration and Refugee Service (LIRS), United Hebrew Immigration and Assistance Service (United HIAS), the International Rescue Committee (IRC), the American Council for Nationalities Services (ACNS), Travelers' Aid–International Social Services (TAISS), and the Tolstoy Foundation. These nine organizations had a long tradition of resettling immigrants in the United States. The IATF solicited other organizations to resettle Vietnamese. This was the first time any of these had worked resettling immigrants. The Chinese Consolidated Benevolent Association and various states (New Mexico, Washington, Maine, Oklahoma, Nebraska, Iowa), one county (Jackson County, Missouri), and one city (Indianapolis) were contracted to serve the same functions as the VOLAGs. Their role was to find organizations or individuals to serve as sponsors and to deal with problems in immigrant-sponsor relations as they arose until resettlement was considered complete.

What a completed resettlement entailed was never clear. Obviously it involved getting Vietnamese out of the camps to sponsors, but it extended in theory beyond this to monitoring the sponsorships until the immigrant was considered self-sufficient and the sponsorship relation was no longer needed. The vagueness of the definition of VOLAG responsibility meant that agencies or states could choose to remain involved with immigrants as long as they cared to or had the resources to do so. They could also choose to serve the immigrants according to their means and definitions of responsibility. For example, an immigrant could turn to his or her sponsor for assistance in getting medical or dental care or some item like a car or a bed they felt was necessary. The sponsor could refuse or refer the immigrant to either the voluntary agency which arranged the sponsorship or to state welfare authorities in the case of medical care and daily sustenance. The VOLAG, if it either had the funds or had defined its responsibilities in such a way as to disperse funds for these purposes, might provide the money or refer the immigrant to the government. Initially the government held the VOLAGs responsible for disbursements that individual sponsors were unable to make. The VOLAGs reacted vehemently against a role definition that made them replace the state as the source of welfare funds.

The one role common among the VOLAGs was responsibility for finding Vietnamese a sponsor and, should that sponsorship become untenable, to find another for the immigrant until he or she were self-supporting and self-sufficient.

How to Get a Sponsor

Vietnamese immigrants had very limited control over who would sponsor them and where they would relocate in the United States. When Vietnamese entered the camps they either chose or were assigned a VOLAG which would handle their resettlement. Vietnamese could influence the choice of a sponsor that VOLAGs found for them only if they personally knew of Americans or Vietnamese residents of the United States who were willing and able to sponsor them. If they knew such persons, they could request the VOLAG to arrange a sponsorship. Many Vietnamese, especially in May and June of 1975, were sponsored in this way as Americans who were former employers, lovers, and/or friends stepped forward with offers of assistance. U.S. government agencies and several corporations sent representatives to the camps to "gather up" former employees. It was not uncommon for camp newspapers to run items requesting some agency's or corporation's former employees to identify themselves so they could be sponsored. The following ads appearing in *Dat Lanh* were typical.

> DAO. AF: Former Employees
> Former Vietnamese Employees of the Defense Attache Office, Air Force Division, are invited to write to:
>> John Rustall
>> DOD Material Distribution Study Group
>> Hoffman Building No. 2, Room 2 N47
>> 200 Stovall Street
>> Alexandria, Virginia 22332[17]

> LSI Employees
>> Lear Siegler (LSI) Employees in Nha-Trang.
>> Please call collect Jim Carie (301) 466-4130

> ATTENTION
> Former Saigon Employees of
>> R.M.K. (Raymond, Marion & Khuston)
>> Philco-Ford
>> PAE (Pacific Architecture and Engineering)
>> DMJM (Daniel, Mann, Johnson & Mendenhall)
>> Television Associates
> Please contact Jane Stanley, Sponsorship Coordinator Center, Bldg. 5-115, Room 34-B[18]

Vietnamese who accepted these sponsorship offers often found jobs working with their former employers. Chase Manhattan Bank, for example, not only sponsored all former Vietnamese employees and their families, they reassigned them jobs similar to ones they held in Vietnam. Other employers could not always do the same.

Vietnamese also arranged their own sponsorships with relatives in the United States. These usually were with daughters, nieces, or sisters who had married American servicemen while they were in Vietnam. In some cases immigrants phoned or wrote their relatives from the camps and arranged for a sponsorship offer to be made. A second type of sponsorship arranged among Vietnamese residing in the United States and those who came at the time of the American evacuation was done through the Catholic Church and its Vietnamese clergy. Many Vietnamese priests were in the United States before the collapse of the Saigon government; several had been in the country for many years. Immigrant priests usually were sponsored out of the camps by the church through USCC. These priests were then assigned to parishes both in and out of the camps. Many like Father L., a long-time resident of the United States, went to the camps (in the case of Father L. to Fort Chaffee) to search for family members and former neighbors. Father L. returned to his duties in an eastern city where he generated sponsors—parishes in his diocese—for the family members, neighbors, and former parishioners he had located, close to 200 people in all.[19] Father L. was not an isolated case. In New York City, Father D. M. generated sponsorships in much the same way for individual immigrants he identified in his travels through the camps. In the case of both priests, this was a "gathering together of souls" to establish ethnic parishes.[20]

Many Vietnamese found sponsors through the American connections they had before they came to the country. Through May and June the VOLAGs' major work consisted of doing paper work generated by having ready-made sponsors for individual immigrants and their families. Resettlement agencies like IRC checked sponsorship offers by telephone only, merely verifying the intent of individuals who made such offers to make good on them.[21] There was little reticence among Vietnamese about accepting the sponsorships which they themselves had arranged.

Not many immigrants had contacts with Americans, as chapter 3 pointed out. For those who were not former employees of American corporations or the American government, not Catholics, or not related to Americans or resident aliens, sponsorships had to be arranged by the VOLAGs. Vietnamese choice in the matter was reduced to accepting or rejecting offers by individuals they did not know or groups whose religious orientations seemed foreign or hostile. This was particularly the case with Vietnamese Catholics who simply could not understand why Protestant churches would wish to take responsibility for them unless they intended to convert them to their religious beliefs.

Until late August 1975 Vietnamese could freely reject sponsorship offers—and many did—basing their decisions often on considerations considered trivial by Americans who arranged the sponsorships. Most often Vietnamese told Americans that climate was their sole reason for rejecting resettlement offers, alleging that Maine, New Hampshire, Minnesota, and the like, were too cold for them. Many social workers felt this objection could be overcome by explaining to immigrants that houses were heated and that clothing would keep them warm. A second reason that social workers said Vietnamese gave for refusing resettlement offers was fear of racial prejudice. The latter was comprehensible to case-workers who understood, perhaps better than Vietnamese, the ethnic/racial tensions in American society.[22]

Few Americans, however, understood Vietnamese reticence in accepting any sponsorship Americans generated for them. They alleged that Vietnamese had developed a sense of security in the camps. At Fort Indian Town Gap, Pennsylvania, they called this "Gapitis," claiming that the camp had become a "little Vietnam." Hesitancy to accept a sponsorship was simply a sign of illness, peculiar to immigrants. This was clearest in articles appearing in *Dat Lanh*, Fort Indian Town Gap's daily newspaper. One, entitled "Gapitis? a . . . . Gapitis??? Gapitis, Gapitis," began:

> Observers at the Gap report a growing incidence of psychological illness which is only rarely seen in America. They have dubbed it "Gapitis." This unusual "disease" afflicts only inhabitants of refugee centers. The symptoms are a growing reluctance to think of life outside the camp, fear of sponsors and *spending one's time concocting reasons not to leave.* (Author's italics.)[23]

The remedy to the "disease" was simple and indicated more than anything else American conceptions of how Vietnamese thought. It consisted of talking to individuals who were "stricken" by the malady, pointing out

> that life in America is basically a good life: there is no war. There is no want. There is very little fear. There is freedom. There is opportunity. There is education. There is happiness.
>   Life in the camps leads nowhere if it doesn't lead out. Both the camp and the sponsorship arrangements are only stages in the bridge that has brought you from Vietnam and *which will lead you to your free life as an American*.[24] (Author's italics.)

For Americans, it was simply "arbitrary" or an illness on the part of Vietnamese to hesitate in accepting any sponsorship offer, regardless of the nature of that offer or Vietnamese understanding of what they as Vietnamese wanted in resettlement. Many Vietnamese refused to accept sponsorships because they meant family separations. VOLAGs often split extended families into several households and resettled these households in disparate parts of the country.[25]

Fear of isolation from other Vietnamese was another reason that immigrants turned down sponsorship offers. Many Vietnamese were unwilling to resettle either alone or in a household of five or six persons in rural areas of states like Nebraska, Iowa, or Texas unless other Vietnamese families were located close by. Fear of exploitation also figured prominently in refusals to accept a sponsorship. Many offers, as is documented later in this chapter, were tied to employment, and Vietnamese became aware of the hazards of the sponsor and one's employer being the same person or organization. Finally, Vietnamese may have considered the sponsor-immigrant relation inappropriate among total strangers. That Vietnamese reticence about accepting sponsorships was related to the way anonymous sponsorship offers were generated and "matched" to a particular immigrant and/or family is best substantiated by looking at how they were arranged and what offers consisted of.

Generating Sponsorships and Matching Them to Vietnamese

Sponsors for Vietnamese did not "grow on trees," as *Dat Lanh* rightly pointed out. Most had to be generated, although a few offers to sponsor Vietnamese were forthcoming without much prodding. These initially involved requests which several resettlement workers labeled as "single guys looking for single girls" and as part and parcel of a search for cheap domestic labor.[26] These requests, most resettlement workers claimed, were ignored, especially the ones with sexual overtones, which many had. The offers connected with household help—maids, butlers, etc.—were shelved by many resettlement workers, only to be reopened in late October and in November when sponsorship offers became scarce.[27]

Random sponsorship offers were not the only ones made. The camps were not totally isolated from American society. Although Vietnamese could not leave without a sponsor, Americans could enter the camps, as did the thousands of volunteers who staffed recreation programs, the English language classes, day-care programs, and the other jobs set up for volunteers coordinated by the Red Cross, the YMCA, and the Salvation Army. Many of the people who worked at the camps sponsored a Vietnamese family, usually one whose acquaintance they had made while working in the camps. Volunteers at the camps also involved friends and neighbors in their community in sponsoring refugees. Sometimes the volunteers would arrange the sponsorship for refugees they had met in the camps.

The degree to which volunteers working in the camps developed a sponsorship network is best illustrated by the areas in which Vietnamese resettlement was greatest. By 31 December 1975, 27,199 had been sponsored by individuals in California. Most of the refugees were relocated in southern California (Camp Pendleton was located near San Diego); 7,159 Vietnamese were relocated in Pennsylvania (Fort

Indian Town Gap was near Harrisburg); and 2,042 were placed in Arkansas (Fort Chaffee was outside of Fort Smith).[28] The Pennsylvania figures, more than the Arkansas and California figures, show the effect of the volunteers. Pennsylvania's climate is scarcely hospitable to Vietnamese, accustomed to year-round temperatures in the high seventies. Few job opportunities could have attracted Vietnamese to the state since Pennsylvania was one of the eastern states hit hardest by recession and unemployment. Personal contact through Fort Indian Town Gap is probably the only thing that could explain the number of people offering sponsorships irrespective of job opportunities, and Vietnamese accepting them.

Most sponsorships were generated through two networks: one was the national job market, through which the Department of Labor and the IATF functioned; the other was through American religious, immigrant, and community organizations. The IATF collected information on Vietnamese skill levels during the in-processing described in chapter 4, and fed this into a computer bank, matching job vacancies (listed with state employment offices) with immigrants' skills.[29] Once a "match" had been made, the IATF, through its sponsorship coordinating center, would contact an individual, club, business, or church and encourage them to sponsor a Vietnamese family on the basis that some member of that family would readily find employment. Sometimes the IATF would contact business concerns, like a paper mill, a chicken processing plant, or a candy factory, and ask them if they were willing to employ as well as sponsor a Vietnamese. The IATF often did not need to ask, as business concerns initiated recruitment for skilled and unskilled labor. The IATF also generated occupational profiles of Vietnamese for city, county, and state governments to interest them in sponsoring refugees. People from Nebraska, for example, came to Fort Indian Town Gap and Camp Pendleton looking for M.D.s. The state sponsored refugee M.D.s interested in the Nebraska program and gave them a salary while sending them to programs preparing them for the Educational Commission for Foreign Medical Graduates examination. This was done on the provision that once the M.D.s passed the exam and were licensed to practice, they would remain in Nebraska for ten years. New Mexico and Maine were other states that sent representatives to the camps to recruit skilled persons.

So closely were sponsorship offers connected to employment that listings of resettlement opportunities appearing in camp newspapers read like the want-ad section of a newspaper. *Dat Lanh* listed these in its column, "Sponsorships Available." The following are typical of the sponsorships listed:

> Two or three mechanics, one of whom should speak some English. The sponsor is a Datsun car dealer in Georgia. The position offers free housing, assistance with food and regular salary.[30]

> Workers for greenhouses in Maryland and North Carolina. Free housing, food assistance, and wages.[31]

> Two machinists, one of whom should speak English, for a position in Pennsylvania. Free housing and food. Starting wage at $2.10 per hour. If good job performance, can increase to $4.00 per hour.[32]

> Three men with skills needed to fill job and sponsorship offer. Experience in carpentry, auto mechanics or other laboring skills acceptable. Sponsor will provide job, room and board in his own home.[33]

> Two fishermen needed for job in Florida. Position pays $2.10 per hour with sponsorship. Housing to be provided in new house trailer plus farm animals and garden. Work on tropical fish farm. Should be able to sex-sort and count fish.[34]

> Family up to 8 people to go to Springfield, Oregon. Sponsor would train refugees to work in his hairdressing salons. Also jobs available as fruit pickers.[35]

Single man for Charlton, Massachusetts. Live with a large family. If desires can work in shoe factory for minimum wage.[36]

Will take one family of 5 or less persons. A position is open for a janitor with some English and a cook with some English.[37]

Will take 4 single persons, two (2) to be nurse's aides and two (2) to be workers in a laundry or kitchen of a retired individual's home. This would be a live-in sponsorship. The salary is $2.00 per hour, or $65/month plus room and board.[38]

Individual Sponsorship—Man and wife, owners of a nursing home in Sharon Hill, Pennsylvania, want to sponsor three single ladies ages 18 to 30. The couple will provide means for training in nursing and part-time employment at the nursing home.[39]

Such ads did not go unheeded. At Fort Indian Town Gap, a considerable number of young men were sponsored out to a Poughkeepsie, New York, candy manufacturer who paid each adult $2.10 per hour. Similarly, the sponsor of thirty single men operated a poultry processing plant in which his "refugees" worked for the same minimum wage figures. In both cases room and board as well as the immigrant's start-up expenses, supposedly the obligation of the sponsor, were deducted from salaries.[40]

Sponsorship by an employer was not a peculiar outgrowth of policies at Fort Indian Town Gap. At Fort Chaffee similar sponsorships were arranged. Between 10 June and 11 November, 11 families totaling 55 persons were relocated in Jonesboro, Arkansas, sponsored by Frolics Footwear to work in the company's factory; another 11 families totaling 100 persons went to Kingsport, Tennessee, sponsored by a garment factory; over 76 families with 690 persons were directly sponsored by poultry-processing companies in Oklahoma to work in their plants; another 16 families containing 42 persons were sponsored by a meat packing plant in Wichita, Kansas.[41] Although the IATF issued no statistics on the number of sponsorships that involved employer-employee relations, the chief of the sponsorship coordinating center at Fort Indian Town Gap estimated that a "large proportion" of sponsorship offers were of a "contract labor nature," connected to, as time showed, jobs that paid about or below the minimum wage.[42]

The IATF had no procedures for safeguarding refugees against exploitation in the sponsorship program. It was willing to promote offers of work at jobs paying less than minimum wage rates. After all, the IATF did resettle individuals in situations where they were sent to work at $2 an hour (which is below the minimum wage of $2.10 per hour). Further, it also promoted sponsorship offers that, while connected to employment, paid either minimum wages or above. Still, the salaries offered to refugees in the sponsorship arrangement were considerably below the going wage rate for Americans doing comparable work. The *Dat Lanh* ad offering a sponsorship to skilled machinists (cited earlier in this chapter) advertised a beginning wage of $2.10 per hour that could be increased to $4 per hour. Skilled machinists in this country, however, usually command a beginning wage of $5 per hour.

The IATF also did not inquire into working conditions of jobs Americans offered refugees they sponsored. The case of a Vermont poultry processor who sponsored over twenty-five men from Fort Indian Town Gap illustrates this. The plant's owner had a long history of unsavory labor practices which came to the IATF's attention only after half the Vietnamese sponsored by him left both his employ and the state of Vermont. Previously the plant had employed mentally retarded persons from the Brandon Training School in Vermont. In 1973 the state terminated this arrangement because of poor plant safety and sanitary conditions. In that same year the owner established what he called a "training program" to teach Koreans, whom he arranged to import through the U.S. Immigration and Naturalization Service

(INS). The program was supposed to teach Koreans the poultry business. INS, when it investigated, refused to grant entry permits for the so-called program, alleging that no program in fact existed. In 1975, the year the IATF encouraged Vietnamese to accept sponsorship by the poultry processor, the State of Vermont issued the plant twenty-two citations for violations of health and safety laws designed to protect employees. Despite these questionable working conditions, the IATF continued to send Vietnamese to Vermont, even after half the persons whom they sent left, complaining about their work and their sponsor.[43]

While many sponsors were generated through the national labor market by the IATF, the voluntary resettlement agencies—USCC, LIRS, CWS, IRC, AFCR, ACNS, Tolstoy Foundation, United HIAS, and TAISS— used their national networks of church and civic organizations to find sponsors for Vietnamese. Religious-based organizations like USCC, LIRS, CWS, and United HIAS all had social service agencies scattered throughout the U.S. and contacts with local congregations. Several published booklets that promoted the idea of becoming sponsors which they distributed to churches. The USCC worked through the diocesan structure of the Catholic church in a similar way.[44]

The religious-based VOLAGs, for the most part, were experienced in resettlement work and attempted to avoid sponsorships by individuals, which they believed put too much pressure on the sponsor, or by corporations because of the potential for exploitation. They attempted to depend almost exclusively on congregations for sponsorships and were the organizations that generated the sponsorship offers in *Dat Lanh* that read:

> The following sponsorships are available at Church World Service. . . . All but Nos. 9, 25, and 30 are group sponsors.
> 1. Ellington, Connecticut   5 to 7 people
> 2. Mt. Joy, Pennsylvania   Family of 4
> 3. Altoona, Pennsylvania   7 to 8 people

4. Hatboro, Pennsylvania   4 to 6 people
5. Chewsville, Maryland   8 to 10 people[45]

New Castle First Methodist Church wants any type of family interested in living in New Castle, Pennsylvania.[46]

First Baptist Church, Holyoke, Massachusetts, will take two (2) families up to six persons each.[47]

Neshaniuny Warwick Presbyterian Church will take 3 (three) families. Will be placed with families of the congregation of the church.[48]

Congregational sponsorships, to some extent, were not job offers, they were offers to help Vietnamese settle in the community where that congregation was located. The prime consideration was not employment of the individual or his/her particular skills so much as it was the number of people the congregation thought it could support over an extended time if need be.

The denominational/religious organizations were not the only ones to attempt to resettle Vietnamese with groups rather than with individuals or the immigrant's prospective employer. Several of the secular organizations like the TAISS and ACNS had extensive national networks. ACNS, for example, is a federation of International Houses scattered throughout the U.S. ACNS used the International Houses as sponsors for Vietnamese as the houses proved capable of providing for them. The houses themselves also generated local sponsors through civic organizations like the Rotary Clubs.[49]

Less capable of generating group sponsorships were the secular agencies like IRC, the Tolstoy Foundation, and the AFCR, which are not based on local organizational structures. They relied primarily on individual, rather than group sponsorships, developing those through appeals to members and contributors. In the case of AFCR, sponsorships were generated through individuals the organization had helped to resettle in earlier immigrations.[50] The ability of these organizations to generate sponsorships on their own was limited because of their lack of extensive national local organizations that could act as sponsors like churches or Jewish social service agencies. They came to rely on sponsorships distributed to them by IATF and its employment roster. Many of the sponsorship offers specifying wages and jobs were handled through the Tolstoy Foundation. It was the Tolstoy Foundation which resettled the Vietnamese with the poultry processor in Vermont and the candy factory in Poughkeepsie. This is not to imply that secular organizations exclusively engaged in corporate or individual sponsorships, for religious organizations like USCC were also involved in such sponsorships. Rather, it is to state that resettlement with groups like congregations was rarer for these kinds of organizations.

Regardless of the way in which a sponsorship was generated, each organization had procedures to "match" Vietnamese with an offer. Most organizations interviewed immigrants registered with them for between thirty minutes and an hour per family within the first week that the immigrants were in the camp. These interviews gathered information on family composition; the educational and occupational backgrounds, skills, English proficiency, and age of each family member; the number of potential salaried workers in the family; where the family wished to resettle in the U.S.; and whether they knew anyone in the country who might want to sponsor them (relatives, former employers, friends, etc.).[51]

On the basis of this information, a caseworker at the agency surveyed sponsorship offers available, looking for ones that would suit the immigrant. Suitability was usually determined, according to caseworkers, on the basis of language, job skills (if any) specified by sponsors, and number of people for whom the sponsor was willing to take responsibility. The caseworker then came up with five or six Vietnamese families or individuals who "fit the bill" and one by one asked for their willingness to accept the offer. Those who indicated acceptance, if they exceeded the number of people requested by the sponsor, had their dossiers sent to the sponsor for the sponsor to make the choice. Rarely did sponsors and immigrants meet face to face before the immi-

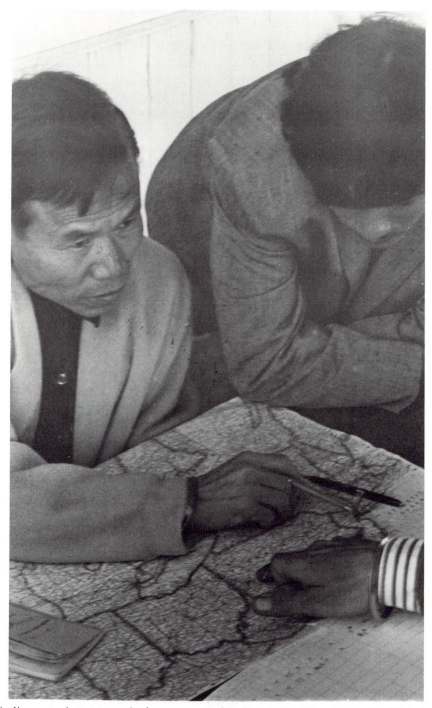

Finding out what state you've been sponsored to. Fort Indian Town Gap. *Fred Friedman*

grant was sent to the sponsor's home. At best, one caseworker estimated, only 50 percent of those resettled met their
sponsors before they agreed to the arrangement.[52] When
Vietnamese and sponsor met before sponsorship arrangements were made final, the meeting between the two was
described by caseworkers who sat in on it as a "kind of
pregnant silence." Vietnamese concentrated their questions
in such meetings on the sponsor's family.[53] For Vietnamese
perhaps a better sign of how the sponsorship would fare was
the sponsor's family life rather than job potential or climate.

Matching, then, was arbitrary, based on American requirements and Vietnamese ability to meet them rather than
American ability to meet Vietnamese needs. Vietnamese
could say either "yes" or "no" to sponsorship offers caseworkers proposed to them. Before August, each immigrant
had total freedom to accept or reject any offer as often as he or
she pleased. By September Vietnamese were told they had but
two "turn-down options" on sponsorship offers for reasons
involving something other than their medical condition or
their impending family reunification. If Vietnamese turned
down sponsorship offers that caseworkers had arranged
more than twice, "counseling" was arranged. By October at
Fort Indian Town Gap, a sponsorship review board was
established to pressure Vietnamese into accepting sponsorships. As the IATF explained it:

> Camp authorities, given the responsibility of placing
> thousands of refugees into those American communi-
> ties, cannot allow the final refugee sponsor match up to
> be changed lightly. The decision has recently been
> made, therefore, that any refugee rejecting a sponsor
> must appear before the camp's sponsorship review
> board to show sufficient cause for the rejection.[54]

Whether Vietnamese liked it or not, they were going to be
resettled on the terms set by the IATF, on the time schedule
decided by the IATF, in sponsorships that the IATF found
acceptable. The review board existed to force Vietnamese
acquiescence. Often the voluntary agencies disagreed with

such policies, but, as I pointed out in chapter 4, they found themselves pressed into conforming to the IATF's requirements as the lesser of evils.

Resettlement: Its Fruits as of December 1975

The sponsorship program resettled 129,792 Vietnamese within the United States by 31 December 1975. Table 5 shows the number of Vietnamese resettled by agency. Table 6 gives a state-by-state breakdown of refugee resettlement. Table 5 indicates that the VOLAGs handled most of the sponsorships. Of the 129,000 or so Vietnamese who settled in the United States, 114,871 were found sponsors through the VOLAGs; less than 5,000 were resettled through state and local governments. Between 8,000 and 10,000 immigrants resettled without sponsors. These were persons (listed in table 6 as "unknown") who had over $4,000 per family member in liquid assets upon arrival in the United States or who were resettled directly by their employers from Vietnam.

Table 5 also shows that the USCC resettled close to half of all immigrants. This reflects in part the religion of Vietnamese and the contacts USCC had in Vietnam for many years. Second in the number of immigrants resettled was IRC, also well known among immigrants for its work in Vietnam over the past twenty years. IRC was the only secular organization to work with this large a volume of immigrants; 89,382 of all immigrants were resettled by church-affiliated voluntary agencies.

The number resettled by state and local agencies, as table 5 shows, is very small; yet it is significant if only because of the role it played in speeding up the work of the voluntary agencies. Initially these state and local agencies committed themselves to resettling a much larger number of people. As of September 1975, for example, the state of Washington stated a resettlement goal of 2,000; Maine, 300; Oklahoma, 1,000.[55] In October, New Mexico committed itself to resettling 500 persons and received an HEW retraining grant as well as the $500 per capita resettlement grant.[56] These states sponsored only 1,570, 167, 373, and 184 persons respectively (see table 5). The initially large numbers the states agreed to

Table 5
Immigrant Resettlement by Agency

Voluntary Resettlement Agencies	Number of Immigrants Resettled
United States Catholic Conference	52,100
International Rescue Committee	18,600
Church World Service	17,864
Lutheran Immigration and Refugee Service	15,897
United HIAS Service	3,531
Tolstoy Foundation	3,270
American Council for Nationalities Services	2,200
American Fund for Czechoslovak Refugees	832
Travelers Aid International Social Services	577
Voluntary Resettlement Agencies Total	114,871

State and Local Agencies

Department of Emergency Services State of Washington	1,570
Governor's Task Force for Indochinese Resettlement Employment Security Commission State of Iowa	633
Department of Institutions, Social Aid and Rehabilitative Services State of Oklahoma	362
Division of Community Services State of Maine	167
Governor's Cabinet Secretariat State of New Mexico Planning Office	184
Jackson County, Missouri Don Bosco Community Center (Kansas City, Missouri)	234
City of Indianapolis Indianapolis Red Cross American Red Cross	80
Chinese Consolidated Benevolent Association of Los Angeles	838
Chinese Consolidated Benevolent Association of New York	72
Church of Jesus Christ of Latter Day Saints Salt Lake City, Utah	580
State and Local Agencies Total	4,720
Total	119,591

Source; HEW Task Force for Indochinese Refugees, Report to Congress,

15 March 1976 (litho), pp. 92, 101-102.

resettle merely stood as an "efficiency" threat to the VOL-AGs. As pointed out in chapter 4, the IATF put considerable pressure on the VOLAGs to clear the camps and force immigrants to accept offers VOLAGs and Vietnamese might have had qualms about. The alternatives to VOLAGs were the states and they were touted as such to the VOLAGs. In the end, the states' role was minimal in resettlement, but probably larger as a means for speeding up the private agencies' work.

Table 6 presents a breakdown by state of Vietnamese settlement in the U.S. as of 15 December 1975, the time the camps closed. This state-by-state breakdown shows a concentration of Vietnamese in California, where 27,199 found sponsors. The next largest concentrations of Vietnamese were in Texas (9,130); Pennsylvania (7,159); Florida (5,322); Washington State (4,182); Illinois (3,696); New York (3,689); and Louisiana (3,601). This pattern reflects several things. The concentration in California is a result of several factors. Before the fall of Saigon and the details of American government policy toward refugees from Vietnam were worked out, Vietnamese were often flown to Travis Air Force Base in California and released directly into American society. Before Saigon fell, congressional representatives from California were complaining that the state had become a dumping ground for Vietnamese and urged the government to send immigrants elsewhere.[57] The second factor contributing to heavy resettlement in California was the presence of Camp Pendleton, the first of the holding centers on the U.S. mainland to open and the largest of the centers. Local contacts with immigrants led to many sponsorship offers as Camp Pendleton, staffed by a host of volunteers, was at one point inundated by American news media and curious private citizens. The third factor that led to a Vietnamese concentration in California was Vietnamese preference. The climate seemed hospitable and, since large numbers of Vietnamese had already settled there from the early influx into the country, many Vietnamese anticipated less isolation there than, say, in Nebraska, New Mexico, or Wisconsin.

The concentrations of Vietnamese in Texas, Pennsylva-

Table 6

Number of Immigrants Resettled

by State as of 31 December 1975

State	Total	State	Total
Alabama	1,262	Nevada	338
Alaska	81	New Hampshire	161
Arkansas	2,042	New Jersey	1,515
Arizona	1,059	New Mexico	1,040
California	27,199	New York	3,806
Colorado	1,790	North Carolina	1,261
Connecticut	1,175	North Dakota	448
Delaware	155	Ohio	2,924
District of Columbia	1,254	Oklahoma	3,689
Florida	5,322	Oregon	2,063
Georgia	1,331	Pennsylvania	7,159
Hawaii	2,039	Rhode Island	223
Idaho	412	South Carolina	759
Illinois	3,696	South Dakota	545
Indiana	1,785	Tennessee	922
Iowa	2,593	Texas	9,130
Kansas	1,897	Utah	559
Kentucky	967	Vermont	150
Louisiana	3,602	Virginia	3,733
Maine	375	Washington	4,182
Maryland	2,319	West Virginia	195
Massachusetts	1,169	Wisconsin	1,821
Michigan	2,200	Wyoming	115
Minnesota	3,802	Guam	778
Mississippi	488	American Samoa	1
Missouri	2,669	Puerto Rico	1
Montana	198		
Nebraska	1,211	Unknown	8,182
		Total	129,792*

Source: HEW Task Force for Indochinese Refugees, Report to Congress, 15 March 1976 (litho), p. 29.

*Includes 115 immigrants at a "Half-way House" in Philadelphia. Does not include 822 children born to immigrants in the U. S.

nia, and Florida reflect, as did that in California, the effect of the location of the resettlement camps. Texas and Oklahoma are adjacent to Arkansas and Fort Chaffee; Fort Indian Town Gap was located in west central Pennsylvania, four hours' car drive from Binghamton, New York, or Philadelphia, Pennsylvania; Eglin Air Force Base was in Florida. Communities in the vicinity of the camps were sources of sponsorships—and, in the case of Florida and Texas, the climate seemed more amenable to Vietnamese and it became clear to most refugees that should they accept sponsorships in those states, they would not be totally isolated.

The Vietnamese resettlement pattern reflected to some extent connections with Americans Vietnamese had before coming to the U.S. The large number of Vietnamese in the Washington, D.C., Virginia, and Maryland areas (altogether 4,306) is a product of Vietnamese-American government ties established through the years of American involvement in the war. Defense contractors and American government agencies, the former employers of Vietnamese while the war raged, were concentrated in the D.C. area. They became their employees' sponsors. Further, Vietnamese who were already in the United States before the fall of the Saigon government were also from this area, either as members of the South Vietnamese embassy and trade and cultural missions to the United States or as defectors from them. As resident aliens, they could and did sponsor immigrants whom they knew.

Much of the resettlement pattern among states reflects Americans resettling Vietnamese. The resettlement of Vietnamese in states like Wisconsin, Minnesota, North Carolina, Ohio, Indiana, and Wyoming are examples of the contacts of American voluntary agencies. The states of the northern Midwest were places of greatest contact for organizations like LIRS. LIRS placed 1,791 Vietnamese in Minnesota and 708 in Wisconsin where Lutheran congregations were strong.[58] This is true of most of the resettlement outside the states in or around the camps or in the D.C. area. Where the VOLAGs had ties, Vietnamese were resettled. Similarly, Vietnamese were resettled where corporations needed unskilled labor or labor with skills Vietnamese possessed. In

Florida, Texas, and Louisiana they became nonunion farm labor and were employed in the fishing industry; in other areas they plucked and processed chickens, made candy or clothes, or provided custodial care in nursing homes, hospitals, etc.

How much does the resettlement indicated in table 6 represent the scattering of Vietnamese as a fulfillment of government policy? Table 6 only partially answers this question, for it shows that Vietnamese were scattered throughout the U.S. in all regions, with the smallest numbers going to the plains and mountain states of the Midwest and the northernmost states of the eastern seaboard. Over half the immigrants were resettled in states where they numbered less than 3,000. They were spread throughout the country, unlike the Cubans who, in the Cuban refugee program, were concentrated in Florida in general and Miami in particular.

Table 6 does not show the extent to which Vietnamese resettled in the urban areas of a particular state. Because of this table 6 may hide the formation of Vietnamese communities in American cities. The IATF and the VOLAGs have rarely released information relating to this. Table 7 shows that Vietnamese families tended to resettle in urban areas, concentrated in 17 U.S. cities, with the greatest number in Los Angeles and San Francisco. The 4,500 or so families in these cities represent at a minimum close to half the Vietnamese resettled in California. The table can be considered at best an estimate since it is a projection of relocation as of 15 September 1975, rather than actual relocation by city. Yet it shows that in state after state, Vietnamese tended to cluster in urban areas. In Florida, for example, where 5,322 persons relocated, at least 3,000 were in the city of Jacksonville (if one figures about 2.5 persons per family, in families over 2 persons, which is by no means the average size of Vietnamese families). Similarly in Texas, where 9,130 Vietnamese resettled, at least 2,400 persons went to Dallas while another 894 went to San Antonio.

Resettlement in groups within urban areas could not be avoided by the U.S. government. Resources—jobs, voluntary agencies, churches—capable of supporting immigrants simply were more plentiful in cities than in rural or small town America where most Americans do not live. Further, the seventeen cities listed in table 7 as the final destinations of Vietnamese tended to be cities where the recession hit least hard and unemployment was less. Because the northeastern United States was most severely hit by the recession, Vietnamese were drawn to places like Jacksonville, Dallas, New Orleans, and San Antonio. They resettled there because jobs were available, because local churches and families— relatively untouched by the country's economic situation— had greater resources and employers were looking for labor. It is little wonder, then, that most rural states (Mississippi, North Dakota, Wyoming, Utah) took few Vietnamese as did the American northeast, with the exception of Pennsylvania.

Vietnamese were dispersed, but this dispersal was uneven. Although it seemed relatively even *among* states (except for California, Pennsylvania, Texas, and Florida), it was uneven *within* states, providing a picture of an urban resettlement. Vietnamese, in short, were scattered only relative to other immigrations. The resettlement did, in fact, lay a basis for Vietnamese communities spread throughout seventeen cities in the United States; it did not provide a groundwork for one Vietnamese community that could exert a power on its own, like the Cuban community of Miami. In this sense, Vietnamese were resettled in every instance, except in California and the cities of Los Angeles and San Francisco, in such relatively small numbers that they lacked the power to make themselves a "problem" except insofar as the American government cared to define them as one. Without money, for Vietnamese the only way to the power to control their futures was through numbers—and the resettlement pattern initially militated against this.

Resettlement: Procedures, Patterns, and Sponsors— A Concluding Note

The last refugee camp closed down in mid-December 1975 as Vietnamese were sent off to sponsors throughout the United States. The resettlement of Vietnamese, as this chap-

Table 7

Projection, Final Family Distribution to 17

Most Popular Destination Areas as of 9 September 1975*

City	Number of Families Over 2 Persons	Percent of Families
Los Angeles	2,499	18.0
San Francisco	2,028	14.6
Jacksonville	1,244	9.0
Dallas	973	7.0
Washington, D. C.	957	6.9
Philadelphia	795	5.7
Seattle	733	5.3
New York	633	4.6
Minneapolis, St. Paul	561	4.1
Chicago	530	3.8
Denver	478	3.5
New Orleans	453	3.3
Columbus (Ohio)	437	3.2
Oklahoma City	419	3.0
Knasas City, Kansas	384	2.8
San Antonio	379	2.7
Little Rock	351	2.5
Total	13,854	

Source: Interagency Task Force on Indochina Refugees, Report to the Congress, (litho) 15 September 1975, p. 14.

*Of the 37,844 families finally resettled 16,819 were one-person families. The rest were over 2 persons. This table leaves about 5,171 families unaccounted for.

ter has shown, was handled in such a way as to minimize Vietnamese control over their futures and silently and invisibly to integrate them into American life. The latter imperative was probably stronger than the former, although one implied the other. The sponsorship requirement attached to Vietnamese resettlement was one means by which government involvement could be minimized. The mode of resettlement involved American private citizens, organizations, and corporations taking responsibility for the immigrants and relieving the government of difficulties arising from 129,000 or so persons entering the U.S. in a time of economic recession. The sponsorship program became closely related to employment opportunities: Vietnamese were resettled by their employers into jobs, most of which paid the minimum wage or less, placing most immigrant families on a cash income considerably below the poverty level. Given the resettlement grant per refugee and the government's initial refusal to make medicaid and other welfare disbursements, there were few ways to avoid this. Even some of the most well-meaning congregations found themselves involved in sponsorships attached to jobs. The financial responsibilities of sponsorship were great and the languages and work skills of most Vietnamese were not necessarily conducive to their finding jobs readily on their own.

Vietnamese participation in making decisions about their initial resettlement and the sponsorship program was minimal. Vietnamese did not resettle in America; they were resettled. They were pushed out of the camps by Americans into the arms of sponsors Americans believed suitable and reliable. It was only after the camps closed down that Vietnamese reaction to the program became evident, as did the weakness of resettlement policies pursued by the IATF. After 15 December 1975, Vietnamese began to regroup, to make known their feelings about the resettlement and the pressures the IATF and American government had placed upon them over the previous six months. They moved out of the northern U.S. and isolation from other Vietnamese into the southern U.S. and into large communities of Vietnamese. Further, they abandoned their original resettlement employ-

Part 3

Into the Lower Classes

Chapter Seven

The Vietnamese in America

What became of the Vietnamese when they left the resettlement camps? How did they adjust to American society and how did American resettlement policies and practices affect this adjustment? In addressing these questions I have chosen to concentrate on Vietnamese entry into the American economy because it is one of the most important aspects of survival in this country. Jobs and the income they yield to a large extent set the range of options individuals have for determining their futures. In the case of many Vietnamese immigrants, the types of work they were able to find and the income that work yielded presented a set of adjustment problems relating not so much to living in a new cultural milieu as to living within a new and lowered socioeconomic situation. Cabinet ministers, generals, lawyers, radio station managers, etc., found themselves faced with employment as cooks, waiters, bell boys, dishwashers, and janitors. This newfound class position in the short run did much to precipitate emotional crises.

Despite the importance of Vietnamese in the American work force and adjustment problems it has presented to many immigrants, work does not represent the entire range of adjustments Vietnamese have had to make living in the United States. Many immigrants did not have to accommodate to lowered class and economic positions because they

were able to find work that was comparable to the work they
had in Vietnam in both status and income. This was far more
the case with Vietnamese who had not been part of their
country's managerial, governing, or professional elite, but
who in Vietnam had been unskilled labor or blue collar
workers in fields like mechanics or the machine trades.
Although these persons may not have had to cope with a new
and lowered socioeconomic status, they still had to deal with
living in American society. American lifestyles for many of
these people impinged on their own. This was particularly
so for immigrants whose recent roots lay in rural Vietnam.
Urban, industrial society was totally foreign to them. Vietnamese, regardless of their social and economic backgrounds, all coped with cultural changes—in family structure and cohesion, in language, in beliefs, and in identity—
which were inevitable because they now lived in America,
not in Vietnam. Further, their initial resettlement in the
country scattered Vietnamese to such an extent that at first
they had to accommodate to American life on their own
without the intermediary of a Vietnamese community.

The types of cultural change Vietnamese have experienced
cannot yet be described because Vietnamese have been in the
United States for such a short period. At the time of this
writing, less than two years after the fall of Saigon, Vietnamese are beginning to reshape their own destinies, in
many cases developing a community that was denied them
in the government's resettlement program. The formation of
a Vietnamese-American community is discussed only in the
broadest terms because it is a new development and one
which in the long run will mediate changes or encourage
persistence in immigrants' cultural and social life.

For the reasons I have outlined above, I am concerned here
almost exclusively with Vietnamese in the American economy and the kinds of social and emotional problems this has
presented to many immigrants. It should be emphasized at
the outset that the integration that I describe in this chapter
is short term. Whether Vietnamese currently integrated into
America's economically marginal populations will remain
in such a position is not at all clear. What is clear is that in

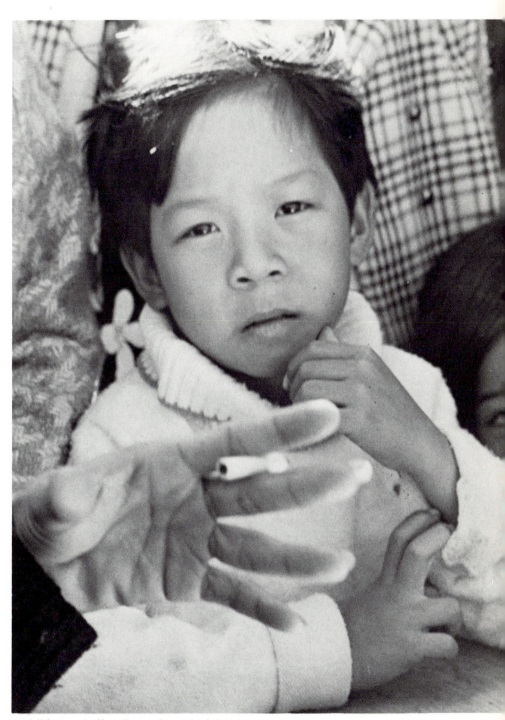

A child. Fort Indian Town Gap. *Fred Friedman*

the short run Vietnamese have become part of the American lower classes because of the time in which they came to the country and U.S. government policies. Further, many Vietnamese have resisted these economic roles, in many instances using the American welfare system to keep from remaining the working poor.

I begin my discussion of Vietnamese life in the United States with two portraits of resettlement. Both of them illustrate the dramatic class adjustments many immigrants have had to make. The two cases are typical of most immigrants as the statistical summaries of employment patterns and welfare assistance which follow them will indicate. The degree to which immigrants were sponsored into American lower classes is to some extent clear in these portraits. It is, however, more evident in the survey of government programs for Vietnamese that follows the portraits and statistical summaries.

Adjustment to America: Two Portraits

Adjusting to life in America was not solely a question of learning to cook food available in supermarkets or use mass transit, refrigerators, etc. It involved coping with new status and with Americans who, under the terms of the sponsorship program, took responsibility for immigrant families, something that Vietnamese heads of households were accustomed to doing on their own. I have chosen to illustrate some of the difficulties in living in America through two case studies: one involves a family of seven which adjusted well to America; the other is a family of eight which had difficulties. Both cases illustrate sponsor-immigrant tensions as well as the immense adjustment to lower class status many immigrants experienced. The cases are transcribed from a tape-recorded interview with an American who was intimately involved with these particular immigrants.* These

---

*These case studies were related to me in an interview with E. R., New York City, 21 September 1976, V.I.C., tape 77, side 1, tape 78, sides 1 and 2, tape 79, side 1. The individual who provided me with the case studies that follow has checked the manuscript for accu-

resettlement cases probably represent successful ones. The sponsorships did not break down, as did many; they did not involve employer-employee relations; and the resettlement agency, sponsor, and the American government consider these immigrants self-supporting, contributing members of American society. In short, the cases went relatively smoothly and are not examples of resettlement that did not work out.

Case One: The H. Family

The H. family was Catholic, originally from North Vietnam. The family had spent less than two months at Fort Chaffee before it found a sponsor, an American organization which had been active in medical assistance in Vietnam.

The H. family consisted of seven persons: a husband, wife, and five children ranging in age from two to eleven years. The father had worked as a radio communications expert in Vietnam, running a communications office in one of the provinces. His position had been managerial rather than technical. Mr. H. spoke English, although he spoke it so fast that his sponsors often "hadn't the foggiest idea what he was saying when he spoke English."[1] He had been to the United States several years earlier for training at Fort Monmouth, New Jersey, as part of a U.S. military assistance program. Mr. H. was about forty years old and well educated. Mrs. H. was about thirty-five years old and had worked as a teletype operator for the same corporation as her husband until 1975, when her fifth child was born. She spoke very good English and apparently understood the language well. In Vietnam, they were comfortable middle-class people who owned their own house and a car.

The H. family arrived in their resettlement location from Fort Chaffee in mid-August 1975. They were met at the airport by several members of their sponsoring organization.

---

racy. However, that individual does not agree with my interpretation of the material and wishes to be disassociated from my conclusions. E. R.'s reasons can be found in V.I.C., Box 9, letter of 9 February 1977.

The family came with luggage and "an enormous picture of the Virgin Mary that was done in mosaic tile they had taken all the way from Vietnam with them."[2] The family was taken from the airport to the home of one of the members of the sponsoring organization who lived in the suburbs of a large metropolitan area.

Within the first two days of their arrival, the job search began.

> H.'s family arrived on a Tuesday. J. brought H. into [the city] on Thursday for job interviews. Because in the meantime we [the sponsors] had been lining up interviews, we knew a little bit about him, so we wrote letters to all the communications type organizations as to whether he could get a position dealing with radio technology. And we really didn't know exactly what his experience was. The next morning after he arrived, T. [a member of the sponsoring organization] sat down with him and tried to get him to write out exactly what he did, how long he worked, for what company. And he was a manager. He had worked his way up the managerial scale in Vietnam. But he was not a technician as much as an overseer at that point in his life. So we really didn't know what we could do for him.
>
> So on Thursday he pounded [the streets] and went on job interviews. . . . He had very little success. First, his English was hard to understand and he was under tremendous nervous strain himself. He had just got plopped down in [the suburbs]. . . . Within two days we knew we were not going to get Mr. H. a job in communications. [One of the members of the sponsoring organization] had various contacts from her years of working . . . for a brokerage firm. So she started making phone calls and a week later we got him a job as a stock transfer clerk at one hundred and ten dollars a week for one of the brokerage firms through her friend. Not that they hired him per se instead of someone else more deserving. . . . It seems they [the brokerage firm] have an

enormous turnover of personnel in that one little area and they had young people in there and they stay a few months and leave whatever happens to them. In any case, they kind of liked the idea of having a husband with a wife and family. They thought he would be much more stable. And it was a trial period. They said that if within three months he worked out, they would increase his salary because they knew no man could raise a family of seven on $110 per week.[3]

H. worked at his job for over a year. Within that time he got three raises that brought his salary up to $140 per week. He stayed at the job partly because he wanted some kind of work and partly because his sponsors "wanted him to work there a full year if it were possible . . . not for a future, but just so he would have it on his employment record that he worked for an American company and had a good record."[4]

The H. family, according to his sponsors, has been able to live on his $140 per week. The household budget was supplemented by food stamps. According to his sponsor, H. came to his resettlement location with about $700, all of which was given to him by his resettlement agency when he left Fort Chaffee. This money was put immediately in a bank account for emergency needs. H. and his family lived in the suburbs with the member of the sponsoring organization for about a month and a half. Their room and board were taken care of by the sponsors and each member of the family was given clothing by the sponsors.

When the family moved into their own home, the housing was found by the sponsoring organization, a member of which described the two-bedroom apartment as follows:

> And we found this marvelous housing project out in . . . off X Street that was a garden apartment complex that had gone downhill in the last ten years and got named quite obviously a slum. The city had put money into it and some private organization had put some money into revitalizing it. [A member of the sponsoring organization] through various means was able to get the

> owners to rent apartments to Vietnamese. And at the point the H. family came, we had several Chase Manhattan families that Chase had airlifted out. . . . Chase, I believe, was one of the corporations involved in funding the housing project.

> So an apartment [in it] normally runs at about $200 a month; we got it at $160. And to get into the housing project you had to have a job. . . . They [the owners] wanted the breadwinner to have a regular job and not to have some sponsor supplement the rent payments, because they knew that would not be a long-term thing. So until H. was in his job long enough and we felt he was going to stay for a period of time, we didn't move them in.[5]

The H. family's start-up expenses for the new apartment were met by his sponsor. In this case, however, a Vietnamese Catholic priest who had helped arrange the sponsorship intervened, either out of general concern for the family with whom he was friendly, or out of a desire to build a base within a potential Vietnamese community. The Father took the family to a resettlement agency other than the one which had found the H. family a sponsor, knowing full well that this particular agency gave a large cash sum for immigrants moving into their own apartments. That resettlement agency, unbeknownst to the sponsors, gave the family a total of $200 per person, or $1,400, which the family's resettlement agency was compelled to reimburse the agency giving the grant. This money helped keep the family off supplemental welfare. A member of the sponsoring organization claimed that the money

> didn't help the family at all. The money was over their head like a sword. They moved into their apartment in September. We immediately tried to apply them for supplemental assistance through welfare for food stamps and medicaid. As soon as they saw that he had a bank account, no way, because he had more than

enough money to supplement his salary take home pay with his savings. And they all said come back when he doesn't have that much money.[6]

In addition to the money the family had gotten from the resettlement agencies, the family got assistance from its sponsor. Members of the sponsoring organization donated furniture for their home. "The only thing new they had to buy were two sets of bunk beds because it was a two bedroom apartment and they had four older children in one room, the larger bedroom, and they took the baby, the two year old, in with them."[7]

The family lives now in the housing project, still off welfare, on Mr. H's $140 a week. The children are enrolled in public school since their parents could not afford to pay tuition for the local parochial school. About 60 or 70 Vietnamese children go to the same school, located about a block away from the housing project.

Case Two: The K. Family

The K. family, like the H. family, was Catholic. It found its sponsor through a Vietnamese Catholic priest who had come to the United States earlier. They arrived in the urban area where they had been relocated in September 1975.

The family consisted of eight persons: Mr. K., his wife, his wife's sister, and five children. Mrs. K. was between seven and eight months pregnant when she left Fort Chaffee. Mr. K. was about thirty-five years old. He spoke good English. He had been a pilot in the Vietnamese air force. Before he served in the military, he worked as a tailor and part time as an electrician. Mrs. K. spoke no English at all and had been occupied solely in raising her five children, the eldest of whom was eight years old. Mrs. K.'s sister spoke very good English. She had been a secretary for an American company in Vietnam.

The K. family was housed at first with an American who had a large apartment close to a hospital where Mrs. K. would have her baby. The apartment was close to a park. The sponsoring organization did not attempt to find Mr. K.

a job immediately. As one of the persons involved in the sponsorship put it:

> We didn't get K. a job right away because [the person in whose apartment they lived] was working, we did not have a member close at hand who was non-working during the day to help them get back and forth from [their home] on a bus to the hospital. So we decided that Mr. K. wouldn't get a job until after the baby was born. We figured his need was helping his wife at this stage. Since he also had a [medical] problem, you couldn't start a job and then have to run to the hospital and ask for time off since it couldn't be done on a Saturday. So K. was used more as a messenger in assisting his family at that point. He was not a productive wage earning head of family.[8]

For over a month K. did nothing other than attend to his family. A month later his sixth child was born. During this period, his sponsors tried to help him plan for a job:

> We sat down and talked with Mr. K. about what he wanted to do since we had this waiting period. We knew we would never find him a pilot's job. We just automatically ruled that out, with his agreement, we didn't dictate to him that you wouldn't be a pilot, if we had thought there was a chance. We wrote letters to every single airport in the . . . area from the tiny ones to the big ones saying, "Is there any position for someone with his background?" Either we got no reply or "no's" back in letters. He then said he wanted to—he's a very handy guy, very multitalented. He did tailoring when he was younger. So we wrote letters to the garment center and that really didn't come through either. He was an electrician. We spoke to someone in the electrician's union. With no actual work experience—he had had jobs at it and could do things like rewire his house in Vietnam—that was out. So he said he wanted a job as an auto-mechanic. He's very good with his hands and we

felt that this was something that could be a career for
him. . . . So we found a . . . school. . . . And we got them
to waive their tuition for $1,000 for a four months
automotive course. And we paid for his train fare out to
the school.

And after the baby was born, I think the baby was born
on Wednesday. On the next Monday K. was on the train
to the school. It was a really grueling trip. He had to go
from [his apartment] by train to A—— station to get on
the —— railroad. He had to go to J—— and change
trains there. . . . It was a long trip. He got up very early
to make this commute. But we [the sponsors] paid for
the whole thing and gave him lunch money and he
attended the school.

So he started in training school, okay. The first day he
was there he had gone in to see the placement man and
they had arranged for him to join one of the classes. He
decided that he wanted to take air conditioning and
refrigeration repair.[9]

While Mr. K. was going to school, most of his family's
expenses were being paid by his sponsor. For four months he
and his family lived with a member of his sponsoring
organization. During these months, his sister-in-law had
found a job. While at Fort Chaffee awaiting resettlement, she
had run into some Americans she had known in Vietnam
who told her that she should look them up if she came to the
city and they would help her find a job. Within a week of her
arrival in that city with her sister's family, she began working as a secretary downtown at $115 per week.

The K. family went through a great deal of strain in their
first five months of life outside the camps. They were living
with an American. Mr. K., accustomed to being head of
household, found that many decisions were taken out of his
hands. The only financially independent member of the
family was his sister-in-law who was not the head of the
household. The strains became clearest around Christmas-

time and erupted over the issue of presents for the children.

> Christmas came and [the sister-in-law] from what I understand, which was a custom in Vietnam as the children's aunt, gave each of the children money. And, of course, she was working, she could afford to do it.
>
> And, of course, we [members of the sponsoring organization] had had presents for everybody from the membership. But Mr. K. couldn't give his family anything. He had gotten his $100 apiece [resettlement grant] so he had $700 for his family and [the sister-in-law] had $100 for herself. But we had been trying to keep that money for when they really needed it when they were out on their own. And that presented a slight rift in the family as a unit. Here was sister-in-law giving money to his children and he couldn't give them any presents himself. He could have, I thought afterwards—we all thought afterwards—taken money from the bank account and gone out and gotten small gifts. I don't think we ever really thought that far as to whether the heads of family should supply their children with Christmas presents. We just assumed that they should save their money for better things. And it was probably a mistake on our part which we learned to regret thereafter.[10]

Not only was the fact of unemployment disrupting the family, so was the fact that the family was living with one of their sponsors. Tensions arose between Mr. K. and the man the family was living with, particularly over the relationship between the host and Mr. K.'s children. At the end of five months, the sponsoring organization decided to move the family to its own apartment which happened to be in the same housing project into which the H. family had moved. K.'s sister-in-law parted from the family and moved into her own apartment nearer to her job, partly because she wanted more independence. The rest of her family moved into its own two-bedroom home, with its rent, gas, electricity, and food paid for by the sponsors.

The sponsoring organization over five months had tried to prepare Mr. K. for a skilled trade and had supported his family of six children during the time. At the end of five months, it appears, their resources gave way and, try as they did, they were unable to sponsor K. into a career.

> K. graduated from school. Not top in his class. . . . We could not get him a job in the air-conditioning field and [a member of the sponsoring organization] wrote letters to everybody. There was just nothing. So what to do with K.? He wanted to go on welfare. We said "No. No way are we going to survive." As a sponsor we could not see it, we knew that it was not the alternative, morally and ethically. We had spent a fortune on this guy and welfare was not the answer. We eventually got him a job in maintenance.[11]

Try as a sponsor might have, the economic situation in the United States simply did not allow K. to get a skilled job that would have some kind of future to it. The sponsor felt frustrated over the situation, trying hard to both retrain the immigrant and provide for his family. For K., as for H., coming to America meant adjusting to a lower status, something that K. resisted but could not avoid.

Vietnamese at Work in America

How typical the cases of K. and H. are becomes clearest on examining the type of work and salaries paid to immigrants. Immigrants underwent considerable class and occupation change in moving from Vietnam to the United States. For the most part, when employed, Vietnamese found jobs at the lowest end of the American occupational spectrum. The work they found was often temporary and tended to offer little or no possibility for advancement. Wages for Vietnamese were the lowest in the country. Many immigrants worked for less than $2.39 per hour, the U.S. minimum wage as of 1976. For Vietnamese families, averaging five persons (see chapter 3), more than one wage earner per family became a necessity since full-time employment for one person in most cases put such a family at the poverty level and dependent on welfare. This, as I will show, became an insurmountable difficulty for families which consisted solely of husband, wife, and children under sixteen years of age.

Vietnamese, when they left the camps, did not automatically find work. As of December 1975, 64.5 percent of all immigrant males over the age of sixteen were employed; 14.1 percent were unemployed; while another 21.3 percent were not in the work force. In the same period 28 percent of women over sixteen years of age were employed, 12 percent were unemployed and 60 percent were not in the work force. The difference in initial employment rates by sex is due to the fact that with the resettlement of Vietnamese in nuclear families with young children, women tended to stay at home to care for them. In the cases of the H. and K. families discussed earlier, sponsors assumed women would care for the children and put no pressure on the wives to enter the job market. H.'s wife, a skilled teletype operator with fine English language skills, probably had a better chance at a well-paying job in the U.S. than her husband. Over 57 percent of immigrant women who worked were heads of households.[12]

As of December 1975, not all Vietnamese employed worked a full forty hours per week. Only 79.9 percent of the men and 64.5 percent of the women employed worked full time; 19.7 percent of the men and 33.7 percent of the women listed as employed had part-time jobs.[13]

The wages for which immigrants worked were not always up to the minimum wage. Of those who worked forty hours or more a week, 36.9 percent grossed $50 to $99 per week in wages (or between $1.25 and $2.50 per hour). About 58.4 percent clearly earned more than the minimum wage, for their weekly gross pay was between $100 and $199.[14] Most of these persons were making closer to $100 per week than $140 per week. Of those with full time employment 1.4 percent made less than $50 per week. Only 62 percent of all Vietnamese employed made $2.50 per hour or $100 per week.[15] Vietnamese families averaged five persons. A yearly gross salary of $5,200 put that family considerably below the poverty level if there was but one wage earner per family. A family of five in the U.S. was considered subsisting at poverty level if it had an income of approximately $9,594 per year. A family of seven subsisted at poverty level at an annual income of $13,199. Only families of two persons had incomes above poverty level with incomes of $5,200 per year.[16]

Most Vietnamese who found jobs like K. and H. found jobs outside areas in which they had previously worked and which were considerably lower on the occupational scale. A 1975 Interagency Task Force survey, which has been the source of the statistics cited above, made this clear. Of immigrants who had worked in managerial, professional, technical, and business positions in Vietnam, 73 percent found themselves in blue collar jobs in the U.S., 17 percent became clerical and sales personnel, and only 10 percent went into jobs equivalent to those they held in Vietnam.[17] The survey estimated that 85.4 percent of persons who were white collar workers in Vietnam became blue collar workers in the U.S. Former blue collar workers experienced downward occupational mobility, but nowhere near as drastically as did Saigon's former elite. Of immigrants who had worked in blue collar jobs in Vietnam, 44.7 percent did not find skilled work for which they had been trained; rather, they joined the ranks of American unskilled workers.

No complete statistical information has been compiled as to what specific jobs Vietnamese hold. United HIAS, as of 12 February 1976, did list the kinds of jobs held by members of the 113 Vietnamese families they resettled in Los Angeles. United HIAS estimated that of the 152 employable adults among these families, 98 had full time jobs. "Most are finding semiskilled and unskilled jobs," United HIAS reported, working as sewing machine operators, busboys, bakers' helpers, factory laborers, warehousemen, store clerks, and office clerks. One immigrant was employed as an apartment manager, another was an auto mechanic.[18] Their situation was about the same as that of Laotian immigrants in Los Angeles that United HIAS had resettled. Of the 30 Laotian families in the city, only three had a weekly income over $140 per week: one individual worked as a miner, another as a mechanic. The third family with an income in excess of $140 per week had two wage earners. Most Laotian immigrants in the Los Angeles area earned between $100 and $140 per week, working on state highway maintenance crews and as janitors, factory laborers, and clerks.[19]

There is little reason to believe that the types of jobs HIAS-sponsored Vietnamese found are any different from those taken by Vietnamese other agencies sponsored. IRC, ACNS, LIRS, CWS all described Vietnamese employed in entry level jobs as waiters, busboys, janitors, dishwashers, low-level clerks and secretaries, day laborers, factory workers. Very few Vietnamese held managerial or technical jobs; even fewer held professional posts. Even as of November 1976, only 6 percent of Vietnamese employed made wages within range of $5 per hour or more (or $800 per month, or $9,600 per year).[20]

The degree of downward occupational (and therefore social and economic) mobility most immigrants experienced is dramatically illustrated by jobs individuals worked in the U.S. compared to ones they held while in Vietnam. (See table 8.)

The jobs Vietnamese held were not only lower-level, poorly paying jobs, they were jobs that held out little opportunity for advancement. Dish washing, busboy, janitorial, secretarial, and day laborer positions do not lead to better paying, more skilled work. Dishwashers rarely become restaurant managers; janitors don't manage businesses, day laborers don't become skilled workers unless, of course, they quit their jobs and train for a more skilled type of work. This point was all too clear to many Vietnamese, for when the Interagency Task Force on Indochinese Refugees surveyed reasons for the large job turnover among immigrants and their dissatisfaction with jobs they held, Vietnamese replied that they were not satisfied with the jobs they had or jobs they were offered because these jobs held no opportunity for advancement (47 percent) or the jobs were temporary (46 percent) and not in line with their training (63.1 percent). Low salaries were mentioned less frequently as the reason for dissatisfaction. Most Vietnamese indicated they were willing

Table 8

Jobs Held in Vietnam Versus in the U. S.

Job Held in Vietnam	Job Held in U. S.
Director General, South Vietnamese Ministry of the Interior	Yard work
Air Force Colonel	Newspaper Delivery Night Watchman
Medical Doctor	Limousine Driver
Aide of Nguyen-Cao-Ky	Judo Instructor, YMCA (Part-time) Night Clerk
Medical Doctor	Dish Washer
Bank Manager	Janitor at a bank
Professor of Literature	Furniture Assembler
Three Star General, ARVN	Maitre d'
ARVN Chief of Staff	Waiter
Colonel, ARVN	Garbage Collector

Source: Mark Shanahan, "Vietnamese Refugees--A Year Later," Devils Lake Journal (Maryland), 26 July 1976, IRC Clipping File; "A Refugee's New Life Chopping Onions," San Francisco Examiner and Chronicle, 23 May 1976, IRC Clipping File; "Former Viet Driver, General: Both Face Money Problems," Washington Post, Sunday, 14 September 1975, pp. D1, D2; Douglas E. Kneeland, "Resettlement Nearing End, But Not Refugee Problems," New York Times, 24 November 1975, pp. 1, 23.

to accept low paying jobs if they led to something better.[21] The problem was that jobs they held were ones that offered little chance for regaining the occupational status and income that they had had in Vietnam.

Vietnamese could not "live" on their wages, especially if families had but one wage earner. H.'s seven-person family could hardly be expected to live long on the $140 a week (or $560 a month) he was grossing as of September 1976, especially with the rent of $160 a month he was paying. This became increasingly clear to immigrants as they entered the work force. As a result, more than one wage earner per household entered the work force whenever possible and many Vietnamese families came to rely on welfare. The number of wage earners per household depended on what part of Vietnamese families were resettled together within a household. Vietnamese families, while large, also tended to have many young children. The H. and K. families were typical, containing as both did schoolchildren no older than 11 or 12 years of age who were incapable of taking full charge of infants. Few Vietnamese households with small children had three or more adults in them so that two salaries could be drawn and one adult left in charge of the children. This was made more unlikely as resettlement occurred in households based on American nuclear rather than Vietnamese extended families, and as the cost of living and household tensions mounted in such a way as to drive out adult wage earners not part of the nuclear family. The K. family was a good example of this. The sister-in-law simply could not tolerate living with the family nor the family with her, especially if it meant that nine persons would be crammed into a two-bedroom apartment. The sister-in-law could do better on her own on the $115 a week she earned.

Despite the difficulties of having more than one wage earner per family, in many immigrant families more than one person per household entered the job market. A look at immigrants resettled by one agency in the Washington, D.C., area (table 9) shows both the increasing trend toward more than one person per household entering the work force and the decrease in size of the average household.

The entry of more than one wage earner into the work force resulted in smaller household sizes. This only in part signaled the break-up of what was left of extended families, it also marked disruptions in the nuclear family. Women increasingly entered the work force. In September 1975, 28 percent of immigrant women over 16 years of age worked; a year later 45 percent worked, many at jobs better paying than men's and ones that had more potential for advancement.[22]

Table 9
Number of Wage Earners Per Household

	Number of Immigrant Residents Resettled by Agency per one Employed	Average Resident Household Size
9 January 1976	4.5	3.4
12 April 1976	3.3	3.3
23 April 1976	2.9*	3.3
4 June 1976	2.0*	3.3
17 August 1976	3.0*	3.2

Source: Indochinese Refugees, Confirmed Employment, International

Rescue Committee, Xerox.   SUNY/Buffalo Archives, Carton 4.   Inter-

view with L. W., Comptroller, International Rescue Committee,

21 September 1976, V. I. C., Tape #72, Side 2.

*Average of more than one person employed per family

This has led to some marital disputes as women apparently have exerted more control over the family economy than they had previously and many of their spouses have become despondent over not only their lowered economic position but also changing power relations in the family. Family separations have resulted from this state of affairs. It is not clear how many have occurred, but there have been enough to cause concern among immigrants themselves.[23]

Despite the presence of more than one wage earner per household, many Vietnamese families found themselves unable to be self-supporting. Two wage earners, bringing in a salary of $600 to $800 per month, if there are seven children, living in most metropolitan areas in the U.S. are still subsisting below the poverty level: their income is only $9,600 per year and a poverty-level income for such a family is over $13,000 per year.[24] Many Vietnamese households found themselves unable to make ends meet even on two salaries. Mr. T., a former chauffeur employed by the U.S. military while he was in Vietnam, illustrates this. He, his wife, and his two eldest children all found some work. He worked two part-time jobs and his wife and sons also worked part-time jobs. Their combined take-home monthly wages were $500 a month (or $6,000 per year).[25]

In October 1975, 42 percent of immigrant households had a yearly income of less than $2,500, 45 percent of less than $5,000.[26] By October 1976, household income had risen considerably due to the larger numbers of wage earners per household. Twenty percent of all refugee families earned less than $5,000 a year while another 35 percent earned less than $10,000 per year.[27] Immigrants had two possibilities to make ends meet: either rely on subsidies from their sponsors or go on welfare. They tried both.

As of December 1975 about 30 percent of all immigrants received some form of welfare, either cash assistance or medicaid. By 29 February 1976, 31,189 of the 128,186 persons resettled in the U.S. with whom the government still had contact were receiving cash welfare assistance. This was 24.3 percent of all immigrants. Another 21,310 immigrants were receiving medical assistance only. Altogether, this meant that close to half of all immigrants were on some type of welfare.[28] The number of people on welfare receiving cash assistance as well as medical assistance mounted between 29 February and 1 June 1976. Nationally the number of immigrants on welfare had risen 16 percent. The increase was uneven across the states. The number of immigrants on cash assistance grew by 63 percent in the state of Connecticut, 139 percent in Louisiana, 123 percent in South Dakota, 71 percent in Arkansas, 84 percent in Wisconsin, 61 percent in Ohio, 24 percent in Texas, and 25 percent in Washington. This was offset by only small increases in states with large immigrant populations like California, where the number of Vietnamese on cash assistance went up only 11 percent, and decreases in states like Mississippi (down 33 percent) and Maine (down 32 percent).[29] The unevenness of the increases to some extent reflects states' willingness to enroll people on welfare as well as it does Vietnamese movement from one area to another. It also shows the general trend of shifting support for immigrants from individual sponsors to the federal government. This was to be expected since with time sponsors found themselves unable to assume major medical expenses or responsibility for indefinitely subsidizing Vietnamese households, even those in which adults were gainfully employed. As sponsors' resources gave way, Vietnamese turned to the federal government for aid.

To some extent the increase in welfare recipients reflects some Vietnamese reactions to their prospective place in the American occupational structure. Mr. K., one of the cases discussed in detail at the beginning of this chapter, wanted to go on welfare after it became clear to him that he would probably end up in a low-paying job despite the four-month retraining program he had struggled to attend. His willingness to go on welfare was in part a response to newfound lower-class status and the realization that he might never be able to better himself. Only his sponsors' intervention prevented him from going on welfare. Other Vietnamese went on welfare not only as a rejection of the newfound status, but also they realized that going on welfare yielded them as much income as the full-time employment that they could get and gave them an opportunity to retrain for jobs with greater chances for advancement. Nguyen-Dinh-Tri, a construction contractor in Vietnam, who resettled in Camus, Washington, with his wife and eight children is a good example of this. Tri, his 16-year-old son, and his wife all found jobs working at the minimum wage for a woolen mill. Between the three of them they managed to earn about $990 a month, slightly more than equivalent welfare benefits for a family of nine if one includes medicaid and food stamps. Tri and his son quit their jobs after a short while when they found that other Vietnamese in the area lived as well as his family lived on their three full-time jobs. Those who went on welfare, Tri discovered, had time to learn English and skilled trades and were able after a few months to interview for better-paying jobs that had a future, which Tri's job as a truck loader did not. Tri went on welfare and enrolled in English language classes and a job retraining program. He sent his son back to school. This was done over the protests of Tri's sponsors and resettlement agency.[30]

American officials became alarmed over the increasing enrollment of immigrants on welfare and in spring 1976 HEW, which had assumed the role of the Interagency Task Force in coordinating programs for immigrants, held a series of regional meetings to discuss refugee problems. These HEW discussions and the programs that emanated from them show that the government pressured Vietnamese into accepting downward occupational mobility. Welfare provisions adopted since fall 1976 and selected programs HEW developed tended to channel Vietnamese into entry-level jobs which held little promise for advancement. The government did this in the hopes of relieving itself of responsibility for the immigrants. To have done differently would have required massive expenditures that the government, in a time of financial crisis and recession and with memories of the cost of the Cuban program, was unwilling to make.

Government Policy and Immigrant Downward Occupational Mobility

Has U.S. government policy helped channel Vietnamese into American lower-class jobs and income? Would Vietnamese have inevitably ended up in this country's lowest occupational and income group considering the time they came to the U.S.? Perhaps this question is unanswerable. Vietnamese did arrive in the country at a time of severe unemployment and economic recession. Many American skilled workers had difficulty finding and keeping jobs commensurate with their skills. The economic recession to a great extent limited what economic roles would be open to Vietnamese. The resettlement policies adopted first by the Interagency Task Force on Indochinese Refugees and then followed by its HEW successor, however, did little to counter the effect of the recession on Vietnamese. The government saw resettlement first and foremost as a private affair between sponsor and immigrant in which the sponsor provided for immigrants' every need without help from the federal government. At first the federal government even refrained from providing medicaid for extraordinary medical expenses unless it could be documented that the sponsorship had broken down. Sponsorships became job-related. When they were not, there was intense pressure on the part of the sponsor to get the immigrant employed in any job to give the sponsor financial relief. In case after case sponsors ended up pressuring Vietnamese to take any job simply because the sponsor could not afford to support an immigrant family through an interim job retraining, English language learning period. The cases of H. and K. presented at the beginning of this chapter illustrate this. Within two days H.'s sponsors had arranged job interviews; within a week they had placed him in his job as a stock transfer clerk for $110 per week and, according to the member of the group sponsoring him through whose words the case was related, the sponsor strongly advised him to stay in that job. The case of K. was more complex. His sponsors were none too happy at his attempts to retrain himself. While they tried to get him a job in his field and helped him to attend an air-conditioning and refrigeration course, they were frustrated at their inability to find him a job to his liking. In the end, they found him a janitorial position.

Economic pressure motivated a good many sponsors to place Vietnamese in any job, regardless of that job's potential for advancement or whether it would actually yield sufficient income to support the immigrants. The channeling of Vietnamese into low-income employment was a product of the support resettlement agencies could give immigrants which, in turn, stemmed from financial provisions the U.S. government made for resettlement. The U.S. government allocated only $500 per immigrant, to be administered through the resettlement agencies. This sum was paltry, for the costs involved were clearly much higher— closer to double or triple that cost per individual, assuming that that individual became self-supporting within a month. A United Hebrew Immigration and Assistance Service (HIAS) representative estimated that $5,000 per person was a more realistic grant, if one wanted to resettle the immigrants

in jobs and income brackets acceptable to them. Because the
federal government's grant was so small and had to be
divided between resettlement organizations and immigrants,
the resettlement organizations also put pressure on immigrants to take what they could get as far as jobs and welfare
were concerned. They openly discouraged immigrants from
quitting jobs they had, realistically assessing that within the
resources available to immigrants and resettlement agencies,
there was little more that could be done. The resettlement
agencies were to some extent influential since they had given
appreciable help to immigrants, often supplying rent depos-
its, paying for dental and medical care not covered by
medicaid, etc.

The resettlement grant and overall policy were not the
only factors channeling immigrants into the lower classes.
The government allocated minimal funds for programs that
would have taught immigrants English or retrained them.
In fiscal year 1975/76, $22,427,232 was allocated to the
education of immigrants, $3,700,000 of which went to
language training and primary and secondary education in
the camps; $12,431,960 of the sum was spent in direct aid to
school districts and state education bureaucracies for school-
aged children ($1,027,644 went to California alone). Less
than $5,000,000 went to adult education—language train-
ing, job retraining or postsecondary education.[31] (This
includes the $250 per month stipend for retraining dentists
and the stipends for medical retraining—the only two clear-
cut job retraining programs HEW has sponsored.) If the sum
allocated to adult education were divided equally only
among heads of households, only $150 per person was
provided by the federal government. Larry McDonough, the
head of the HEW Task Force on Indochinese Refugees,
estimated in a memo to the secretary of HEW that an
allocation of $325 per adult was necessary just to teach
immigrants English. The initial HEW grant, he argued,
assumed only 108 hours of instruction per person although
it was clear that most immigrants needed between 200
and 576 hours of instruction to learn functional English.[32]
Not only did the federal government fail to provide ade-

quate funding for job retraining and English language instruction for adults, it actually embarked on a campaign to bypass such programs by insisting that jobs were available for Vietnamese and that they should be encouraged to take such jobs, regardless of what these jobs entailed or whether they would provide enough income to make an immigrant self-supporting. This policy became clear in April 1976, at the time of rapid increase of immigrants on cash assistance. The New York Regional Office of HEW was the first to come up with a specific program. According to that region's director of the HEW Task Force on Indochinese Refugees, the program was conceived on the assumption that there were plenty of jobs available for which no special vocational skills are required, nor would immigrants necessarily need to speak English well to function in them. The New York program, the director maintained, had only one component: locating jobs in a systematic fashion for immigrants by canvassing both employers and immigrants. Retraining programs and English language courses, according to him, had little value. First, he argued, no one learns English in formal schooling; second, too many supportive services, like retraining programs, created dependence so that Vietnamese would refuse to stand on their own. They also encouraged "unrealistic" aspirations among immigrants. Too many, he complained, want to go to college, buy cars, live the good life.[33]

The New York region's program embodied its director's philosophy. It involved nothing more than setting up an employment placement office that encouraged immigrants to pursue job leads and accept job offers. Employees of the office interviewed immigrants in their homes, helped them develop resumes, set up job interviews, etc. In all, after about four months of operation fifty persons got jobs, all of which required unskilled labor and paid between $2.30 and $2.80 per hour.

While the New York/New Jersey region had the most highly developed job placement service, other regions in which welfare roles swelled emulated this approach. At a 31 March through 1 April 1976 workshop on Indochinese

resettlement held in Seattle, Washington, HEW officials and
Vietnamese immigrants disagreed over whether government
programs should emphasize job placement or job retraining
and language instruction. The Vietnamese attending the
workshop vociferously supported the latter approach over
HEW objections.[34] A similar approach was taken by HEW
Region 9 on the West Coast. Its director in his report, written
15 August 1976, urged a New York region approach, bol-
stered by changes in welfare eligibility requirements that
would make accepting any job offered an immigrant a
condition for receiving government assistance of any kind.[35]

By September 1976, HEW had proposed a series of revisions in welfare regulations concerning refugees which in
essence supported regional efforts to place Vietnamese in
any job and make them stay in those jobs. The revisions deny
any welfare benefits—food stamps, medicaid, or cash
assistance—to unemployed immigrants over age eighteen
unless they have registered for a job with state employment
services and accept whatever job or on-the-job training
opportunity is found for them. Additionally, the revisions
deny welfare to individuals over eighteen if they quit jobs
found for them within thirty days of their initial employment or are fired at any time for willful misconduct.[36] These
revisions went into effect November 1976. Their effect will be
to further pressure Vietnamese into accepting, and remaining in, the country's lowest paying jobs. The new welfare
provisions could also affect future generations' chances for
betterment. Eighteen-year-olds, under the revisions, would
be subject to the same job placement pressures as their
parents, unless without special assistance they find their way
into postsecondary education.

The federal government has not abandoned English
instruction for Vietnamese; it has, however, modified its
provisions, doling out again for 1976/77 the last $5 million it
intends to allocate for such training. (This is at least 20
percent below what McDonough, the director of the HEW
task force, estimated necessary to teach functional English to
immigrants.) Under new HEW provisions, English language instruction is to be job-related only. It will no longer

be directed at trying to develop fluency in reading, writing, and speech; rather it will aim solely at teaching passable English suited to functioning at a job. HEW has not necessarily worked out the specifics of job-related English language instruction. However, it has invited proposals for such instruction and has implied through its criticism of postcamp English training that it will not support English as a Second Language programs directed at all non–English speaking residents in the U.S. as it did in 1975/76. Rather, it would favor programs designed specifically for Vietnamese immigrants who were to enter the work force. The proposed revisions in welfare eligibility require any immigrant over eighteen, as a condition even for receiving supplemental benefits, to attend these English classes. Failure to do so would mean immigrants were no longer eligible to receive benefits.

The federal government projected that its responsibility for immigrants from Vietnam and other parts of Indochina would be ended by September 1977. At that time, the government believed or wished to believe, their resettlement would be over and they would no longer need special assistance. Whatever help they needed, it was assumed, would be the same as that required by any other poor Americans. In short, by September 1977, as far as the federal government was concerned, there would be no Vietnamese refugees or immigrants; rather, there would be only poor residents of America, some of whom happened to have been born in Vietnam.

that may be, does help set the context for understanding
future Vietnamese responses to life in this country. Mapping
these responses is the task of future students of this immigration. It is clear from this survey of American policies and
programs that Vietnamese responses will not necessarily
follow the lines that Americans perhaps have hoped they
would, because Vietnamese are Vietnamese, not Americans,
and because of the situation in which many Vietnamese now
find themselves.

From the onset of this immigration Americans have not
been able to predict or control Vietnamese actions, despite
the fact that Americans have by and large set the context
within which Vietnamese have had to act. This was apparent
in the course of the evacuation of Saigon as well as in the
resettlement of Vietnamese in the U.S. The gulf between
policies and outcomes is to some extent a result of the
differing imperatives upon which Vietnamese and Americans have acted. Vietnamese actions, especially in leaving
their country, had their roots in Vietnamese history and
society, and not necessarily in American policies. Given this,
the Americans' planning of the evacuation of Saigon was
doomed. Americans could no more control which Vietnamese would leave their country than they could have controlled the entire course of Vietnamese history. Vietnamese
became refugees because of long-standing divisions in their
own society, many of which stemmed from the events of the
past hundred or more years. Americans did not create the
gulfs that had arisen between Catholics and non-Catholics,
rich and poor, urban and rural dwellers, westernized and
nonwesternized Vietnamese, Saigon government bureaucrats and the masses, although American involvement in
Vietnam over the past decades helped reinforce them. These
cleavages in Vietnamese society and the animosity that
resulted from them motivated the flight of most refugees.
There was little Americans could do to allay Vietnamese
fears, real and imagined, of bloodbaths and battle zones. The
American propaganda machine had for years, along with the
Saigon government, fanned such fears. No American policies set in April 1975 could prevent Vietnamese from acting

on these fears and commandeering boats or fighting for places on planes leaving Vietnam. Not only was the U.S. government powerless to control Vietnamese actions, it could not even insure that Americans in Vietnam would follow directives set in Washington. Many Americans in Vietnam in 1975 had spread the rumors of bloodbaths sure to follow the collapse of the Saigon government. They themselves honestly believed that such purges were about to occur and acted on their own instincts rather than on American policies in helping Vietnamese refugees.

The impulses born of the Vietnamese context, rather than the American context, explain why the Vietnamese who left their country were not the people that so many congressmen and senators thought "we should have gotten out." Rather, they were Vietnamese who thought they should have gotten out. For this reason, Vietnamese who immigrated represented a less homogeneous group than most Americans would have supposed, for, while among them were South Vietnam's governing, military, and professional/technical elites, there were also persons who were relatively uneducated and unurbanized, who lacked exposure to western culture into which they came when they moved from Vietnam to America. Vietnamese immigrated to the United States for varying reasons and with different degrees of preparation for American life and of anticipation of what that life would be. How they would adjust or adapt became a matter of concern for American officials who were acting on imperatives set by the American context, particularly by the economic recession. For the U.S. government the issue was how to integrate this diverse population of immigrants rapidly into American society. Such integration depended on the Vietnamese elite adjusting to a lower social and occupational status within American society than they had held in Vietnam. It also depended on those who came from the Vietnamese countryside or the lower classes becoming acquainted with western, urban industrial society. The American government hoped that Vietnamese would enter American society without greatly affecting American politics and economic life. This set of imperatives led to the government's policy of dispersing Vietnamese throughout the country.

Once the Vietnamese left their own country, they became subject to American control more than they had ever been before, despite the years of American intervention in their country's internal affairs. Adjusting to American imperatives and control was part of the painful process of becoming an immigrant. The camps were places where Americans promoted such an adjustment. For most Vietnamese the camps were the first American-controlled environment in which they had lived. Living space, food, recreation—all were created by Americans for Vietnamese in the resettlement centers. Vietnamese roles in the camps were more or less passive. Americans set the terms of life; Vietnamese could only react to what Americans proposed to do with and for them.

The camps were also places where Vietnamese were introduced to life in America. There they were systematically exposed to American culture and told how to behave in American society and what to expect from it. In the camps' educational programs Vietnamese were taught about American families, teenage subculture, American food, houses, credit buying, and jobs that awaited them. Not only did the programs, for children and adults alike, inform Vietnamese of how Americans lived, they also attempted to mold Vietnamese expectations of their own lives in America. The elementary school, for example, prepared Vietnamese children to live in a household consisting of their mothers, fathers, and siblings and not a household consisting of grandmother, grandfather, aunts, uncles, and cousins as they had lived in Vietnam. Those outside the nuclear family became, in the words of the school curriculum, "other people who live with me," equated with maids and cooks. Similarly the school prepared Vietnamese teenagers for American adolescent culture and for severing themselves from their parents' households at the age of eighteen. Adults' expectations also became a target of English language classes in which drills and lessons offered Vietnamese a range of occupational choices more suited to American reality than the individual immigrant's past work and class experience or his or her expectations of occupational roles in the U.S. Survival English's list of jobs exemplified this as Vietnamese were assured they could live in the U.S. on the salaries of nurse's aides, clerks, etc.

The cultural orientation in the camps not only tried to shape or reshape immigrants' expectations of life in America, it also, perhaps unwittingly, perhaps consciously, proposed new roles and cultural norms for Vietnamese. The role of women presented in the camps was one directly out of an American, rather than Vietnamese cultural context, as were familial and social roles of the good neighbor, the good child, the good father. These roles were sometimes imposed on Vietnamese as Americans equated them with English language fluency and getting a job, the bare essentials for survival in America.

It is indeed ironic that while cultural orientation programs in the camps tried to inform Vietnamese about life in the U.S., mold their expectations of it, and to some extent change their behavior and thought, Americans who designed and ran these programs had little conception of what they were doing, beyond a vague feeling that Vietnamese needed to be informed about American life and that the programs performed this function. Not only were Americans often unconscious about what they were doing, many did not agree with one another about what aspects of American life Vietnamese should be introduced to, or what they should know in order to "adjust" to the country. To some elementary school teachers and curriculum specialists, adjustment was knowing about families and school behavior; to some secondary school teachers it meant preparing Vietnamese to fit into a preset adolescent culture of dope and problems with the law; to some teachers of adults it meant being able to converse amicably with suburban neighbors; to others it entailed being clear on behavior appropriate to one's sex; while to still others it meant being able to break out of sex role stereotypes. Within the camps, in short, Vietnamese were presented with varying aspects of American culture and encouraged to adapt to them, regardless of whether those aspects conflicted either with one another or with Viet-

namese life-styles and modes of thought. Americans cannot
be faulted too greatly for doing this, for in this society there is
little consensus about what an American way of life is.
Further, many Americans had little knowledge of Vietnamese culture and no Vietnamese-American culture existed
that would have mediated conflicting values and roles
presented by Americans in the way that ethnic cultures have
done in the past for previous immigrant groups whose
immigration stretched over decades.

Although cultural orientation in the camps tried to reshape Vietnamese expectations of life in America and Vietnamese behavior and attitudes, it is by no means clear that
the camps' programs were successful in doing so. Many Vietnamese were confused by what Americans told them. Some
simply avoided the programs. Many adults saw little utility
in the English classes or the public school in the camps and
refused to either attend classes themselves or send their
children to them. MPs were sent into barracks to round up
children for the schools and barracks leaders had to stress
continually that it was illegal not to send children to school.[1]
In the elementary school, many children sat passively,
scarcely comprehending what was expected of them because
they did not understand the English language. Some even
were unaware that they were supposed to refrain from
speaking Vietnamese.[2]   Children were not the only immigrants reticent about entering American society or unable to
comprehend what Americans were preparing them for.
Many adults never bothered to attend classes or orientation
sessions despite the fact that they were urged to do so. To
some extent, this reflected behavior as refugees rather than
immigrants, since in many cases it signified that Vietnamese were avoiding facing up to the reality that they were
going to live in the United States and had left Vietnam
permanently. Many Vietnamese who attended cultural
orientation sessions went to be informed as much as possible
about American life, but refused to conform to behaviors
that they felt conflicted with their own or, if they did, clearly
did not internalize that behavior, preferring to do what was
asked of them for the time being. The fisherwomen were a

good example of such conformity. They did repeat the phrase "I am a housewife" as instructed by their well-meaning teacher. However, they laughed when they understood what the words they had enunciated actually meant. In adult English classes, many Vietnamese, when asked to vent their inmost feelings in front of strangers, simply sat stony-faced and would only tell the "facts" of their existence—where they were born, their jobs, and where they were now; they refused to say how they felt about these "facts."

In short, because Americans presented a set of expectations of life in the U.S. and promoted certain types of cultural and social behavior does not mean that Vietnamese accepted such expectations and conformed to the behavioral models presented them. All it means is that Americans acted out of their own cultural context and Vietnamese sorted through what was presented them as they were able or as they pleased and attempted to make their own choices to the extent they were able.

The camps were transitional institutions. If it were not clear to Vietnamese that they had traveled from a Vietnamese world to an American one from their experience with camp governance, routines, and programs, resettlement policies drove this point home. Resettlement was according to American imperatives, on the basis of patterns Americans, rather than Vietnamese, deemed acceptable. Where one was resettled depended in large part on Vietnamese ability to fit into a local job market, on whether household size conformed to an American sponsor's specifications, or on Vietnamese having an American connection. Vietnamese could enter the country officially only if they met American demands, not Vietnamese ones. From the perspective of most Vietnamese, if they had a choice resettlement would have led to the establishment of a Vietnamese community within the U.S. Those who could, tried to have themselves resettled in this fashion, using their own connections, particularly the network of Vietnamese Catholic clergy and relatives already in the U.S. to do so. Many Vietnamese, however, at first were in no position to resettle on their own terms. Rather, they relied on American decisions about their fate.

The mixture of resettlement by Vietnamese and American networks is apparent in the pattern of resettlement as of December 1975. Many Vietnamese communities were formed in places like Los Angeles, San Francisco, and the Washington, D.C. area. These were places where there were Vietnamese before the fall of Saigon, where there were Americans who had worked with Vietnamese in Vietnam, and where there was a Vietnamese clergy.

Vietnamese, outside the camps, faced a very different world from the one most had expected or had been accustomed to all their lives. Until Vietnamese left the camps, they perhaps had not yet fully understood that they were to become members of American society—immigrants and not refugees. The world outside the camp made this unavoidable. The adjustment to American society began in earnest and the kinds of problems it presented to individual immigrants varied depending on that immigrant's social class and status in Vietnam. Members of Vietnam's ruling circles and professional/managerial elite found that moving from Vietnam to the United States meant total loss of socioeconomic status as they ended up in jobs on the lowest end of the American occupational scale. The jobs which many found offered little possibility for regaining their former class positions since they were jobs without advancement possibilities. The American government offered little assistance to Vietnamese who resisted being channeled into the American lower classes; on the contrary, its policies encouraged such channeling.

The kinds of problems Vietnamese faced in adjusting to the United States varied in intensity by individual immigrant, depending on his or her prior exposure to western urban life and on previous class backgrounds. Vietnamese who had had prior exposure to western urban life, who had worked for Americans, or who spoke English before they left Vietnam probably experienced less culture shock than individuals who had come from rural areas and had had little contact in Vietnam with Americans and their life-styles. Rural Vietnamese had no conception of the U.S.; many had assumed that their flight from Vietnam would entail moving out of village-based communal life—and especially for rural Vietnamese Catholics—from a life centered on the church and the village priest. Doubtless these immigrants faced two kinds of adjustment: the adjustment from rural to urban life-styles which they would have no doubt have faced had they been refugees from rural to urban Vietnam; and the adjustment from a Vietnamese society and culture to an American one. The members of Vietnam's elite had to deal only with the transition from Vietnamese to American urban society.

Refugees with rural backgrounds had to deal first with alien cultural and social institutions; they did not have to adjust to changed socioeconomic class positions. Like immigrants whose origins were in the urban lower classes, as were the rank and file of the Vietnamese military, moving from Vietnam to America meant in many cases moving into affluence relative to their life-styles in Vietnam, despite the fact that they were channeled into low-status and low-income jobs in the American occupational structure. If these persons did not find themselves materially and socially better off in the U.S., neither did they find their class positions lowered. Unskilled workers in Vietnam found themselves jobs as unskilled workers in the U.S.

Vietnam's former managerial and technical elite, while perhaps better acquainted with Americans and their life-styles than rural or lower-class Vietnamese, lost power, prestige, and income moving from Saigon to this country. Most had to cope with the reality that in the United States they could no longer enjoy the middle- or ruling-class positions they held at home. A Vietnamese cabinet minister, for example, had little usefulness for Americans—as a cabinet minister. His skills equipped him to earn a living in the U.S. only as an unskilled laborer. Not only were people like him placed into the American lower classes, but they were placed there on an equal, if not lower, footing than other Vietnamese over whom they had once ruled. Adjusting to American culture was essentially adjusting to a change in class position.

Even had Vietnam's former elite anticipated loss of power and prestige in terms of their ability to rule a nation-state, many had anticipated being able to play such a role in the context of a Vietnamese community within the United States. Nguyen-Cao-Ky illustrates such expectations on the part of Vietnamese political leaders. When he first arrived in the U.S. he set himself up in a mansion worthy of a political leader in Alexandria, Virginia. From his headquarters, he toured the camps with his staff, trying to establish his leadership of the refugee community. Ky failed in his aspirations in part because a Vietnamese community failed to materialize. American policy to disperse Vietnamese throughout the country was responsible for this. Ky then was reduced to living in his mansion in isolation, becoming painfully aware he no longer led anyone.

All Vietnamese coming out of the refugee camps faced the loss of any Vietnamese society. Resettlement was first arranged so that most Vietnamese began their life in America isolated from one another. Because U.S. government policy had this effect in the months immediately following resettlement does not mean that Vietnamese accepted such isolation for long. Since early in 1976, Vietnamese have been resettling themselves out of the various places where they had been sponsored into areas more to their liking, which are places where there are other Vietnamese. This movement has been into urban areas in general and particularly to the cities of Los Angeles and to a lesser extent San Francisco, where the largest numbers of Vietnamese had initially been resettled. As of December 1975, about 27,199 Vietnamese had been resettled in California, concentrated in Los Angeles and San Francisco.[3] By February 1976, a mere two months later, about 1,000 more Vietnamese appeared in California; by 1 July 1976, the number had gone over 30,000 and the International Institute of Los Angeles estimated that by the end of 1976 that city alone would have a Vietnamese immigrant population of 40,000.[4] Within six months after the camps closed Vietnamese were regrouping. The number of Vietnamese in California and the Los Angeles area is probably greatly underestimated because many Vietnamese have moved there without informing either their sponsors, resettlement agencies, or the U.S. Immigration and Naturalization Service (INS). As of December 1975, for example, INS could not account for the whereabouts of 8,000 Vietnamese immigrants.

The movement to California in general and to Los Angeles in particular is not the only regrouping of Vietnamese in the United States. On the whole, immigrants have moved from small cities and towns in which they were placed into larger metropolitan areas. To some extent this movement is one from northern to southern states; to a greater extent, however, it is a movement into Vietnamese communities. This shift also became evident within a month after the camps closed. By February 1976 Vietnamese left rural midwestern states like Kansas, Kentucky, New Mexico, North Dakota, and Oklahoma, areas in which few Vietnamese had been resettled. Within two months about 600 Vietnamese moved out of these states. Other states which Vietnamese left in the same two months were likewise rural and were places where few immigrants had first been resettled. These states were North Carolina, South Carolina, Mississippi, and New Hampshire.[5] The early movement tended to be southward, with states like California, Texas, and Louisiana receiving relatively large numbers of immigrants. The Vietnamese population of Texas alone rose by 1,000 persons. This southward movement apparently accelerated after the winter of 1975, with Texas and Louisiana, particularly the cities of New Orleans and Dallas, receiving immigrants from northern and midwestern states.[6]

The degree to which the movement represented Vietnamese desires to form a community rather than to move to warmer climates is reflected in intrastate movement. In several northern states, the Vietnamese population has shifted from small towns to large metropolitan areas. New York State's Vietnamese population, for example, has stayed relatively stable, even growing slightly, but within the state Vietnamese have moved into the New York City metropolitan area and out of small towns and cities in which few Vietnamese had been relocated. The city of Buffalo, for example, originally welcomed close to 800 Vietnamese; by spring 1977 that population had fallen below 200. Several of those leaving Buffalo went to Louisiana; others, however, went to New York City. Between December 1975 and February 1976, over 400 Vietnamese moved into New York State. Similarly, the same number moved into Illinois, concentrating in the Chicago area.

The regrouping of Vietnamese within the United States began as family reunification.[7] In the camps Americans divided many extended Vietnamese families, used to living together under one roof, into households comprising elements of nuclear families—mother, father, and children— and resettled them in disparate parts of the country.[8] The push out of the camps meant separation of these units. Once out of the camps, many simply abandoned their sponsors to reconstitute their households as they had existed in Vietnam regardless of whether such a move meant unemployment and/or going on welfare.[9]

Reunification of extended families triggered Vietnamese regrouping. However, some of the movement of Vietnamese into communities was part of a conscious effort of former Vietnamese leadership to reassert itself in the context of an American-Vietnamese community. This was evident in the Vietnamese clergy's activities in this country. In Vietnam, especially among northern Catholic villages transported south after 1954, the priest had combined political and religious leadership, being at once teacher, spiritual guide, mayor, and judge of villages. Many, as I have pointed out earlier, came from Vietnam with their entire parishes and, with the help of Vietnamese priests already in this country, sought to resettle those parishes intact. Failing that, they attempted, through the same means, to reestablish or create new Vietnamese parishes. The Vietnamese influx into New Orleans represents a new resettlement by Vietnamese priests who, through manipulating the Catholic church's resources, were able to gather up their flocks from disparate parts of the country, including from as far north as western New York. The Vietnamese concentration in New Orleans, if it sustains itself, is in essence a return to Vietnamese Catholic village structures within urban America. Many Vietnamese wholeheartedly support the priest's initiatives in reestablishing their communities, which are often considered by Vietnamese part of their extended families.[10]

Elsewhere the reestablishment of communities has been less conscious, less manipulated by a traditional Vietnamese leadership. Vietnamese, both rural and urban, former elite and poor, moved for differing reasons closer together to lay the groundwork for the emergence of an ethnic community within the United States which the American government had taken such great pains to try to prevent.

Not only have Vietnamese moved closer together, reversing the American-sponsored diaspora, they have begun organizing themselves into a community within as well as between urban areas. Since December 1975 an estimated 100 organizations of Vietnamese and Cambodian immigrants have been formed. Most of these organizations are local, confined to immigrants within an urban area. Some are purely social, providing places for Vietnamese to meet together; others like the Vietnamese Mutual Assistance Group of Birmingham, Alabama, and the San Diego, California, Vietnamese Alliance have confined their activities to job placement; and still others, like the Boulder, Colorado, Vietnamese Alliance, emphasize bicultural programs such as English language tutoring of school-age children in a project called "The Americanization of Nguyen," as well as recreation and a series of Vietnamese cultural events (dinners, folk songs, establishing libraries of books in Vietnamese about Vietnam's culture and language).[11] Some of the Vietnamese self-help organizations are not entirely autonomous or even Vietnamese-run, but rather function under the aegis of sponsoring organizations like the Indiana International Center of Indianapolis; the Appleton, Wisconsin, Valley Interfaith Refugee Committee; or the American-Vietnamese Association of Kansas City, Missouri. Their role tends to be confined to fostering immigrant-American mutual understanding and assisting Vietnamese integration into American life. Other voluntary organizations function through the Catholic church, like the Vietnamese Association of Riverside and San Bernardino, California, and the Vietnamese Catholic Parish Committee of San Diego, California, both presided over by Vietnamese priests.

The strength—and role—of these organizations over the long run are not clear. Their proliferation indicates that Vietnamese, as immigrants, feel they need each other in America: to help them assimilate into American culture, to preserve their cultural heritage, and to form the basis for the emergence of a Vietnamese-American culture in the future. The context now for Vietnamese is America, and they have clearly been transformed from refugees to immigrants.

Notes

Notes

A Note on Abbreviations

Most of the documentation for this book is unpublished, consisting of taped interviews, correspondence with individuals involved with the immigration, mimeographed reports, dittoed instructional materials I collected at Fort Indian Town Gap, mimeographed camp newspapers, and the like. Unpublished materials and the tapes on which this book is based have been deposited with the Archives of the State University of New York at Buffalo and form the Archives' Vietnamese Immigration Collection. The collection is open to serious scholars of immigration. Throughout this book I have referred to materials in this collection. In the notes, reference to the collection appears as V.I.C. (Vietnamese Immigration Collection). A detailed description of the sources used is given in the section following these notes.

Chapter 2: Leaving Vietnam

1. See "La Guerre Est Finie," *Newsweek*, 5 May 1975, pp. 22–29.

2. Interview with G.N., deputy civilian coordinator, Fort Indian Town Gap, 25 September 1975, tape no. 8, side 1, V.I.C. G.N. had been a senior AID official in Vietnam for fifteen years and left Vietnam in the American evacuation in April 1975. The surprise over the rapid collapse of the

Saigon government was expressed by other Americans who were working for the U.S. government in Vietnam. See interview with B.L., Fort Indian Town Gap, tape no. 37, sides 1 and 2 (B.L. worked with the consul general in Da-Nang); R.D., Fort Indian Town Gap, 25 September 1975, tape no. 10, side 2; tape no. 11, side 1 (R.D. was with AID in Vietnam also), V.I.C.

3. U.S. Congress, Senate, Committee on the Judiciary, Subcommittee to Investigate Problems Connected with Refugees and Escapees, *Hearings, Indochina Evacuation and Refugee Problems, Part I: Operation Babylift and Humanitarian Needs*, 94th Cong., 1st Sess., 8 April 1975. See especially p. 90.

4. See, for example, Senate Subcommittee to Investigate Problems Connected with Refugees and Escapees, *Refugee Problems in South Vietnam, Report Pursuant to S. Res. 49*, 89th Cong. 1st Sess. (Washington, D.C.: Government Printing Office, 1966). This trend is also clear for people who fled from the advancing NLF and North Vietnamese armies. Refugees around the Vung-Tau area of South Vietnam in March and April 1975 were found, for the most part, to be both Catholic and persons who had fled south in 1954. See Le-Thi-Que, A. Terry Rambo, and Gary D. Murfin, "Why They Fled: Refugee Movements During the Spring 1975 Communist Offensive in South Vietnam," *Asian Survey*, 16, no. 9 (September 1976): 855–63.

5. See Milton Osborne, *The French Presence in Cambodia and Cochinchina: Rule and Response, 1860–1905* (Ithaca, New York: Cornell University Press, 1969).

6. Examples of such persons that I interviewed are B.T., graduate of Lycée Albert Sarraut and the Indochinese University of Hanoi, former director of the Collège de Can-Tho, and minister of primary education in the South Vietnamese government (V.I.C., tape no. 31, side 2) and Mr. V., a graduate of Ecole Pellerin, a prestigious Catholic private *lycée* in Hanoi, whose father was a high ranking official in the colonial radio broadcasting network (V.I.C., tape no. 14, side 2; tape no. 15, side 1). For statistics on schooling in colonial Vietnam see Gail P. Kelly, "Franco-Vietnamese

Schools, 1918 to 1928" (Ph.D. diss., University of Wisconsin, 1975), chap. 2.

7. The reasons underlying South Vietnam's refugee problems were enumerated by Senator Edward Kennedy. See U.S. Congress, Senate, Committee on the Judiciary, Subcommittee to Investigate Problems Connected with Refugees and Escapees, *Hearings, Indochina Evacuation and Refugee Problems, Part II. The Evacuation,* 94th Cong., 1st Sess., 15, 25, and 30 April 1975. On p. 19 Kennedy laid the blame for the refugees on American and ARVN firepower: "Regarding why refugees flee, we have official surveys taken—not conclusions made by this committee, but [by officials in the Department of State] who have gone around to refugee camps during the time I have been chairman of the Refugee Subcommittee and quite clearly the overwhelming conclusion is that refugees leave areas where they think the greatest threat to their own security comes from, and the principal firepower in this war has not been initiated by the other side."

8. See, for example, interview with T.V.Q., Fort Indian Town Gap, 25 September 1975, tape no. 5, side 1, V.I.C. See also Senate Subcommittee to Investigate Problems Connected with Refugees and Escapees, *Indochina Evacuation and Refugee Problems, Part IV. Staff Reports Prepared for the Use of the Subcommittee,* 94th Cong., 1st Sess., 9 June 1975, especially part I, pp. 4–5; Le-Thi-Que, Rambo, and Murflin, "Why They Fled," pp. 855–63. The motivation to escape from the war is clear in the movement of refugees within South Vietnam before 1975. See U.S. Congress, Senate, Committee on the Judiciary, Subcommittee to Investigate Problems Connected with Refugees and Escapees, *Refugee Problems in South Vietnam,* 89th Cong., 1st Sess., 1966. M. R. Lemburg, "The Refugee Problem in South Vietnam," *Proceedings of the First Melbourne Southeast Asian Pugwash Conference,* 1967, pp. 112–17. Don Luce, "No Way Home, Vietnam's Refugees," *Christian Century,* 84 (11 October 1967): 1279–81. On the atmosphere in Saigon just before the U.S. evacuation, see Tiziano Terzani, *Giai Phong: The Fall and Liberation of Saigon* (New York: St. Martin's Press, 1976), especially chaps. 1 and 2.

9. See interview with T.V.Q., Fort Indian Town Gap, 25 September 1975, tape no. 5, side 1; N.H.,26 September 1975, Fort Indian Town Gap, 26 September 1975, tape no. 7, side 1; B.T., Fort Indian Town Gap, 30 October 1975, tape no. 31, side 1; D.T.N., Fort Indian Town Gap, 30 October 1975, tape no. 32, V.I.C. See also Terzani, *Giai Phong*, chaps. 1 and 2, and John Pilger, *The Last Day* (New York: Random House, Vintage, 1976).

10. Examples of such propaganda are Douglas Pike, *Viet Cong: The Organization and Techniques of the National Liberation Front of South Vietnam* (Cambridge, Mass.: M.I.T. Press, 1961); *La politique aggressive des Viet Minh communistes et la guerre subversive communiste au Sud Viet-Nam* (Saigon: Government of the Republic of South Viet-Nam, July 1962); Robert B. Rigg, "Catalog of Viet Cong Violence," *Military Review* (December 1962); Hoang Van Chi, *From Colonialism to Communism: History of North Vietnam* (New York: Praeger Publishers, 1964).

11. See especially interview with G.N., Fort Indian Town Gap, Pennsylvania, 25 September 1975, tape no. 8, sides 1 and 2; tape no. 9, side 1, V.I.C. (G.N. had worked with the State Department in Saigon before becoming deputy civilian coordinator of the refugee camp). Interview with R.D., Fort Indian Town Gap, 25 September 1975, tape no. 10, side 2; tape no. 11, side 1,V.I.C.

12. Letter from Tham-Ngoc-Lien to Patricia, 28 May, 1975, V.I.C., Box 9. The same rumor appears in Terzani, *Giai Phong*, chaps. 1 and 2.

13. "Refugees: A Cool and Wary Reception," *Time Magazine*, 12 May 1975, pp. 24, 26. A second poll had similar results. See Richard T. Schaefer and Sandra T. Schaefer, "Reluctant Welcome: U.S. Response to South Vietnamese Refugees," *New Community*, 4, no. 3 (Autumn 1975): 366–70.

14. Talcott is quoted in "Refugees: A Cool and Wary Reception," *Time Magazine*, 12 May 1975, p. 24.

15. Senate Subcommittee to Investigate Problems Connected with Refugees and Escapees, *Hearings, Indochina Evacuation and Refugee Problems, Part II. The Evacuation*, 94th Cong., 1st Sess., 15, 25, and 30 April 1975; Senate

Subcommittee to Investigate Problems Connected with Refugees and Escapees, *Indochina Evacuation and Refugee Problems, Part IV. Staff Reports Prepared for the Use of the Subcommittee*, 94th Cong. 1st Sess., 9 June and 8 July 1975, especially pp. 1–2.

16. Senate Subcommittee to Investigate Problems Connected with Refugees and Escapees, *Indochina Evacuation and Refugee Problems*, 94th Cong., 1st Sess., 15 April 1975, executive session, especially pp. 28, 29, and 35; 25 April 1975, pp. 54, 57; pp. 82 and 83 (testimony of Rev. John Schauer, Church World Service [CWS], protesting what appeared to be government policy).

17. Interview with W.C.K., 16 September 1976, New York City, tape no. 70, sides 1 and 2; tape no. 71, sides 1 and 2; interview with J.C., Fort Indian Town Gap, 17 October 1975, tape no. 27, sides 1 and 2; tape no. 28, side 1, V.I.C.

18. The planning began after the fall of Da-Nang on 27 and 28 March. Those Americans who managed the barge evacuation of Da-Nang were called to Deputy Ambassador Jacobson's office to discuss the plans for a pullout from Saigon immediately after they arrived at Cam-Ranh Bay around 2 April. See interview with B.L., Fort Indian Town Gap, 31 October 1975, tape no. 36, side 2, tape no. 37, sides 1 and 2, V.I.C.

19. Fox Butterfield, "How South Vietnam Died—By the Stab in the Front," *New York Times Magazine*, 25 May 1975.

20. Interview with W.C.K., New York City, 16 September 1976, tape no. 70, side 1; interview with B.L., Fort Indian Town Gap, tape no. 37, sides 1 and 2, V.I.C.

21. Habib's testimony was in executive session and can be found in Senate Subcommittee to Investigate Problems Connected with Refugees and Escapees, *Indochina Evacuation and Refugee Problems, Part II. The Evacuation*, 94th Cong., 1st Sess., 15 April 1975.

22. Ibid., pp. 31, 41. The 25 April figures come from the same volume, p. 54.

23. Senate Subcommittee to Investigate Problems Connected with Refugees and Escapees, *Indochina Evacuation and Refugee Problems, Part II. The Evacuation*, 94th Cong.,

1st Sess., 15, 25, and 30 April 1975, p. 71.

24. Senate Subcommittee to Investigate Problems Connected with Refugees and Escapees, *Indochina Evacuation and Refugee Problems, Part IV. Staff Reports Prepared for the Use of the Subcommittee*, 94th Cong., 1st Sess., 9 June and 8 July 1975, p. 2.

25. Interview with J.C., October 17, 1975, Fort Indian Town Gap, tape no. 27, sides 1 and 2, V.I.C. At the time I interviewed this individual, he had left the army and was a caseworker for one of the resettlement agencies at the refugee camp. He had served as a military adviser in Bien Hoa Province in Vietnam in 1966/67, returned to Vietnam in 1969/70 to assist with the training of Vietnamese defectors from the Viet Cong, and then later served in Vietnam as a district adviser. While attached to the Joint Chiefs of Staff he went to Vietnam in 1975 to get a Vietnamese family out of the country and then, with his mission completed, returned to Saigon to help handle the evacuation and the processing of Vietnamese to join it.

26. Senate Subcommittee to Investigate Problems Connected with Refugees and Escapees, *Indochina Evacuation and Refugee Problems, Part IV. Staff Reports Prepared for the Use of the Subcommittee*, 94th Cong., 1st Sess., 9 June and 8 July 1975, p. 2.

27. Ibid.

28. Much of this is based on an account of the events leading to the fall and evacuation of Da-Nang by B.L., who was witness to these events and helped arrange the barge evacuation of the city. See interview with B.L., 31 October 1975, Fort Indian Town Gap, tape no. 36, side 2; tape no. 37, sides 1 and 2, V.I.C. See also Philip A. McCombs, "We Are All Brothers and Sisters," *Washington Post*, 13 April 1975. McCombs describes looting of civilians by the ARVN along the road from Quang-Tri and Hue, Qui-Nhon, etc. Interestingly, his account of refugees points out that those he interviewed were originally from North Vietnam and were Catholic, bearing out much of what I pointed out earlier in this chapter.

29. Interview with Dr. D., Fort Indian Town Gap, 31

October 1975, tape no. 39, V.I.C.

30. Interview with V.L., Fort Indian Town Gap, 31 October 1975, tape no. 37, sides 1 and 2, V.I.C. (edited transcript).

31. Terzani, *Giai Phong*, p. 51; Senate Subcommittee to Investigate Problems Connected with Refugees and Escapees, *Indochina Evacuation and Refugee Problems, Part II. The Evacuation*, 94th Cong., 1st Sess., pp. 54, 55.

32. Interview with B.L., Fort Indian Town Gap, 31 October 1975, tape no. 37, side 2, V.I.C. (edited transcript).

33. Ibid.; Senate Subcommittee to Investigate Problems Connected with Refugees and Escapees, *Indochina Evacuation and Refugee Problems, Part IV. Staff Reports*, 94th Cong., 1st Sess., p. 5.

34. Senate Subcommittee to Investigate Problems Connected with Refugees and Escapees, *Indochina Evacuation and Refugee Problems, Part II. The Evacuation*, 94th Cong., 1st Sess., 15, 25, and 30 April 1975, p. 59. One refugee interviewed at Fort Indian Town Gap reported paying such a sum to get out of the country. See interview with N.T.L., Fort Indian Town Gap, 25 September 1975, tape no. 5, side 2, V.I.C.

35. Habib in his testimony of 30 April 1975 to the Subcommittee to Investigate Problems Connected with Refugees and Escapees claimed that over three thousand Vietnamese came out this way on about one hundred Vietnamese Air Force planes. Ibid., pp. 106–7. Several Vietnamese interviewed at Fort Indian Town Gap who came out this way claimed that pilots charged $10,000 per person.

36. Interview with N.T.D., Fort Indian Town Gap, Pennsylvania, 30 October 1975, tape no. 31, side 2, tape no. 32, V.I.C.

37. Interview with B.T., Fort Indian Town Gap, 30 October 1975, tape no. 31, side 2, tape no. 32, V.I.C.

38. Interview with T.V.Q., Fort Indian Town Gap, 25 September 1975, tape no. 5, V.I.C. I am indebted to John Stephens for a verbatim translation of this tape from Vietnamese to English for use in this book.

39. Interview with B.L., Fort Indian Town Gap, 31

October 1975, tape no. 37, side 2; tape no. 38, side 1, V.I.C.
B.L. interviewed the returnees for the U.S. government in
Guam.

40. Senate Subcommittee to Investigate Problems Connected with Refugees and Escapees, *Indochina Evacuation
and Refugee Problems, Part IV. Staff Reports*, 94th Cong.,
1st Sess., p. 5.

41. Ibid., p. 6.

Chapter 3: Who Immigrated: A Profile

1. The form is reproduced in Senate Subcommittee to
Investigate Problems Connected with Refugees and Esca-
pees, *Indochina Evacuation and Refugee Problems, Part IV.
Staff Reports*, 94th Cong., 1st Sess., 9 June 1975, pp. 63–64.

2. Interview with J.M., assistant coordinator for human
services, HEW, and C.W., Department of Labor, and department coordinator of human services, Fort Indian Town
Gap, 20 November 1975, tape no. 44, sides 1 and 2; interview
with L.F., public affairs officer, Fort Indian Town Gap, 20
November 1975, tape no. 41, sides 1 and 2; tape no. 42, side 1,
V.I.C.

3. Data on the military is taken from "Refugee Statistical
Data," Fort Indian Town Gap, Pennsylvania, October 1975
(mimeographed), Box no. 4, V.I.C.

4. The procedure for defining families was explained to
me by several persons working at Fort Indian Town Gap in
family reunification services provided by the American Red
Cross, the Lutheran Immigration and Refugee Service
(LIRS), and the United States Catholic Conference (USCC).
See interviews with J.F., LIRS caseworker, Fort Indian
Town Gap, 19 November 1975, tape no. 40, sides 1 and 2;
J.C., caseworker, USCC, Fort Indian Town Gap, 17 October
1975, tape no. 28, side 1; N.B., head of Reunification Services, American Red Cross, Fort Indian Town Gap, 15 October
1975, tape no. 20, side 1; N.C.B., reunification service
worker, American Red Cross, Fort Indian Town Gap, 15
October 1975, tape no. 20, side 1, V.I.C. N.C.B. claimed that
even in the case of nuclear families, only up to seven persons
could be reunited to constitute a family except for unat-

tached minors. The individuals in these interviews explained how families were defined by the Immigration and Naturalization Service (INS); they did not necessarily agree with the INS definition of family or household.

5. My information about number of children per family was obtained from Alan Carter, senior civilian coordinator, Fort Indian Town Gap, in an interview conducted on 26 September 1975, tape no. 13, side 1, V.I.C.

6. Interviews with N.T.D., Fort Indian Town Gap, 30 October 1975, tape no. 32; Mrs. A., Fort Indian Town Gap, 26 September 1975, tape no. 13, side 2; T.V.Q., Fort Indian Town Gap, 25 September 1975, tape no. 5, side 1; unidentified southern woman, Fort Indian Town Gap, 16 October 1975, tape no. 17, side 1.

7. Interview with L.F., public affairs officer, Fort Indian Town Gap, 20 November 1975, tape no. 41, sides 1 and 2; tape no. 42, side 1, V.I.C.

8. Memo from senior civilian coordinator, Fort Indian Town Gap, IATF to SECSTATE, WASH DC/IATF, UNCLASSIFIED, SUBJECT: WEEKLY PROFILE, 14 November 1975 (typescript), p. 3, V.I.C., Box 4.

9. Indian Town Gap Refugee Data Sheet, October 1975 (typescript), V.I.C., Box 4. See also interview with L.F., public affairs officer, Fort Indian Town Gap, 20 November 1975, tape no. 41, sides 1 and 2; tape no. 42, side 1, V.I.C.

10. Interview with Dr. D., Fort Indian Town Gap, 31 October 1975, tape no. 38, side 2; tape no. 39, side 1, V.I.C.

11. Interview with L.F., public affairs officer, Fort Indian Town Gap, 20 November 1975, tape no. 41, sides 1 and 2; tape no. 42, side 1, V.I.C.

12. See Gail P. Kelly, "Franco-Vietnamese Schools, 1918 to 1938" (Ph.D. diss., University of Wisconsin, 1975), chap. 2.

13. Joseph W. Dodd, "Aspects of Recent Educational Change in South Vietnam," *Journal of Developing Areas*, 6, no. 4 (July 1972): 555–71.

14. P.H.M. Jones, "Vietnam at School," in Wesley R. Fishel, ed., *Vietnam: Anatomy of a Conflict* (Itasca, Ill.: F.E. Peacock, 1968), pp. 548–60.

15. Dodd, *Recent Educational Change*, pp. 559–61.

16. Interview with N.T.D., Fort Indian Town Gap, 30 October 1975; Dr. D., Mr. L.N.V., 26 September 1975, Mr. T.V.Q., 25 September 1975.

17. "Refugee Demographic Characteristics," Camp Pendleton, 16 September 1975, p. 3 (mimeographed), V.I.C., Box 4. Language in the South Vietnamese schools is discussed in Jones, "Vietnam at School," Fishel, ed., pp. 548–60.

18. The estimate of the percent of Vietnam's doctors and medical personnel which came to this country was made by U.S. Senator Fong. See Senate Subcommittee to Investigate Problems Connected with Refugees and Escapees, *Indochina Evacuation and Refugee Problems, Part IV. Staff Reports*, 94th Cong., 1st Sess., 9 June and 8 July 1975, part 2, p. 47. The numbers employed by U.S. firms can be found in the same volume, p. 168.

19. Senate Subcommittee to Investigate Problems Connected with Refugees and Escapees, *Indochina Evacuation and Refugee Problems, Part II. The Evacuation*, 94th Cong., 1st Sess., 15, 25, and 30 April 1975, p. 28.

20. Interview with E.R., New York City, 21 September 1976, tape no. 78, sides 1 and 2; tape no. 79, side 1, V.I.C.

21. HEW Refugee Task Force, *Report to the Congress* (lithograph), 15 March 1976, p. 28, V.I.C. Box 2.

Chapter 4: Being Processed

1. Interagency Task Force on Indochina Refugees, *Report to Congress*, 15 September 1975, Annex C, Reception Center Guidelines, p. 17. V.I.C., Box 2.

2. Ibid., p. 2.

3. The Task Force's senior members as of September 1975 were Julia V. Taft (director) on loan from HEW; Robert Keely (deputy director) from the Department of State; James J. Wilson, Jr., from the Department of State; Foster Collins from the Department of the Treasury; Roger E. Shields from the Department of Defense; Lt. General Maurice F. Casey from the Joint Chiefs of Staff; General Leonard F. Chapman, commissioner of the Immigration and Naturalization Service of the Department of Justice; Fred Zeder, Department

of Interior; Maurice Hill, Department of Labor; Don Wort-man, HEW; Abner Silverman, Housing and Urban Develop-ment; General Benjamin Davis, Department of Transporta-tion; Arthur Z. Gardiner, East Asia Bureau, Agency for International Development; Fernando Oaxaca, Office of Management and Budget; Edward E. Rusk, chief of East Asia Logistics, Intelligence Community. Ambassador L. Dean Brown of the Middle East Institute was initially appointed director of the Task Force on 18 April. He resigned on 27 May when Ms. Taft assumed the post.

4. This is discussed in detail in chapter 6.

5. The background information on these officials was gathered in interviews. The information on MacDonald came from interview with B.D.V., coordinator, Indochina program, IRC, New York City, 17 September 1976, tape no. 71, side 2; on Thorne from W.M.T., consultant, Indochina program, Church World Service (CWS), New York City, 20 September 1976, tape no. 74, sides 1 and 2; on Carter from Carter himself in an interview on 26 September 1975, Fort Indian Town Gap, tape no. 13, side 1; C.C., area coordinator, Fort Indian Town Gap, 21 November 1975, tape no. 47, side 1; the information on Clifford Nunn was obtained from an interview with him at Fort Indian Town Gap, 25 September 1975, tapes no. 8 and 9, V.I.C.

6. Robert DeVecchi, "Notes" (Fort Chaffee), typescript and handwritten, about forty pages. DeVecchi headed the IRC operation at Fort Chaffee until July 1975. He was kind enough to allow me access to the diary he kept while working at the camp. He wrote about this problem in entries marked 2 June and 14 June. See also, *Report of the Intera-gency Task Force on Indochina Refugees, 2 May–20 De-cember 1975*, Fort Chaffee, Arkansas, 14 January 1976, V.I.C., Box 2.

7. Governor Brown's hostility to Pendleton and his fears about having to deal with large numbers of Vietnamese in his state is common knowledge and becomes evident in congressional hearings dating from 15 April. See testimony of Rep. Mineta of California on 25 April 1975, Senate Subcommittee to Investigate Problems Connected with

Refugees and Escapees, *Hearings, Part II. The Evacuation*, 94th Cong., 1st Sess., 15, 25 and 30 April 1975. See also interview with W.M.T., Indochina Program, CWS, New York City, 20 September 1976, tape no. 74, sides 1 and 2, V.I.C.

8. See Robert Scheer and Warren Hinckle, "The Vietnam Lobby," in Marcus G. Raskin and Bernard Fall, eds., *The Vietnam Reader: Articles and Documents on American Foreign Policy and the Viet Nam Crisis* (New York: Random House, Vintage, 1965), pp. 66–81.

9. Interview with L.F., public affairs officer, Fort Indian Town Gap, 20 November 1975, tape no. 41, sides 1 and 2, tape no. 42, side 1, V.I.C.

10. *Report of the Interagency Task Force, 2 May–20 December 1975*, Fort Chaffee, 14 January 1976, pp. III-22-24.

11. This is very clear in interviews with voluntary agency personnel. See interview with K.S., field director, American Fund for Czechoslovak Refugees (AFCR), Fort Indian Town Gap, 26 September 1975, tape no. 12, sides 1 and 2; W.K., director, American Council for Nationalities Service (ACNS), New York City, 16 September 1976, tape no. 70, sides 1 and 2, tape no. 71, side 1; W.M.T., consultant, Indochina Program, C.W.S., New York City, 20 September 1976, tape no. 74, side 1, V.I.C. DeVecchi, "Notes," p. 36. See entry of 18 June in which DeVecchi writes, "The papers announced that Don MacDonald, head of the Task Force here, would quit in mid-July. I suppose he's done some good things and I know he's meant well, but his 'body count' mentality and 'let's look at the big picture' approach reek of all that went wrong for one and one-half generations in Vietnam. One feels that no two cultures ever so poorly understood each other as our two. We keep thinking that if only the Vietnamese could 'get it together' all would be ok but their idea of 'getting it together' is in no way related to ours."

12. A complete listing of those recruited can be found in *Report of the Interagency Task Force, 2 May–20 December 1975*, Fort Chaffee, p. IX-H-75.

13. A description of the rule can be found in Interagency

Task Force, *Report to Congress*, 15 September 1975, p. 6.

14. See interview with E.W., caseworker, USCC, Fort Indian Town Gap, 17 October 1975, tape no. 28; A.Z., caseworker, IRC, Fort Indian Town Gap, 16 October 1975, tape no. 23, side 1; tape no. 24, sides 1 and 2, V.I.C.

15. E.W., caseworker, USCC, Fort Indian Town Gap, 17 October 1975, tape no. 28, side 1, V.I.C. Similar feelings were expressed by resettlement agency personnel in other camps. See Robert DeVecchi, "Notes," p. 24. See entry of 2 June in which he writes: "Luncheon meeting with Task Force people. Once again they are stressing body counts and replacements, thinking figures and systems, not people and needs."

16. Detailed descriptions of Red Cross work at Fort Indian Town Gap can be found in interviews with the following individuals who worked with the Red Cross: R.F., field director, American Red Cross (ARC), Fort Indian Town Gap, 26 September 1975, tape no. 15, side 1; N.B., head of Reunification Services, ARC, Fort Indian Town Gap, 15 October 1975, tape no. 20, side 1; N.C.B., Reunification Services, ARC, 15 October 1975, tape no. 20, side 1; P.B. and T.H., Red Cross office of higher education, Fort Indian Town Gap, 15 October 1975, tape no. 20, side 2, tape no. 21, side 1; A.V., recreation director, Red Cross Recreation Center, Fort Indian Town Gap, 19 November 1975, tape no. 40A, side 2.

17. L.F., public affairs officer, Interagency Task Force, Fort Indian Town Gap, 20 November 1975, tape no. 41, V.I.C. The senior civilian coordinator shared such a view. See interview with Alan Carter, senior civilian coordinator, Fort Indian Town Gap, 26 September 1975, tape no. 13, side 1, V.I.C.

18. This description of the day-to-day governance of the camps is based on descriptions provided by: L.F., public affairs officer, Fort Indian Town Gap, 20 November 1975, tape no. 41; C.C., area coordinator, Fort Indian Town Gap, 21 November 1975, tape no. 47, sides 1 and 2; tape no. 48, side 1; M.T., area coordinator, Fort Indian Town Gap, 20 November 1975, tape no. 42, sides 1 and 2, V.I.C.

19. C.C., area coordinator, Fort Indian Town Gap, 21 November 1975, tape no. 47, sides 1 and 2, V.I.C. A description of the Chaffee governance system and the Vietnamese mayor and council can be found in *Report of the Interagency Task Force 2 May–20 December 1975*, Fort Chaffee, pp. IX-B-61-62. The area coordinators at Fort Indian Town Gap had visited Fort Chaffee and Camp Pendleton and were critical of their systems of governance. See, particularly, interview with M.C., area coordinator, Fort Indian Town Gap, 20 November 1975, tape no. 42, sides 1 and 2, V.I.C.

20. Criteria for selection were described in detail by C.C., area coordinator, Fort Indian Town Gap, 21 November 1975, tape no. 42, sides 1 and 2, V.I.C.

21. B.L., area coordinator, Fort Indian Town Gap, 31 October 1975, tape no. 38, side 1, V.I.C.

22. C.C., area coordinator, Fort Indian Town Gap, 21 November 1975, tape no. 47, side 2, V.I.C.

23. M.C., area coordinator, Fort Indian Town Gap, 20 November 1975, tape no. 42, V.I.C.

24. This person maintained this attitude a year later while he was serving as a HEW regional coordinator in follow-up work on the refugees. See interview with M.C., New York City, 20 September 1976, tape no. 76, V.I.C.

25. This role was discussed in an interview with B.L., area coordinator, Fort Indian Town Gap, 31 October 1975, tape no. 38, side 1. One immigrant discussed how he had been "encouraged" to accept particular sponsorships by area coordinators. See interview with Mr. H., Fort Indian Town Gap, 11 December 1975, tape no. 56, sides 1 and 2, V.I.C.

26. This analysis of the area coordinators' role is in part based on interviews I conducted with various individuals at Fort Indian Town Gap and on my own observations while on field trips in that camp. See interview with L.F., public affairs officer, Fort Indian Town Gap, 20 November 1975, tape no. 41, sides 1 and 2; B.L., area coordinator, Fort Indian Town Gap, 31 October 1975, tape no. 38, side 1; group interview with P.D., caseworker, USCC, and teacher, Adult Night School; E.W., caseworker, USCC, and counselor, Adult Night School; and Pvt. R.B., information specialist,

U.S. Army, Fort Indian Town Gap, 20 November 1975, tape no. 42, sides 1 and 2; interview with K.A., superintendent of schools, Fort Indian Town Gap, 20 September 1975, tape no. 9, side 2, tape no. 10, side 1, V.I.C. The only Americans outside of camp management I met or heard of at Fort Indian Town Gap who spoke Vietnamese and had lived in Vietnam for a period of time were an IRC caseworker who left the camp in October 1975, the U.N. representative who also did volunteer work for the American Red Cross, and a USCC caseworker who had been a career officer when he served in Vietnam for three years. This last individual could not speak Vietnamese fluently and needed an interpreter for his work.

27. Most interviews with Vietnamese at Fort Indian Town Gap showed that the refugees were anxious to live with other Vietnamese and wanted to turn down sponsorship offers if those offers meant living isolated from their countrymen. See, for example, interview with N.V.S., Fort Indian Town Gap, 14 September 1975, tape no. 3, side 2, V.I.C. Mr. S. blurted out in the middle of the interview, which was conducted in Vietnamese, "We hope in the future we will be able to live close together in our new country." Similar feelings were expressed by other Vietnamese. See 25 September 1975, tape no. 4, side 2, V.I.C. (unidentified former soldier, ARVN); interview with Mr. T.V.Q., thirty-year-old Catholic, former government official, Fort Indian Town Gap, 25 September 1975, tape no. 5, side 1; interview with N.T.L., Fort Indian Town Gap, 16 October 1975, tape no. 18, side 2, V.I.C.

28. Interview with W.K., director, ACNS, New York City, 17 September 1976, tape no. 20; C.W., United HIAS, New York City, 21 September 1976, tapes no. 81 and 82, V.I.C.

29. This description of "in-processing" is based on field observations at Fort Indian Town Gap, September–November, 1975; interviews with J.M. and C.W., both HEW employees responsible for "in-processing" at Fort Indian Town Gap, 20 November 1975, tape no. 44, side 1, V.I.C.; *Report of the Interagency Task Force, 2 May–20 December 1975*, Fort Chaffee, pp. IX-A-55-60, V.I.C., Box 2.

30. There are several articles in *Thong Bao*, Camp Pen-

dleton's daily newspaper, and in *Dat Lanh*, Fort Indian Town Gap's daily, which allude to this. See especially "Sponsorship: Door to the U.S.," *Dat Lanh*, Bo 4, So 2 (25 October 1975), pp. 1–4.

31. Interview with L.F., public affairs officer, Fort Indian Town Gap, 20 November 1975, tape no. 41, V.I.C.

32. Interview with T.V.Q., Fort Indian Town Gap, 25 September 1975, tape no. 5, side 1, V.I.C.

33. "Dien! Rat Nguy Hiem: Xin dung Cau them day vao trai," *Dat Lanh*, Bo 1, So 27 (23 June 1975) p. 1. See also *Tuan Le Phong Hoa Tu Ngay 5-11 Thang Muoi* ("Fire Prevention Week," 5–11 October), V.I.C., Box 3. The latter is a pamphlet written especially for children at the Fort Indian Town Gap School that tells about fire safety and overloading circuits in barracks.

34. The story of Mr. V. comes from an interview with him and with individuals at the Red Cross. Interview with Mr. V., Fort Indian Town Gap, 26 September 1975, tape no. 14, side 2, tape no. 15, side 1; R.F., field director, American Red Cross, Fort Indian Town Gap, 26 September 1975, tape no. 15, side 1, V.I.C.

35. Field notes, New York City, 18 September 1976.

Chapter 5: Being Taught About America

1. Interview with N.V.S., Fort Indian Town Gap, 15 September 1975, tape no. 3, side 2, V.I.C.

2. Interview with R.S., curriculum coordinator, secondary school, Fort Indian Town Gap, 29 October 1975, tape no. 30, side 1; K.A., Superintendent, K–12 School Program, Fort Indian Town Gap, 25 September 1975, tape no. 9, side 2, tape no. 10, side 1, V.I.C.

3. See Gail Kelly, Ronald Goodenow, and John Stephens, "The Education of Vietnamese in Refugee Camps," 8 December 1975, station WBFO, Buffalo, New York. Tapes of this broadcast are available in the SUNY/Buffalo Archives, WBFO Archives. The broadcast included excerpts from an English class for children at Camp Pendleton. The class was taught by a Vietnamese.

4. HEW Refugee Task Force, *Report to Congress*, 15

June 1976, p. 80.

5. Interview with P.J., resource specialist, English as a Second Language and Foreign Language Education, K–12 and Adult Education Program, Fort Indian Town Gap, 17 October 1975, tape no. 26, side 2; K.A., superintendent, K–12 School Program, Fort Indian Town Gap, 25 September 1975, tape no. 9, side 2, V.I.C. Apparently 700 teachers had applied for these jobs.

6. Background information on the staff of the school at Fort Indian Town Gap was obtained from the following: P.J., resource specialist, English as a Second Language and Foreign Language Education, K–12 and Adult Program, 17 October 1975, tape no. 26, side 2; B.G., curriculum coordinator, grades 4–6, Fort Indian Town Gap, 16 October 1975, tape no. 21, side 2; R.S., curriculum coordinator, secondary school, Fort Indian Town Gap, 29 October 1975, tape no. 30, side 1; V.L., guidance counselor, elementary grades, Fort Indian Town Gap, 16 October 1975, tapes no. 23, 25; H.M.B., curriculum coordinator, K–3, Fort Indian Town Gap, 17 October 1975, tape no. 26, side 1; K.A., superintendent, K–12 School Program, Fort Indian Town Gap, 29 September 1975, tape no. 9, side 2; B.C., language arts specialist, K–6, Fort Indian Town Gap, 20 November 1975, tape no. 46, side 1; R.A.K., primary school principal, Fort Indian Town Gap, 25 September 1975, tape no. 8, side 1, V.I.C.

7. See interviews with N.T.D. and B.T., school aides, Fort Indian Town Gap, 30 October 1975, tape no. 31, side 2, tape no. 32, sides 1 and 2, tape no. 33, side 1, V.I.C.

8. Teachers' in-service, Fort Indian Town Gap, 17 October 1975, tape no. 26, side 2, tape no. 27, side 1; interview with B.S., teacher, grade 4, Fort Indian Town Gap, 16 October 1975, tape no. 22, side 2, V.I.C.

9. Ibid. Teachers' conversations at the in-service meeting made this clear. In it teachers complained about how students simply didn't understand a word they said and joked about the "speak English only" policy of the school. Tape no. 26, side 2; 17 October 1975, V.I.C.

10. See Interagency Task Force, *Report to Congress*, 15 September 1975, pp. 65–71, V.I.C., Box 2.

11. The goal of the schools was articulated in the Interagency Task Force, *Report to Congress,* 15 September 1975, p. 65, and by various curriculum coordinators. See, for example, interview with H.M.B., curriculum coordinator, K–3, Fort Indian Town Gap, 17 October 1975, tape no. 26, side 1; R.S. and P.H., curriculum coordinators, secondary school, Fort Indian Town Gap, 20 November 1975, tape no. 45, sides 1 and 2, tape no. 46, side 1, V.I.C.

12. See "School Curriculum—Fort Indian Town Gap," especially for grades K–3, 4–6, weeks of 22–26 September, 29 September–3 October, V.I.C., Box 3. This is also described in detail by the curriculum coordintor of K–3. See also interview with H.M.B., curriculum coordinator, Fort Indian Town Gap, K–3, 17 October 1975, tape no. 26, side 1, V.I.C.

13. Interview with B.G., curriculum coordinator, grades 4–6, Fort Indian Town Gap, 16 October 1975, tape no. 21, side 2, tape no. 22, side 1, V.I.C.

14. Grades 1–3, "Suggested Schedule," 20–24 October 1975, Fort Indian Town Gap School, "School Curriculum—Fort Indian Town Gap," V.I.C., Box 3. See also grades 1–2, "Suggested Schedule," 13–17 October 1975, V.I.C., Box 3.

15. U.S. Department of Labor, *Manpower Report of the President* (Washington, D.C.: Government Printing Office, 1974). This report indicates that 42 percent of married women in the U.S. work. Of these married women 50 percent had school-age children (ages six to seventeen) and 31 percent had preschool-age children (ages one month to five years).

16. See Ngo-Vinh-Long, ed., *Vietnamese Women in Society and Revolution* (Cambridge: Vietnam Resource Center, 1974); Arlene Eisen Bergman, *Women of Vietnam* (San Francisco: People's Press, 1974).

17. Interview with E.R., New York City, 21 September 1976, tape no. 78, V.I.C.; interview with N.T.D., Fort Indian Town Gap, 30 October 1975, tape no. 31, side 2, tape no. 32, sides 1 and 2, V.I.C. An American who had worked in Vietnam for many years also discussed changing sex role divisions of labor in that country resulting from the war. See

interview with M.C., Fort Indian Town Gap, 20 November 1975, tape no. 42, sides 1 and 2, V.I.C.

18. See "School Curriculum—Fort Indian Town Gap," Box 3, V.I.C. This is a collection of the secondary school (as well as primary school) curriculum guides. The high school curriculum is described in some detail by R.S., curriculum coordinator, secondary school, Fort Indian Town Gap, 29 October 1975, tape no. 30, side 1, V.I.C.

19. Secondary School Curriculum—Fort Indian Town Gap, Topic: Jobs, Lesson 1, Unit 3. Box 3, V.I.C.

20. Secondary School Curriculum—Fort Indian Town Gap, Topic: Youth Culture, Advanced Classes, October 20–24, pp. 2–3, Box 3, V.I.C.

21. Ibid., p. 9, "Dialogue."

22. These remarks were made informally in the teachers' meeting. See teachers' in-service, Fort Indian Town Gap, 17 October 1975, tape no. 26, side 2, tape no. 27, side 1, V.I.C.

23. This particular interchange was taped. See "Tour of Classes," 16 October 1975, Fort Indian Town Gap, tape no. 21, side 2, tape no. 22, side 1, V.I.C.

24. Field notes, Fort Indian Town Gap, 17 October 1975. Unfortunately the tape recorder ran out of tape in the middle of the lesson. However, part of the class was taped and is available at V.I.C. See tape no. 29, side 2.

25. Interview with B.G., curriculum coordinator, grades 3–6, Fort Indian Town Gap, 16 October 1975, tape no. 22, side 1; interview with H.M.B., curriculum coordinator, K–3, Fort Indian Town Gap, 17 October 1975, tape no. 26, side 1; interview with R.S., secondary school curriculum coordinator, Fort Indian Town Gap, 29 October 1975, tape no. 30, side 1, V.I.C.

26. Interview with K.A., superintendent, K–12, School Program, Fort Indian Town Gap, 29 September 1975, tape no. 9, side 2, tape no. 10, side 1; P.H., curriculum coordinator, Pennsylvania Department of Education, Adult Education Program, Day School, Fort Indian Town Gap, 29 October 1975, tape no. 29, sides 1 and 2, V.I.C.

27. P.H., curriculum coordinator, Adult Education Program, Day School, Fort Indian Town Gap, 29 October 1975,

tape no. 29, side 1, V.I.C.

28. See "Functional English, Level II—Intermediate Sequence," Box 3, V.I.C.

29. Survival English, Level II, Intermediate, lesson 4, p. 4; Level I, Unit IV, lessons 3 and 4; Advanced English, Unit 5, reading selection entitled "How to Stretch Your Dollar," Box 3, V.I.C.

30. See especially interview with P.H., curriculum coordinator, Adult Education Program, Day School, Fort Indian Town Gap, 29 October 1975, tape no. 29, sides 1 and 2, V.I.C.

31. I taped one of his classes and it is available at SUNY/Buffalo Archives, V.I.C., classroom observation, Adult Education Program, Day School, Fort Indian Town Gap, 30 October 1975, tape no. 34, sides 1 and 2. The development of this class' curriculum is discussed in an interview with D.M., teacher, Adult Education Program, Day School, Fort Indian Town Gap, 30 October 1975, tape no. 34, side 2, V.I.C.

32. See English Language Services, Inc., *English 900*, books 1–3 (New York: Macmillan, 1976, 16th ed.), book 3, unit 5, p. 49. This class was also taped; see classroom observations, Adult Education Program, Night School, Fort Indian Town Gap, 16 October 1975, tape no. 25, sides 1 and 2; tape no. 35, sides 1 and 2. A discussion of the class and the teacher's attitudes can be found in interviews with P.D., the teacher; interview with P.D., teacher, Adult Education Program, Night School, 20 November 1975, tape no. 43, sides 1 and 2, V.I.C.

33. Interview with P.H., curriculum coordinator, Adult Education Program, Day School, Fort Indian Town Gap, 29 October 1975, tape no. 29, sides 1 and 2; E.W., guidance counselor, Adult Education Program, Night School, Fort Indian Town Gap, 17 October 1975, tape no. 28, sides 1 and 2, V.I.C.

34. Classroom observations, 30 October 1975, tape no. 33, side 2, V.I.C. Field notes, 30 October 1975.

35. D.C., director, Transition America, Fort Indian Town Gap, 16 October 1975, tape no. 17, side 2, V.I.C.

36. Interview with R.F., IRC caseworker who conducted these programs, Fort Indian Town Gap, 26 September 1975,

tape no. 14. A tape of one of the IRC orientation meetings is available. See tape no. 53, side 2 (31 October 1975), V.I.C.

37. Interview with J.H., director of information, Pennsylvania Commission for Women, Fort Indian Town Gap, 29 October 1975, tape no. 30, side 1, V.I.C.

38. Taped class presentation, Women in America, Fort Indian Town Gap, 29 October 1975, tape no. 30, side 2, tape no. 31, side 1, V.I.C.

39. Interview with J.H., director of information, Pennsylvania Commission on Women, 29 October 1975, tape no. 30, side 1, V.I.C.

40. See Judy Klemesrud, "Learning the Ways of America," *New York Times*, Sunday, 26 October 1975, section 1, p. 60; Pennsylvania Commission on Women meeting, 29 October 1975, tape no. 31, side 1, V.I.C.

41. Pennsylvania Commission on Women meeting, 29 October 1975, tape no. 31, side 1, V.I.C.

42. "South Vietnam May Reject Refugees Asking to Return," *Thong Bao*, So 19, 6 June 1975. Until the 5 June issue, the paper carried almost every day a column called "News on Vietnam," which was negative in nature, depicting civil war against the new government, hardships in Vietnam, etc. After 6 June, the column disappeared. The only other items on Vietnam appear in no. 41, 4 July 1975, and on 6 October when refugees sailed from Guam back to Vietnam.

43. Articles of this kind can be found in almost every issue of *Thong Bao* and *Dat Lanh*. See, for example, "New Life: Life in North America: Questions and Answers," *Thong Bao*, no. 47 (June 1975); "New Life: Renting an Apartment or a House," *Thong Bao*, no. 50 (16 July 1975); "New Life: American Ways, " *Thong Bao*, nos. 51, 52, 53 (17, 18, 19 July 1975); "New Life: Welcome to the Supermarket," *Thong Bao*, no. 58 (24 July 1975), etc. Articles in *Dat Lanh* that are similar are "Credit Buying: Sometimes Costly," *Dat Lanh*, 3, no. 31 (18 October 1975): 1–2; "Renting," *Dat Lanh*, 3, no. 49 (22 October 1975): 3; "Experience of Living in America," *Dat Lanh*, 1, no. 28 (24 June 1975): 1–2; "American Way of Life," *Dat Lanh*, 2, no. 20 (5 August 1975): p. 1; "Viet Family is

Working at Learning Our Life Style," *Dat Lanh*, 2, no. 1 (17 July 1975): 1–2; "American Way of Life: Traveling Around Your New City," *Dat Lanh*, 2 (21 August 1975): 1–2; "Employment," *Dat Lanh*, 2, no. 23 (7 August 1975): 1–2.

Chapter 6: Being Sponsored and Resettled

1. Senate Subcommittee to Investigate Problems Connected with Refugees and Escapees, *Indochina Evacuation and Refugee Problems, Part IV. Staff Reports*, Report of 9 June 1975, 94th Cong. 1st Sess., pp. 20–25.

2. HEW Refugee Task Force, *Report to Congress*, 15 March 1976, pp. 30, 31.

3. Interview with the State Department representative, Fort Indian Town Gap, 31 October 1975, tape no. 38, side 2, V.I.C.

4. HEW Refugee Task Force, *Report to Congress*, 15 March 1976, p. 31.

5. *Report of the Interagency Task Force 2 May–20 December 1975*, Fort Chaffee, 14 January 1976, V.I.C., Box 2, pp. II-8 and II-9.

6. Interview with B.L., Fort Indian Town Gap, 31 October 1975, tape no. 37, side 2, V.I.C. This individual interviewed persons who returned to Vietnam prior to their leaving Guam.

7. HEW Refugee Task Force, *Report to Congress*, 15 March 1976, p. 31.

8. Letter of welcome from General Cannon and Mr. Friedman, Fort Indian Town Gap, n.d., p. 2, V.I.C., Box 4.

9. Interagency Task Force, *The Indochinese Refugee Program, Questions and Answers*, pub. 2, July 1975, pp. 4–5.

10. Senate Subcommittee to Investigate Problems Connected with Refugees and Escapees, *Hearings*, 94th Cong., 1st Sess., July 1975, pp. 33–35. A worker with United HIAS estimated much higher resettlement costs, maintaining that about $5,000 per person was needed to help immigrants get established in the country. See interview with C.W., United HIAS, New York City, 21 September 1976, tape no. 81, V.I.C.

11. For example, United HIAS kept $50, passing along about $450 to the sponsor; Travelers' Aid International kept

$100; while LIRS kept the full $500. See Senate Subcommittee to Investigate Problems Connected with Refugees and Escapees, *Hearings*, 94th Cong. 1st Sess., July 1975, pp. 23, 28, 31.

12. See table 2, chapter 3.

13. Senate Subcommittee to Investigate Problems Connected with Refugees and Escapees, *Hearings*, 94th Cong., 1st Sess., July 1975, p. 31.

14. Ibid., p. 112.

15. Ibid., p. 20. The town selectman was quoted in William Claiborne, "Vermont Town Withdraws Welcome Mat—Refugee Family Rebuffed," *Washington Post*, 4 August 1975.

16. ACNS, Resettlement Memo no. 9 from Wells Klein (director, ACNS), 12 June 1975.

17. *Dat Lanh*, Bo 1, So 34 (30 June 1975) p. 2.

18. *Dat Lanh*, Bo 3, So 10 (13 September 1975) p. 4.

19. Interview with Father L., Buffalo, New York, 12 March 1976, tapes no. 68 and 69, V.I.C.

20. A description of Father D.M.'s work in finding sponsorships for individuals he knew in Vietnam can be found in interview with E.R., New York City, 20 September 1976, tapes no. 77 and 78, V.I.C.

21. Robert DeVecchi, "Notes."

22. These reasons were supplied in almost every interview I conducted with caseworkers employed by the VOLAGs. See, for example, interview with M.S., caseworker, Tolstoy Foundation, Fort Indian Town Gap, Pennsylvania, 26 September 1975, tape no. 13, side 2; J.F., caseworker, LIRS, Fort Indian Town Gap, Pennsylvania, 19 November 1975, tape no. 40; C.M., caseworker, USCC, Fort Indian Town Gap, Pennsylvania, 15 October 1975, tape no. 21, side 2, V.I.C.

23. *Dat Lanh*, Bo 2, So 34, 19 August 1975, p. 1.

24. Ibid. Articles like this one abounded in *Dat Lanh*. See, for example, Nguyen Van Phai, "Transition," letter to *Dat Lanh*, Bo 2, So 34, (19 August 1975) p. 2; "Turning a Sponsor Off," Bo 2, So 35 (20 August 1975) p. 1; "Dear Refugees," signed Vu Dinh Hung, Bo 2, So 35 (20 August 1975) p. 2;

"Sponsors Don't Grow on Trees," Bo 2, So 32 (17 August 1975) p. 4; "Don't Be Afraid of Cold Water," Bo 2, So 40 (26 August 1975) pp. 1, 2; "A Coin Has Two Sides," Bo 3, So 13 (16 September 1975) pp. 1–2.

25. Field notes, Fort Indian Town Gap, 16 October 1975.

26. Interview with A.Z., caseworker, IRC, Fort Indian Town Gap, 16 October 1975, tape no. 23, side 2; interview with E.W., caseworker, USCC, 17 October 1975, tape no. 28, 29, side 1, V.I.C.

27. Ibid.

28. HEW Refugee Task Force, *Report to Congress*, 15 March 1976, p. 29.

29. This process was described at length by A.R., chief, Sponsorship Coordinating Center, Fort Indian Town Gap, in an interview on 20 November 1975, tape no. 46, side 2, V.I.C. See also "Sponsorship: Door to the U.S.," *Dat Lanh*, Bo 4, So 2 (25 October 1975), pp. 1–4.

30. *Dat Lanh*, Bo 3, So 49 (22 October 1975), p. 3.

31. Ibid., p. 2.

32. Ibid.

33. Ibid.

34. *Dat Lanh*, Bo 4, So 3 (26 October 1975), p. 3.

35. *Dat Lanh*, Bo 4, So 2 (25 October 1975), p. 4.

36. Ibid., p. 5.

37. *Dat Lanh*, Bo 3, So 22 (25 September 1975), p. 2.

38. Ibid., p. 3.

39. *Dat Lanh*, Bo 3, So 45 (18 October 1975), p. 2; similar offers appear in other issues of *Dat Lanh*. See, for example, "Viec Lam," Bo 4, So 5 (28 October 1975), p. 2.

40. There have been several newspaper articles about these sponsorships because they broke down with so much bitterness. See, for example, John Kifnel, "Recruits Leaving Vermont Chicken-Processing Plant," *New York Times*, 18 November 1975; Richard Severo, "Offer of Work for Vietnamese Turns Sour," *New York Times*, 14 November 1975, Sect. 2, p. 1, 66.

41. *Report of the Interagency Task Force 2 May–20 December 1975*, Fort Chaffee, 14 January 1976, p. IX-H-78.

42. Interview with A.R., chief, Sponsorship Coordinating

Center, Fort Indian Town Gap, 20 November 1975, tape no. 46, side 2, V.I.C.

43. Kifnel, "Recruits Leaving Vermont Plant," 18 November 1975.

44. See, for example, "An Orientation Brochure Prepared for Congregations Resettling Vietnamese Refugees in the U.S.A.," LIRS, n.d., V.I.C., Box 4. This pamphlet contained an "Agreement to Sponsor" form and a letter from Donald E. Anderson beginning: "Dear Pastor, we are turning to you to ask if you can assist us with the resettlement of one or more refugee families."

45. *Dat Lanh*, Bo 4, So 1 (24 October 1975), p. 2.

46. *Dat Lanh*, Bo 3, So 22 (25 September 1975), p. 2.

47. Ibid.

48. Ibid., p. 3.

49. Interview with W.K., director, ACNS, New York City, 16 September 1976, tapes no. 70 and 71, V.I.C.

50. Interview with K.C.S., field director, AFCR, Fort Indian Town Gap, 26 September 1975, tape no. 12, sides 1 and 2, V.I.C.

51. See resettlement forms, IRC, "Interview and Sponsor Information Sheet," V.I.C., Box 4; interview with J.M., assistant field director, USCC, Fort Indian Town Gap, 25 September 1975, tape no. 9, V.I.C.

52. This procedure was described in minute detail by a caseworker with the Tolstoy Foundation at Fort Indian Town Gap on 26 September 1975. See tape no. 13, side 2, V.I.C.

53. Ibid.

54. *Dat Lanh*, Bo 4, So 2 (25 October 1975), p. 2.

55. Interagency Task Force, *Report to Congress*, 15 September 1975, pp. 40–43.

56. Information about the New Mexico Program can be found on tape no. 46, side 2, tape no. 47, side 1, Fort Indian Town Gap, 21 November 1975, V.I.C.

57. See, for example, Senate Subcommittee to Investigate Problems Connected with Refugees and Escapees, *Hearings*, 94th Cong., 1st Sess., 15, 25, 30 April 1975.

58. Indochina Resettlement Program, case load by state,

LIRS, 30 June 1976. Typewritten attachment to letter of Susan J. Severance, assistant to the director of LIRS, to Gail P. Kelly, 13 December 1976, V.I.C., Box 4.

Chapter 7: The Vietnamese in America

1. Interview with E.R., 21 September 1976, V.I.C., tape no. 77, side 1.
2. Ibid.
3. Ibid., tape no. 78, side 1.
4. Ibid.
5. Ibid.
6. Ibid.
7. Ibid.
8. Ibid.
9. Ibid., tape no. 78, side 2.
10. Ibid.
11. Ibid.
12. All these statistics are taken from surveys contracted by the Interagency Task Force on Indochinese Refugees for September and December 1975. A draft of these surveys may be found in SUNY/Buffalo Archives, V.I.C., Box 4. See particularly table 1.
13. Ibid., table 6, "Hours Worked Per Week by Age and Sex."
14. Ibid., table 7, "Hours Worked Per Week by Weekly Wage and Salary Income for Working People."
15. "Nhan Dinh Cua HEW Ve Tinh Trang Dinh Cu," *Doi Song Moi*, 2, no. 10 (October 1976): p. 1.
16. These figures are computed from 1969 data and include a 50 percent adjustment for inflation to meet 1977 dollars (e.g., an annual inflation rate of about 5 percent, which is probably an underestimate of inflation since 1969). See *1970 Census of Population, General Social and Economic Characteristics, PC (1) C 51 Wisconsin*, appendix B, "Table A—Weighted Average Thresholds at Poverty Level in 1969 by Size of Family and Sex of Head, by Farm and Non-Farm Residence," app. p. 30.
17. Interagency Task Force on Indochinese Refugees, Survey, September and December 1975, p. 14.

18. United HIAS, Jewish Family/Vocational Service of Los Angeles, Vietnamese Resettlement Unit, 12 February 1976, V.I.C., Box 4.

19. United HIAS, *Report to Congress,* Indochinese Resettlement Program, 15 August 1976, attached table entitled "Lao Program," V.I.C., Box 4.

20. *Doi Song Moi,* November 1976, p. 1.

21. Interagency Task Force on Indochinese Refugees, Survey, September and December 1975, table 9.

22. "Nhan Dinh cua HEW ve Tinh Trang Dinh Cu," *Doi Song Moi,* 2, no. 10 (October 1976): pp. 1, 15.

23. Interview with T.N., Buffalo, New York, 23 February 1976, tape no. 64; interview with M.T., New York City, CWS, 20 September 1976, tapes no. 74, 75, side 1; interview with L.W., comptroller, IRC, 21 September 1976, tape no. 72, side 2, V.I.C. See also James T. Woolen, "The Struggle to Survive Erodes Refugees' Marriage," *New York Times,* 29 October 1975, p. 21.

24. *1970 Census of Populations,* app. p. 30.

25. "Former Vietnamese Driver, General: Both Face Money Problems," *Washington Post,* Sunday, 14 September 1975, sect. D, pp. 1 and 2.

26. Frances Fitzgerald, "Punch In, Punch Out, Eat Quick," *New York Times Magazine,* 28 December 1975, pp. 8–10, 32–38.

27. "Nhan Dinh cua HEW ve Tinh Trang Dinh Cu," *Doi Song Moi,* 2, no. 10 (October 1976): pp. 1, 15.

28. HEW Refugee Task Force, *Report to Congress,* 15 March 1976, pp. 48, 49, 50.

29. Memorandum to VOLAG directors from Lawrence L. McDonough, acting director, HEW Task Force, 30 July 1976, enclosure A, IRC files, New York City.

30. Andrew H. Malcolm, "Refugees' Early Fortune Turns to Trouble," *New York Times,* 13 September 1975, p. 24. Stories similar to this can be found. See, for example, Kifnel, "Recruits Leaving Vermont Plant," 18 November 1975, p. 24; Severo, "Offer Turns Sour," 14 November 1975, pp. 39 and 74.

31. HEW Refugee Task Force, *Report to Congress,* 15

June 1976, p. 80.

32. Draft memorandum dated 14 January 1976 to the secretary; from Larry McDonough, IRC HEW file.

33. Interview with M.C., director, New York/New Jersey region, HEW Task Force on Indochinese Refugees, 20 September 1976, tape no. 72, side 2, V.I.C.

34. Conference Report, Regional Workshop in Indochinese Resettlement, A Workshop of Resources, Seattle, Washington, 31 March–1 April 1976. Sponsored by the office of the governor, state of Washington, the Washington Association of Churches, HEW, Region X (offset), IRC, HEW files.

35. See *HEW Report on Indochinese Refugee Resettlement*, 15 August 1976. IRC HEW files.

36. See ACNS resettlement memo, no. 82 (attachment), 26 August 1976. Draft, "Indochinese Refugee Assistance Program: Proposed Recommendations to SRS for Policy Revisions and Related Actions." See also *Doi Song Moi*, November 1976, p. 1.

Chapter 8: The Immigration and the Vietnamese

1. Interview with H.M.B., curriculum coordinator, K–3, school, Fort Indian Town Gap, 17 October 1975, tape no. 26, side 1, V.I.C.

2. Tour of classes, taped classroom, Fort Indian Town Gap, 16 October 1975, tape no. 22, side 2, tape no. 26, side 2 (17 October 1975), and tape no. 27, side 1, V.I.C. (The latter two tapes are of teachers' in-service training where the problem is discussed.)

3. HEW Task Force on Indochinese Refugees, *Report to Congress*, 15 June 1976, p. 24.

4. *HEW Report on Indochinese Refugee Resettlement in Region IX, 1 July 1975 to 1 July 1976*, 15 August 1976, IRC HEW files, San Francisco, p. 10.

5. HEW Task Force on Indochinese Refugees, *Report to Congress*, 15 June 1976, p. 24.

6. Ibid. See also interview with M.C., New York regional director, HEW Task Force on Indochinese Refugees, 21 September 1976, tape no. 76; interview with L.W., comptroller, IRC, 20 September 1976, tape no. 72, V.I.C.

7. Interview with W.K., director, ACNS, New York City, 16 September 1976, tapes no. 70 and 71, V.I.C.

8. Field notes, Fort Indian Town Gap, 16 October 1975. I witnessed a caseworker from USCC trying to photograph a large Vietnamese fishing family from coastal Vung Tau. The family numbered more than 30 persons. The family at first refused to come out of the barracks to be photographed until the head of the family was promised that only one photograph would be taken of everybody. The family came out of the barracks and huddled together, refusing to budge as the caseworker tried to take pictures of them in groups of threes and fours. The caseworker told me that he was trying to take pictures of households for the purpose of splitting the family up for resettlement.

9. This is clear since areas with influxes of Vietnamese immigrants also experienced increases in the number of Vietnamese on welfare. In Louisiana, where many Vietnamese have moved since December 1975, the number of Vietnamese on welfare (cash assistance only) rose over 139 percent. See chapter 7.

10. Information about the regrouping of Vietnamese in New Orleans was obtained from Father L. in an interview in Buffalo, New York, 12 March 1976, tapes no. 67 and 68, V.I.C.

11. See "Tuong Than Tuong Tro" ("Helping Each Other"), *Doi Song Moi*, Bo 2, So 7 (February 1976), pp. 1, 18–19. The same issue of *Doi Song Moi* lists the names and addresses of major Vietnamese self-help organizations through the U.S. See "To Chuc Ai Huu" ("Mutual Assistance Organizations"), pp. 16–17. Other articles about these organizations can be found in this HEW newspaper. See "Truong Than Tuong Tro" ("Helping Each Other") (June 1976), p. 10; "Hoi Cho Viet-Nam," September 1976, p. 13; "Dem Van Nghe Viet-Nam," November 1976, p. 17.

Sources

Sources

This book is based on a variety of sources, oral and written, published and unpublished, many of which are not readily available in research libraries in the United States. I have deposited all the oral and unpublished as well as some published materials with the SUNY/Buffalo Archives, 123 Jewett Parkway, Buffalo, New York 14214. These materials make up the Vietnamese Immigration Collection (V.I.C.) and are available to serious scholars of either the Vietnamese immigration or immigration history in general.

I have listed below the sources used in this book, beginning with the oral material available at the SUNY/Buffalo Archives. Wherever materials are on deposit in the V.I.C. there, I have so noted it in this appendix.

I. ORAL SOURCES

I agreed to keep the identity of individuals whom I interviewed at Fort Indian Town Gap, Pennsylvania, at the voluntary agencies, and in Buffalo, anonymous. Below is a list of the persons interviewed by their positions and roles in the immigration and the tape numbers at the V.I.C. containing these interviews.

A. Fort Indian Town Gap

   1. *Camp Management*

Senior civilian coordinator (tape no. 13)

Deputy civilian coordinator (tape no. 8, side 2; tape no. 9, side 1)

a. Area coordinators

B. L., tape no. 36, side 2; tape no. 37, sides 1 and 2; tape no. 38, side 1

C. C., tape no. 47, sides 1 and 2; tape no. 48, side 1

M. C., tape no. 42, sides 1 and 2

b. Information officers

L. F., tape no. 41, sides 1 and 2; tape no. 42, side 1

SSG. K., tape no. 1, sides 1 and 2

c. Task force personnel

In-processing: J. M. and C. W., tape no. 44, sides 1 and 2

Sponsorship coordination: A. R., tape no. 46, side 2

Orientation: N. N. B., tape no. 16, sides 1 and 2; D. C., tape no. 17, side 2

2. *School People and Educational Programs*

a. School administrators

K. A., school superintendent, tape no. 9, side 2; tape no. 10, side 1

R. A. K., primary school principal, tape no. 8, side 1

b. Curriculum coordinators and specialists

A. K., media specialist, tape no. 2, sides 1 and 2

J. E., curriculum specialist, tape no. 2, sides 1 and 2

B. G., curriculum coordinator, grades 3–6, tape no. 21, side 2; tape no. 22, sides 1 and 2

H. M. B., curriculum coordinator, grades K–3, tape no. 25, sides 1 and 2

R. S., curriculum coordinator, secondary school, tape no. 30, side 1; tape no. 45, sides 1 and 2

P. H., curriculum coordinator, adult school, tape no. 29, sides 1 and 2; tape no. 45, sides 1 and 2

P. J., English as a Second Language specialist, tape

no. 26, side 2

B. C., language arts specialist, tape no. 46, side 1

V. L., guidance counselor, tape no. 23, sides 1 and 2, tape no. 24, side 2; tape no. 25, side 1

c. School aides

B. T. and N. T. D., tape no. 31, side 1; tape no. 32, sides 1 and 2; tape no. 33, side 1

d. Teachers

Teachers' in-service, elementary school, tape no. 26, side 1

Elementary teacher, tape no. 22, side 1

D. M., adult school, tape no. 36, side 1; tape no. 34, side 2

P. D., adult school, tape no. 43, sides 1 and 2

R. B., tape no. 43, sides 1 and 2

e. Classes

Mr. B.'s adult education class, tape no. 16, sides 1 and 2

Elementary classes, tape no. 22, side 2

Adult class, tape no. 29, side 2

Adult basic English classes and home economics class, tape no. 33, sides 1 and 2

Adult English class for illiterates, tape no. 34, sides 1 and 2

Intermediate adult English class, night school, tape no. 35, sides 1 and 2

High school class, tape no. 35, sides 1 and 2

3. *Voluntary Agency Personnel*

a. USCC

J. C., assistant director, tape no. 9, side 2

F. P., director, tape no. 12, side 2

C. M., caseworker, tape no. 21, side 2

J. C., caseworker, tape no. 27, sides 1 and 2; tape no. 28, side 1

E. W., caseworker, tape no. 28, sides 1 and 2; tape no. 29, side 1

P.D., tape no. 43, sides 1 and 2

b. IRC

R. D., director, tape no. 10, side 2; tape no. 11, side 1

R. F., sponsorship breakdown caseworker, tape no. 14, side 1

A. Z., caseworker, sponsorship matching, tape no. 23, side 2; tape no. 24, sides 1 and 2

  c. AFCR

K. C. S., field director, tape no. 12, sides 1 and 2

  d. Tolstoy Foundation

M. S., caseworker, tape no. 13, side 1

  e. LIRS

J. F., caseworker, tape no. 40, sides 1 and 2

4. *Red Cross and YMCA Workers*

R. F., field director, ARC, tape no. 15, side 1

B., ARC, family unification worker, tape no. 20, side 1

N. B., ARC, family unification worker, tape no. 20, sides 1 and 2

P. B. and T. H., ARC, college credentials section, tape no. 20, side 2; tape no. 21, side 1

A. V., ARC recreation center director, tape no. 40, side 2

S. and T., recreation workers, YMCA reading room, tape no. 44, side 2; tape no. 45, side 1

5. *Vietnamese Refugees*

Many of these interviews were held in the Vietnamese language. Several are group interviews, because as we interviewed an individual, many people gathered around the tape recorder and joined in the discussion without identifying themselves. In all we recorded conversations with about fifty identifiable persons.

Vietnamese conversation no. 1: two men, one a soldier from South Vietnam, age thirty-eight, and Catholic; the second from North Vietnam, thirty-four years old, Catholic, who gave his occupation as "tailor." Tape no. 1, side 2.

Vietnamese conversation no. 2: twenty people gathered around the tape recorder. The major speaker is a former soldier, age thirty, born in a South Vietnamese city. Tape no. 1, side 2.

Vietnamese conversations no. 3, 4, 5: unidentified

former soldiers, continued from no. 2. Tape no. 1, side 2; tape no. 2, side 1.

Vietnamese conversation no. 6: young men who refused to identify themselves, speaking in northern dialect. Tape no. 2, side 1.

Vietnamese conversation no. 7: Father N. T. L., chaplain, area no. 4, Fort Indian Town Gap. Tape no. 2, side 1.

Vietnamese conversation no. 8: with six young men of northern origin who refused to identify themselves. Tape no. 2, side 2.

Vietnamese conversation no. 9: N. V. S., former officer, ARVN, age forty-five, born in North Vietnam, Buddhist, resident of Bien Hoa before leaving Vietnam. Tape no. 3, side 2.

Vietnamese conversation no. 10: V. V. N., male, former soldier originally from North Vietnam, Catholic, fisherman. Tape no. 4, side 1.

Vietnamese conversation no. 11: T. V. Q., thirty-year-old male, Catholic, born in North Vietnam (Nam-Dinh Province), former government official, received Ph.D. at University of Michigan. Tape no. 5, sides 1 and 2.

Vietnamese conversation no. 12: forty-two-year-old woman from North Vietnam, midwife, interruptions by a former sailor. Tape no. 6, side 1.

Vietnamese conversation no. 13: N. K. H., former journalist, born in North Vietnam. Tape no. 6, side 2.

Vietnamese conversation no. 14: N. K. H. (cont'd); T. V. D., twenty-one-year-old former student; D. V. H., twenty-two-year-old former government official; unidentified forty-year-old former soldier. All speak with pronounced northern accents. Tape no. 7, side 1.

Vietnamese conversation no. 15: unidentified fifty-seven-year-old former policeman, born in North Vietnam, Buddhist. Father was a colonial civil servant. Tape no. 7, side 2.

Mr. V., forty-year-old former policeman, born in North Vietnam, father was head of a Hanoi radio station before 1954. Tape no. 14, side 2 (English).

Vietnamese conversation no. 16: N. N. B. (camp management), born in North Vietnam. Tape no. 16, side 1.

Vietnamese conversation no. 17: T. D., Buddhist monk. Tape no. 16, side 2 (English).

Vietnamese conversation no. 18: sixty-four-year-old South Vietnamese woman, unidentified man. Tape no. 17, side 1.

Vietnamese conversation no. 19: dog butcher; unidentified South Vietnamese male; tailor from North Vietnam; elderly South Vietnamese male. Tape no. 17, side 1.

Vietnamese conversation no. 20: Father N. T. L., chaplain, area 6, Fort Indian Town Gap. Tape no. 18, side 2.

Vietnamese conversation no. 21: N. D. H., newspaper man, northerner. Tape no. 19, sides 1 and 2; tape no. 51, side 1; tape no. 56, sides 1 and 2.

B., former air force pilot, born in North Vietnam. Tape no. 20, side 1 (English).

T. H., former air force pilot. Tape no. 20, side 2; tape no. 21, side 1 (English).

B. T., former minister of primary education, South Vietnam. Tape no. 31, side 2; tape no. 32, sides 1 and 2; tape no. 33, sides 1 and 2 (English).

N. T. D., former university teacher, originally from North Vietnam, Catholic. Tape no. 31, side 2; tape no. 33, sides 1 and 2; tape no. 34, sides 1 and 2 (English).

Dr. D., thirty-five-year-old Vietnamese female M.D., born and raised in Da-Nang. Tape no. 38, side 2; tape no. 39, side 1 (English).

Vietnamese conversation no. 22: D.V. H., twenty-two-year-old former government official, born in North Vietnam. Tape no. 49, sides 1 and 2.

Vietnamese conversation no. 23; Mr. D., northern

male. Tape no. 49, side 2.

Vietnamese conversation no. 25: N. D. H., former Saigon reporter. Tape no. 51, sides 1 and 2.

T. Q. V., middle-aged male, Catholic, former government official, tax bureau, born in North Vietnam. Tape no. 51, sides 1 and 2; tape no. 52, side 1; tape no. 54, side 2; tape no. 55, side 1.

Unidentified men, one a former reporter, the other an ARVN major. Tape no. 53, side 1.

T. V. D., former student. Tape no. 54, side 1.

N. K. T., South Vietnamese male. Tape no. 54, side 2.

Three soldiers, two born in North Vietnam, one born in South Vietnam. Tape no. 57, sides 1 and 2.

P. L., former air force officer, born in North Vietnam, Catholic. Tape no. 59, side 1.

6. *Camp Events (other than school classes)*

"Closing the Gap," WITF, Hershey, Pennsylvania, TV broadcast carrying Pham Duy concert. Tape no. 11, side 1.

HEW's "Transition America." Tape no. 17, side 1.

Mass, area 6 chapel in Vietnamese. Tape no. 18, side 1.

Pennsylvania Commission on Women, "Women in America." Tape no. 30, side 1.

IRC orientation session for Vietnamese. Tape no. 53, side 1.

7. *Interviews with Miscellaneous Americans*

Captain R., Psyops (publisher of *Dat Lanh*). Tape no. 4, side 2.

D. C., HEW's "Transition America." Tape no. 17, side 2.

New Mexico program chief (state sponsorship). Tape no. 46, side 2; tape no. 47, side 1.

K. C., Chinese Benevolent Association (also editor of *Thong Bao* at Camp Pendleton). Tape no. 48, sides 1 and 2.

B. Oral Materials in Buffalo, New York, for which tapes are available:

1. *Vietnamese*
   T. H., president, Vietnamese Club of Buffalo. Tape no. 60, sides 1 and 2; tape no. 61, side 1.
   T. N., teacher of English, Buffalo Board of Education, Adult Learning Center. Tape no. 64, sides 1 and 2.
   Father J. L., priest, Archdiocese of Buffalo. Tape no. 67, sides 1 and 2.
   Father D. L., priest, Archdiocese of Buffalo. Tape no. 68, sides 1 and 2.
2. *Schoolmen*
   J. Y., director, Buffalo Board of Education, Adult Learning Center. Tape no. 66, sides 1 and 2.
3. *English Classes for Vietnamese*
   Adult Learning Center. Tape no. 62, sides 1 and 2; tape no. 63, sides 1 and 2.
   Newman Center. Tape no. 65, sides 1 and 2; tape no. 65a, sides 1 and 2.

C. Interviews Collected in New York City, September 1976

1. *Resettlement Agency Personnel*
   W. C. K., national director, ACNS. Tape no. 70, sides 1 and 2; tape no. 71, sides 1 and 2.
   R. D. V., director, Indochina Program, IRC. Tape no. 72, sides 1 and 2; tape no. 79, sides 1 and 2; tape no. 80, sides 1 and 2.
   L. W., inspector, IRC. Tape no. 72, side 2; tape no. 73, sides 1 and 2.
   M. T., consultant, Indochina Program, CWS. Tape no. 74, sides 1 and 2; tape no. 75, sides 1 and 2.
   E. R., caseworker, IRC. Tape no. 77, side 2; tape no. 78, sides 1 and 2; tape no. 79, side 1.
   C. W., director, Indochina Program, United HIAS. Tape no. 81, sides 1 and 2; tape no. 82, side 1.
   K. P., caseworker, Indochina Program, United HIAS. Tape no. 81, sides 1 and 2; tape no. 82, side 1.

2. *HEW*

> M. C., director, Indochina Refugee Program, New York Regional Office. Tape no. 76, sides 1 and 2; tape no. 77, side 1.

II. UNPUBLISHED MATERIALS

A. Collected at Refugee Camps

At Fort Indian Town Gap I collected many materials which I used in this book, especially as documentation in chapters 4, 5, and 6. These materials are all now available in the Vietnamese Immigration Collection at SUNY/Buffalo. They can be classified as follows:

1. *Refugee statistical profiles,* issued by the IATF at Fort Indian Town Gap (mimeographed), V.I.C., Box 2.
2. *Orientation materials distributed to Vietnamese refugees,* V.I.C., Box 4. Notable among these are:
   a. *Chung Toi Nhang Nguoi My Goc A-Chau,* HEW, GPO stock no. 0324-0043, n.d.
   b. *Your New Country: A Guide to Language and Life in the U.S.A.,* ARC, bilingual, 1975.
   c. *Huong dan ve hai nen Van hoa Hoa-Ky,* IATF, 8 August 1975.
   d. *Vietnamese Refugee Orientation Handbook (Nguoi Ti Nan Viet Nam Sach Chi Dan),* IATF, July 1975, lithographed, 59 pp.
   e. *Tin Tuc Ve Bao Tro Nhung Nguoi Dan Di Cu Ty Dan Di Cu Ty Nan Dong Duong,* HEW, 8 August 1975.
   f. *Tai-Lieu Chi Dan (Information Guide for New Arrivals at Fort Indian Town Gap, Pa.),* 2d ed., lithographed, September 1975.
   g. Letter of Welcome from General Cannon and Mr. Friedman, Fort Indian Town Gap, Pa., lithographed, 24 pp.
   h. *Orientation Briefing On Processing For "Heads of Family,"* lithographed, Camp Pendleton, 21 June

1975, 10 pp.

3. *School instructional materials*, developed and distributed by the primary, secondary, and adult schools at Fort Indian Town Gap, Pennsylvania, V.I.C., Box 3.
    a. "Weekly Curriculum, K–3"
    b. "Weekly Curriculum, grades 3–6"
    c. "Secondary School Weekly Curriculum"
    d. "Survival English"

B. Resettlement Agency Reports, Memoranda, and Files Consulted

1. *The Role of the Voluntary Agencies in the Indochina Refugee Resettlement Program—1975*, draft, xerox, typescript, V.I.C., Box 4.
2. *Resettlement memorandum, ACNS*, 11 April 1975.
3. *ACNS files*, New York City, 21 August 1976.
4. *CWS*
    a. Office Memorandum, 18 November 1975, from John Schauer to William Taylor, subject: "Response to Continuing Needs of Indochinese Refugees Through CWS, Denominations, and Local Churches," xerox, 7 pp., V.I.C., Box 4.
    b. *Church World Service Indo-China Refugee Resettlement Program: Interim Report*, 11 October 1975, mimeographed, 4 pp., V.I.C., Box 4.
    c. *The Role of Church World Service in Developing Communities of Understanding and Support for Indochina Refugees*, interim report no. 2, 21 December 1975, mimeographed, 7 pp., V.I.C., Box 4.
    d. *The Continuing Role of Church World Service in Developing Communities of Understanding and Support for Indo-China Refugees*, interim report no. 3, 29 March 1976, mimeographed, 10 pp., V.I.C., Box 4.
5. *IRC*
    a. HEW file, New York Office (contains various memoranda from Larry McDonough, acting director, HEW Refugee Task Force).
    b. Clipping file, New York office.

    c. "Notes," Robert DeVecchi (Chaffee diary), New York office.

    d. Memo to Carel Sternberg from Robert DeVecchi, subject: "Statistical Information in IRC Cases by Camp and State," 15 January 1976, xerox, 3 pp., V.I.C., Box 4.

    e. "Indochinese Refugees, Confirmed Employment," xerox, V.I.C., Box 4.

6. *United HIAS*

    a. *Statistical Abstract*, 4th Quarter, 1975, vol. 16, no. 4, mimeographed, 22 pp., V.I.C., Box 4.

    b. *Report to the Congress, Indochinese Resettlement Program*, 15 August 1976, typescript, 6 pp. plus tables, V.I.C., Box 4.

    c. *Initial Settlement of HIAS Assisted Migrants in the United States*, January 1–December 31, 1975.

    d. Report, Jewish Family Service of Philadelphia, 28 November 1975, xerox, V.I.C., Box 4.

    e. Questionnaires, Jewish Family/Vocational Service of Los Angeles, Vietnamese Resettlement Unit, 12 February 1976, xerox, 4 pp., V.I.C., Box 4.

    f. Re: Vietnamese refugees: comments on the report of Mr. Robert Gilson, refugee coordinator, region 1, of 28 January 1976, Jewish Family and Children's Service, Boston, Mass., xerox, 2 pp., V.I.C., Box 4.

7. *LIRS*

    a. *An Orientation Brochure Prepared for Congregations Resettling Vietnamese Refugees in the U.S.A.*, c. May 1975, mimeographed, V.I.C., Box 4.

    b. Letter of 13 December 1976, Susan J. Severance, assistant to the director, LIRS, to Gail P. Kelly, 4 pp. typescript (responding to questions on LIRS involvement in the Indochina Program), V.I.C., Box 4.

    c. *Resettlement Policy of the LIRS*, mimeographed, 9 pp. and addendum, V.I.C., Box 4.

    d. "Indochina Resettlement Program—LIRS Caseload by State—30 June 1976," typescript, V.I.C.,

Box 4.
8. *USCC*
   a. USCC Offices, 1 July 1975, V.I.C., Box 4.
   b. Refugees resettled, by diocese, to 14 September 1975, V.I.C., Box 4.
9. *Miscellaneous: HEW, surveys, etc.*
   a. Association for New Americans, Inc., *Report*, New York City, November 1975, mimeographed, 4 pp., V.I.C., Box 4.
   b. *First and Second Wave Surveys to Assess the Status of Vietnamese Refugees*, draft, typescript, 25 pp. plus 38 tables. (This study was commissioned by the IATF but was never printed or released.) V.I.C., Box 4.
   c. "Recommendations to the IATF," no author, n.d., typescript, draft, HEW, 7 pp. (I collected this from the HEW regional director in New York City and believe it is a prelude to the New York/New Jersey Program of April 1976, see below.) V.I.C., Box 4.
   d. *An Approach to Developing Employment Opportunities in the Local Community*, New York/ New Jersey Indochinese Refugee Resettlement Task Force, April 1976, mimeographed, 19 pp., V.I.C., Box 4.

III. GOVERNMENT DOCUMENTS

A. Congressional Hearings

   1. U.S. Congress, Senate, Subcommittee to Investigate Problems Connected with Refugees and Escapees of the Committee on the Judiciary. *Hearings, Refugee Problems in South Vietnam and Laos*, 89th Cong., 1st Sess., 13, 14, 17, 20, July; 4, 5, 10, 18 August; 17, 21, 28, 29, 30 September 1965.
   2. U.S. Congress, House of Representatives, Committee on the Judiciary. *Refugee Problems in Vietnam, India, and Hong Kong, British Crown Colony, H. Res. 593, a Resolution Authorizing the Committee on the Judiciary to Conduct Studies and Investigations*

Relating to Certain Matters Within its Jurisdiction, House report no. 1769, 89th Cong., 2d Sess., 1966.

3. Senate Subcommittee to Investigate Problems Connected with Refugees and Escapees, *Hearings, Civilian Casualty, Social Welfare and Refugee Problems in South Vietnam,* 90th Cong., 1st Sess., 10, 18 May; 16 August; 21 September; 9, 10, 11, 13, and 16 October 1967.

4. Senate Subcommittee to Investigate Problems Connected with Refugees and Escapees, *Hearings, Civilian Casualty, Social Welfare and Refugee Problems in South Vietnam,* 91st Cong., 1st Sess., part 1, 14 and 15 June 1969.

5. Senate Subcommittee to Investigate Problems Connected with Refugees and Escapees, *Hearings, War-Related Civilian Problems in Indochina. Part III—Vietnam,* 92nd Cong., 1st Sess., 22 April 1971.

6. Senate Subcommittee to Investigate Problems Connected with Refugees and Escapees, *Hearings, World Refugee and Humanitarian Problems,* 92nd Cong., 1st Sess., 22 July 1971.

7. Senate Subcommittee to Investigate Problems Connected with Refugees and Escapees, *Hearings, Relief and Rehabilitation of War Victims in Indochina, Part IV. South Vietnam and Regional Problems,* 93rd Cong., 1st Sess., 1 August 1973.

8. Senate Subcommittee to Investigate Problems Connected with Refugees and Escapees, *Hearings, Indochina Evacuation and Refugee Problems, Part I. Operation Babylift and Humanitarian Needs,* 94th Cong., 1st Sess., 8 August 1975.

9. Senate Subcommittee to Investigate Problems Connected with Refugees and Escapees, *Hearings, Indochina Evacuation and Refugee Problems, Part II. The Evacuation,* 94th Cong., 1st Sess., 15, 25, and 30 April 1975.

10. Senate Subcommittee to Investigate Problems Connected with Refugees and Escapees, *Hearings, Part IV. Staff Reports,* 94th Cong., 1st Sess., 8 June and 9 July 1975.

11. Senate Subcommittee to Investigate Problems Con-

nected with Refugees and Escapees, *Hearings*, 94th Cong., 1st Sess., 24 July 1975.

12. U.S. Congress, House of Representatives, Subcommittee on Immigration, Citizenship, and International Law of the Committee on the Judiciary, *Hearings, Indochina Refugees*, serial no. 4, 94th Cong., 1st Sess., 5 and 7 May 1975.

13. U.S. Congress, House of Representatives, Subcommittee on Foreign Operations and Related Agencies of the Committee on Appropriations, *Special Assistance to Refugees from Cambodia and Vietnam*, 94th Cong., 1st Sess., 8 May 1975.

14. U.S. Congress, House of Representatives, Subcommittee on Elementary, Secondary and Vocational Education of the Committee on Education and Labor, *Hearings, to Authorize Funds for Assistance to Local Educational Agencies for the Education of Cambodian and Vietnamese Refugees, and for Other Purposes*, 94th Cong., 1st Sess., 5 November 1975.

B. Public Laws

1. *Migration and Refugee Assistance Act of 1962*, 76 stat. 121.

2. *Indochina Migration and Refugee Assistance Act of 1975*, 20 May 1975.

C. Reports to Congress

Most of the reports listed below are available at the SUNY/Buffalo Archives, Vietnamese Immigration Collection, Box 2. All, except the first one listed, are not generally available.

1. Comptroller general of the United States, *U.S. Provides Safe Haven for Indochinese Refugees, Department of State and Other Agencies, Report to Congress*, 16 June 1975.

2. Interagency Task Force for Indochinese Refugees, *Report to Congress*, 15 September 1975.

3. Interagency Task Force for Indochinese Refugees, 15 December 1975.

4. Interagency Task Force for Indochinese Refugees, *Interagency Task Force on Indochinese Refugees, 2 May–20 December 1975, Fort Chaffee.*
5. Interagency Task Force for Indochinese Refugees, *Report to Congress,* 15 June 1976, V.I.C.
6. HEW Refugee Task Force, San Francisco Regional Office, *Report on Indochinese Refugee Resettlement in Region 9, 1 July 1975 to 1 July 1976,* mimeographed.

IV. PUBLISHED SOURCES

A. Refugee Newspapers

1. *Dat Lanh,* Fort Indian Town Gap, Pennsylvania, June 1975–December 1975, mimeographed, V.I.C., Box 5, bilingual daily, in English and Vietnamese with occasional Cambodian language editions.
2. *Thong Bao,* Camp Pendleton, California, May 1975–November 1975, lithographed, V.I.C., Boxes 6a and 6b, bilingual daily, in English and Vietnamese.
3. *Chan Troi Moi,* Guam, 5 May 1975–27 August 1975, lithographed, V.I.C., Box 7, daily, Vietnamese only.
4. *Doi Song Moi,* Washington, D.C., HEW, November 1975–January 1977, newsprint, V.I.C., Box 7, monthly, bilingual in English and Vietnamese, with four to five pages in each issue printed in Cambodian.

B. Books and Journal Literature

Secondary material on the 1975 immigration is very sparse. In preparing this book I surveyed the American popular press (*New York Times, Washington Post, Newsweek, Time Magazine,* and *U.S. News and World Report*). All carried extensive reports of the ARVN retreat, the refugee flight both within and out of Vietnam, and the refugee camps. The popular press after the summer of 1975 also carried occasional articles on postcamp life. This reportage is too extensive to be covered here. I have included below longer popular articles and books and the very few scholarly articles on the subject that have been published.

1. Anson, Robert Sam, "The Prisons of Our Freedom," *New York Times*, 18 June 1975, pp. 16–30.

2. Austerlitz, Max, "Vietnamizing South Vietnam," *New York Times Magazine*, 25 April 1976, pp. 32–34, 98–103.

3. Chen, Edwin C., "The Last 'New Life Hamlet'," *The Progressive*, November 1975, pp. 20–24.

4. Fitzgerald, Frances, "Punch In! Punch Out! Eat Quick," *New York Times Magazine*, 28 December 1975, pp. 8–11, 32–34, 38–39.

5. Friedman, Fred, "Inside the Vietnamese Refugee Camps, or Call Me Ishmael," *Red Balloon*, no. 11 (spring 1976), 3 pp.

6. "Where is Home? Indochina's Evacuees in the United States,"*Indochina Chronicle*, no. 40 (September 1975), pp. 1–20.

7. Johnston, Tracy, "Torment Over the Vietnam Non-Orphans," *New York Times Magazine*, 9 May 1976, pp. 14–15, 76–78, 86–88.

8. Le-Thi-Que, Rambo, A. Terry, and Murfin, Gary D., "Why They Fled: Refugee Movement During the Spring 1975 Communist Offensive in South Vietnam," *Asian Survey* 16, no. 9 (September 1976): 855–63.

9. Pilger, John, *The Last Day: America's Final Hour in Vietnam* (New York: Random House, April 1976).

10. Schaefer, Richard T. and Schaefer, Sandra L., "Reluctant Welcome: U.S. Response to the South Vietnamese Refugees," *New Community* 4, no. 3 (autumn 1975): 366–70.

11. Sterba, James P., "Captain Midnight Becomes Civilian Ky," *New York Times Magazine*, 11 January 1976, pp. 34–40.

12. Terzani, Tiziano, *Giai Phong: The Fall and Liberation of Saigon* (New York: St. Martin's Press, 1976).